Sounds American

Sounds American

National Identity and the Music Cultures of the
Lower Mississippi River Valley, 1800–1860

ANN OSTENDORF

The University of Georgia Press

ATHENS AND LONDON

© 2011 by The University of Georgia Press
Athens, Georgia 30602
www.ugapress.org

Printed digitally in the United States of America

LIBRARY OF CONGRESS CATALOGING-IN-PUBLICATION DATA

Ostendorf, Ann, 1976–
    Sounds American : national identity and the music cultures of the lower Mississippi
River Valley, 1800–1860 / Ann Ostendorf.
       p.   cm.—(Early American places)
    Includes bibliographical references and index.
    ISBN-13: 978-0-8203-3975-7 (cloth : alk. paper)
    ISBN-10: 0-8203-3975-x (cloth : alk. paper)
    ISBN-13: 978-0-8203-3976-4 (pbk. : alk. paper)
    ISBN-10: 0-8203-3976-8 (pbk. : alk. paper)
    1. Music—Mississippi River Valley—19th century—History and criticism.   2. Music—
Social aspects—Mississippi River Valley—History—19th century.   3. Mississippi River
Valley—History—19th century.   I. Title.
ML200.4.O88   2011
780.976'09034—dc22

                                                                    2010049357

    British Library Cataloging-in-Publication Data available

To Rich

&

For all Haitians and the victims of Katrina
Rebuilding destruction while this was being created

Contents

Acknowledgments

Reflecting back over the years of working on this project, I can now see the process as a necessary stage for my personal and professional development. However, were it not for the constant supportive presence of many people in my life, the struggles of researching and writing this book would have overwhelmed me. I remained motivated by the collegial atmosphere of Marquette University's Department of History, whose faculty continued to express sincere interest in my work and well-being in untold ways. I must mention a few particularly special mentors by name. I am grateful to Phillip Naylor, whose reiteration of the significance of perception in history has inspired me ever since I worked as his teaching assistant. I am especially thankful for James Marten, who always went beyond his duties as chair and director of graduate studies in preparing me for my life as a historian. He took seriously every question or concern I had, and I find myself emulating him in my own professional activities and relationships. Finally, I must thank my adviser, Kristen Foster, for her untiring ability to help defuse my anxieties during this process. The balance between her supportive friendship and scholarly advice has been the perfect combination as I pursue my own potentials. I also thank my fellow graduate students, who consistently found time in their own busy schedules to evaluate my work and push me toward fuller scholarly growth.

The financial support provided by Marquette's History Department, the Cyril Smith Family Fellowship, and the Father Henry Casper S.J.

Memorial Fellowship allowed me to immerse myself in my scholarship, and for this I am grateful. I also thank the administration at Gonzaga University for the financial support to see this project to completion, as well as the friendship and mentoring of my new colleagues during this transition into a new professional family. The Gonzaga University students also deserve my appreciation; their participation in discussions of early United States history has already taught me new ways of thinking and explaining.

Numerous librarians and archivists assisted me, especially the Interlibrary Loan Department at Marquette University's Raynor Memorial Library and Gonzaga University's Foley Center Library. Without them, this would have been a very different project. Others include Lucinda Cockrell and Grover Baker at the Center for Popular Music at Middle Tennessee State University, Deborah Cribbs and Charles Brown at the St. Louis Mercantile Library at the University of Missouri St. Louis, Irene Wainwright at the New Orleans Public Library, Siva Blake and Daniel Hammer at the Historic New Orleans Collection's Williams Research Center, Mimi Miller at the Historic Natchez Foundation, and the entire staff at the Missouri History Museum, Library and Research Center, Tulane University Archives, Mississippi Department of Archives and History, Louisiana State University Library's Special Collections, and the Sainte Genevieve Public Library. I especially thank Dale Cockrell, Frank Nickell, John Keeling, and my long-lost cousin Berndt Ostendorf for their willingness to give of their time to read parts of my work. I also thank all the editors at the University of Georgia Press, but especially Derek Krissoff, whose approachable professionalism has made this first experience with publishing for a young scholar like me much more pleasant than I ever would have expected.

Finally, I thank my family and friends who have put up with me throughout this process. Jodi and Enaya, having two great friends to share the journey with made it all that much easier. The fantastic company of the Maggie Lang, Danielle Carder, and Emily Schall households provided refuge and hospitality during research trips and vacation getaways. I'm sure your vicarious experience of researching and writing has made you all that much more confident in your own career paths. To Mom, Dad, Jill, Mark, and Nick, thanks for empathizing with my work even though it means time away. But my greatest thanks goes out to Rich, for taking care of everything else in my life.

Sounds American

Introduction

It is the belief men betray and not that which they parade which has to be studied.

CHARLES SANDERS PEIRCE, "ISSUES OF PRAGMATICISM"

During the early decades of the new American nation, intellectuals and cultural commentators were concerned with the question of what it meant to be American. More than a desire to differentiate themselves from Europeans, their anxiety arose out of the belief that the nation's members lacked any commonalities beyond the shared revolutionary experience. To them, diversity within the nation potentially threatened to undermine the unity they assumed necessary to ensure the successes of this republican experiment. The newly forming political parties, the variety of religious traditions, the contrasting regional experiences, and the ethnic and racial diversity within the nation, all caused insecurity, and thus became problems with which to be dealt. Because this new nation existed in a process of definition, more so than as a singularly definable entity, the nation's diversities heightened its insecurity as its identity remained in flux. Many wondered, if the character of the United States could not even be defined, what were its chances for survival?[1]

As a result, a resounding call to create an American national culture emerged from an array of thinkers as a way to encourage a cohesiveness that would bind together the varied, changing, and uncertain components of the nation.[2] From voices as diverse as Noah Webster, with his attempt to codify American English soon after the Revolution, to the following generation's cultivation of an American literary culture by the likes of Emerson, Fuller, and Thoreau—all engaged in a dialogue promoting a unique national culture through both explicit and implicit comparisons to what they considered to be non-American ways. The relationship between early Americans' ideas about national identity and that which they considered no longer, not yet, or never to be included in the nation is a component of early American cultural history that requires further study. According to Elisa Tamarkin, a scholar of early American culture, "We need better to examine how nationalism, as a form of feeling, an ideology, and a set of practices, works every bit as seriously at bringing some aspects of the outside in, as it does at keeping others out."[3] We also need to better understand the seeming paradox that American nationalism developed as peculiarly regional processes. National loyalty and regionally distinctive experiences were two components of most early Americans' identities.[4] Yet, which of these diverse experiences could be brought into American culture, and whose ways would be defined as outside the national expression and experience?

The methods these nationalist thinkers used to investigate what it meant, or should mean, to be American, especially the language they used when writing on the topic, reveal that the ethnic and racial diversity of the United States presented a unique issue that needed special consideration as they worked toward developing a national culture. Among their calls for an American language and literature, these self-conscious American nationalists also called for a distinctive American music culture. The language writers used when encouraging the development of a unique national music, as with a national culture in general, exposes their assumptions that a music way was intimately connected to what today would best be called race or ethnicity.

Within this early American music culture, descriptors bound music into clearly identifiable categories embedding the presumption that a music way was a peculiar characteristic of a national, racial, or ethnic group's members. Commentators variously saw music as an inherited biological trait, a product of the environment, the result of one's particular education, or a combination of the three.[5] No matter which characteristic they considered to be strongest, cultural critics believed music to be connected to a person's specific homeland past and shared with others of the same biology, heritage, and experience.

I use "music way" and "music culture" as umbrella terms to include any expression made through or with music, including those performed and printed. Although at times I use the term "American" in the context of purposefully nationalistic writers' style of thinking about the nation, I primarily use it as a designator for that which is happening in the United States in a general way. Thus, although the term "American culture" implied specific racial and ethnic associations (among many others categories) to self-conscious cultural commentators, I employ the term *inclusively* of all people who happened to be living at the time within the United States. As such, my word American does not imply homogenization either as a reality or goal, but rather describes a person inhabiting the unsettled cultural and geographic entity of the early nation. This person was quite often surrounded by, and most likely reacting to, other unsettled people with varying traditions and expectations of their neighbors and nation.

I use the terms "ethnicity" and "race" neither interchangeably, nor precisely distinct from each other. According to Bruce Dain's study of early nineteenth-century race theory, "Racial concepts did not move tidily from a shallow Enlightenment environmentalism to a deep biology; nor were the two positions mutually exclusive. Nurture and nature intertwined." The term "race" would have been used in the early nineteenth century to describe what twentieth-century language attempted to separate into categories of race and ethnicity, as well as a word used to describe in a generic way categories of difference. More frequently, the words "character," "nature," and "characteristic" would have been employed instead of "race" when describing attributes of a particular group of people. The term "ethnicity" would not have been used at all. In order for the distinctions between the various attempts to categorize people within the early republic to appear clear to the reader, I choose the term "race" or "ethnicity" based on today's popularly accepted definitions. In general, I use the term "race" when describing early nineteenth-century assumptions about human difference based on physical or biological traits related to a person's continental ancestry (African, Asian, European, or American), whereas I use the term "ethnicity" to describe the contemporary assumptions of a shared kinship or remembered heritage based on a person's ancestral place of origin. Neither the modern terms "race" and "ethnicity," nor the early nineteenth-century attitudes I attempt to convey with these terms were mutually exclusive, thus making precise differentiation difficult. Much overlap existed between both the concepts and their categorization. In some instances, certain people of African or European descent in the early nineteenth century were described as distinct and classified into categories more similar to what today would be considered an ethnic group, whereas at other times their distinctiveness extended from being nonwhite or nonblack, a particular social and legal distinction of the United States. In other cases, a group that might be spoken of as an ethnicity today, the Irish for example, was assigned traits more closely resembling the modern concept of race.[6]

Because of the fluid yet solidifying meaning of ethnic, racial, and national group membership during the early republic and antebellum eras, these categories must be studied as ephemeral units always moving toward reassignment, a contentious reassignment simultaneously pursued by self and society. According to Dale Knobel in his study *Paddy and the Republic*, scholars of early America should treat ethnic groups in the United States "as perceptual categories, with undoubted roots in linguistic, cultural, and ancestral consistencies, but perpetuated when populations set boundaries around themselves meant to define who belongs and who does not. Looked at this way, 'ethnicity' has a verbal as well as nominative quality; it is a process of giving identity to other and thereby to self." Clarifying the murky edges of one's self-perception in a multifarious world meant naming others to better recognize where oneself belonged. As a result, the self and other were designated different as part of the same process.[7]

Because of this situation, many Europeans on their arrival in the United States made the transition, sometimes simultaneously with becoming an ethnic group, into racial whiteness.[8] This membership reorientation occurred through choices about self but also through decisions made by others, both prior to and during the immigrants' transition into their new home. At the same time, separate African ethnicities were increasingly unified into a racial blackness in early America, at least as defined against whiteness. Yet this African Americanness seemed to incorporate the prior African ethnic groups within its definition without destroying outright other Old World identities within this shaping racial category, especially not according to the group members themselves. Examples from New Orleans's Congo Square, advertisements for slave sales, early American popular music, slave and free black narratives, as well as incidental commentary on slave life and culture in the United States— all reveal a recognition among Americans, black, white, slave, and free, that a connection with one's particular homeland somewhere within the African continent was never completely subsumed by racial blackness despite the legal system of racial slavery one was forced into. Although this movement toward homogenized racial blackness and whiteness had been ongoing within the context of American colonization, it was in no way settled as containing agreed-upon concepts of categorization by all members of either racial group in all parts of the United States. These categories remained in flux during the early republic and antebellum eras, and were reconsidered when new groups arrived in need of assignation by others already present.[9]

Because a person's ethnic identity was shaped not only by self but also by other, many ethnic groups were unique American creations. This was largely true of "Germanness." Germans in America largely became German only on their arrival. Their regional, religious, and other components of identity that may have separated them in Europe were enveloped in America by non-Germans who grouped all German speakers under the common nomenclature. As such, according to Steven Nolt, a historian of the Pennsylvania Germans in the early republic, "creating an ethnic identity and becoming American" were "integrally related processes," a progression that could also be described as "ethnicization-as-Americanization." In this example, language, instead of continental heritage, seemed to have been the assumed ingredient necessary for group cohesion by outside labelers. German speakers, on the other hand, often felt little kinship with these other "Germans" beyond their shared language, hardly enough, they thought, to create a shared community of affiliation in the United States. Interestingly, within some German American communities, the decision to learn and speak English divided the German American population into factions of traitors to, versus conservators of, their homeland culture. This instance highlights the difficulty of discussing ethnic identities and communities in the early nineteenth-century United States: Who gets to choose the boundaries and labels of a group?[10]

The difficulty in studying how early Americans compartmentalized people into categories of ascription is compounded by diverse regional experiences. Hence, the process of organizing one's world changed not only over time and was dependent not only on the newly arriving people who "needed" to be assigned but also on the place where such events were transpiring. It is well known that racial and ethnic categorization within what would become the United States happened differently than in other areas of North, Central, and South America. This was largely the result of different assumptions within the Spanish, Portuguese, French, and British colonial enterprises and homeland cultures.[11] However, it has been less well studied to what extent ethnic and racial categorization occurred uniquely within distinct regions in what would eventually become parts of the United States, despite the varied colonial heritages that made up the nation. Such influencing factors created discrepancies within any concept of race or ethnicity according to time, place, and people, thus making precise definitions of these conceptual categories difficult in the context of early America. This book, however limited, attempts to contribute to the understanding of ethnic and racial categorization by a case study of one particular region, the lower Mississippi River Valley, through studying a source base consisting of the printed works of and about music in the early nineteenth-century United States.

Sounds American is about how Americans, whether they *called* themselves Hanoverian, German, American, Congo, free people of color, white, or several of these simultaneously, thought about themselves in relationship to the diverse and changing others surrounding them within the United States—but only incidentally. This book makes no attempt to describe all of the various self-conscious group identities swirling in and out of existence during the early nineteenth century. Rather, my ultimate goal is to explore how individuals, of whatever heritage or identity, considered those who were not like themselves culturally, whatever that might mean to them. Who became an outsider within the spoken and written language of a self-identified cultural group attempting to define itself within a new and changing environment? How did this process of creating the other in order to better define the self proceed? What does this process of categorizing difference, as opposed to self-conscious attempts to define or express self, tell us subliminally about the self that is doing the defining, as well as the nation within which these opinions are being formed? And, how do these individual attempts at inclusion and exclusion relate to those attempting simultaneously to define while creating an "American"?

Because of the understanding of music's relationship with a people, even if some people defined this relationship differently than others, and because creating and recognizing the distinctiveness of this new nation's character was of particular concern, an examination of how commentators wrote about the music culture reveals inherent assumptions regarding the perception of diversity in America. In this way, a close reading of the print culture considering music in America, even that not explicitly calling for a national music culture, reveals a general concern with the diverse cultural components within the national music culture, and the nation as a whole.

The multitude of musical traditions within the United States remained a dilemma for cultural commentators throughout the early republic and antebellum eras, because these men and women assumed a need for a unified national culture. Diversity within American culture presented a problem to them, since the extant music ways within the nation, including those styles most popular and most lauded, already seemed to be the cultural possessions of someone else. According to the literary theorist Sacvan Bercovitch, "The open-ended inclusiveness of the United States was directly proportionate to America's capacity to incorporate *and exclude,* and more precisely to incorporate by exclusion. The culture seemed indefinite, infinitely processual, because as America it closed everything else out as being Old World and/or not-yet-America." Hence, these ethnically, racially, or nationally identifiable musical forms were removed from the potential of being adequately available as part of a self-conscious American music.[12] The early American nationalists' quest to identify available cultural forms, which could augment the American national culture, is one reason for the obsessive categorization of music ways with racial, ethnic, or national markers. By clearly identifying the German, African, or Irish components of the music culture within the United States, those aspects available to advance an American national culture, considered by necessity as not German, African, or Irish, became known. Because the reality of the American musical *experience* was mostly one of musical pluralism and not cultural nationalism, identifying uniquely American music ways to support a distinctive American culture, as a way to create the necessary cultural unity in an emerging nation of great diversity, remained a nagging and unresolved question for some people during the early national and antebellum eras.

While commentators called for a national music culture, and while nativists worked toward a particularly virulent form of Americanization, the diverse American populace negotiated its way through the varied cultural traditions within different locales throughout the United States in a more benign and often unconscious fashion. While doing so, many people attempted to solidify the fluid boundaries of ethnic, racial, and national identity within the country—although for a different purpose. Americans of all backgrounds pursued techniques to alleviate the disorienting anxiety of an identity crisis induced by the desire yet inability to differentiate the culture of other from the culture of self. By consistently arranging their world into discrete categories of distinctiveness as a way to make sense of the surrounding diversity, assorted Americans participated in an experience shared by others throughout the nation. As such, and somewhat ironically, the experience of categorizing difference became a unifying national phenomenon.[13]

This consistent labeling of cultural forms resulted in the emergence of what I have termed "ethnic music genres" within American music culture. These genres were neither ancient, unchanged cultural forms transplanted into new soil, nor wholly new inventions of this peculiar

American environment. Rather, an adjusted cultural product emerged through the repeated performance and consumption of an ethnically *labeled* musical commodity in the United States. The creation and consumption of ethnic music genres could simultaneously serve multiple and different uses depending on the situation, the propagator, and the consumer of the musical form. The music culture of early America allowed for a consideration of diversity and its threat to national unity, as well as the means to neutralize this threat, through the creation and consumption of ethnic music genres.

This is not a study of the resulting musical product but rather how and why these ethnic music genres were created and the meanings we can extract from this early American cultural habit. Throughout these discussions of ethnic and national music culture and their interactions with each other, it is important to remember Lawrence Levine's admonition that "culture is a process, not a fixed condition; it is the product of unremitting interaction between the past and present."[14] Hence, defining what this music culture was outside of individual moments is nearly impossible; explaining how early Americans perceived and gave meaning to or through their music ways is a more realistic goal. As a result, particular instances of distinct music ways in the United States are chosen for this study as representative of trends within early American culture and should be seen more as illustrative rather than as comprehensive.

This is also why I make no attempt to trace particular musical forms back to their Old World antecedents through various American expressions. Although such a musical ethnography would be interesting and useful, this book is concerned with how people used and gave meaning to and through traditions different from their own—not how traditions changed from Old World to New World or within a diverse regional context. Because my argument pivots on *perceptions* of difference within the United States, and because the accurately understood details of someone else's unfamiliar music and dance styles (the minutiae of ethnographic data) made no difference to most people in early America, such an exploration is not included in this work. A recognition by the reader of the distinction between *perceptions* of ethnicity by outsiders to a tradition and *actual expressions* by members of a particular cultural group is necessary to fully grasp the strand of early American cultural development this book attempts to unravel.

Such explicit concern with identifying ethnic or racial cultural components versus specifically American traits consistently influenced how people considered music in the early United States. Ethnic, racial, and national labels were attached to a wide variety of musical ways in this country, reflecting the contemporary perception of a music way's linkage with a particular group of people.[15] But, not only did these words represent the attitudes of those doing the defining (whether the definer be of a group or outside the group); this language also shaped the attitudes of others exposed to the categorization. The way people spoke, wrote, performed, experienced, and used these music genres reveals a strategy employed to alleviate concern with diversity. Thus, the creation of ethnic genres within the American music culture allowed for a practical way to consider the various and clearly identified cultural groups through exposure to what was *perceived* to be their music ways. At times, this technique might facilitate a safe way to incorporate the foreign into American culture, whereas in other instances it might clearly relegate a people to the status of outsider. Although ethnic music genres *could* allow a fractured nation to deal with difference, not everyone was interested in mediating cultural diversity. This book, however, is a study of the creation of an *available* option for dealing with difference in early America, an especially popular option once ethnic music genres became widespread commodities. This process of creating an American culture while navigating among diversity brought some people in while keeping others out.[16] In either instance, however, the varied American populace was dealing with the diversity surrounding it.

Through the way merchants sold sheet music, music teachers advertised, editors described performances, and many other examples, an attempt to label the unfamiliar in their midst, but also an appeal of this perceived foreignness, emerges. Simultaneous with other responses to the threat diversity posed to national unity, such as nativist rhetoric and the calls for cultural nationalism based on a separation from European ways, existed a "relish for these others."[17] Part of this appeal of foreignness arose out of the desire to understand, or at least neutralize, the difference encountered in one's daily existence. By consuming an ethnic music genre, such as witnessing a performance or purchasing sheet music, the outsider could potentially be made less threatening, better understood, and more available for national membership. In order for this technique to work, an ethnic music genre had to believably represent, although not actually express, the people under consideration. These ethnic music genres were merely "ethnic enough" in their presentation to allow them to appear adequately as a specific culture's product, yet remain available for consumption by members not of the identifiable in-group. So, although an ethnic music way could become an ethnic music genre by outsiders witnessing a public performance of a clearly defined ethnic, racial, or national group and then attaching a corresponding label of identification (think "Irish" jig, "African" chant, or "American" hymn), in fact, through clever marketing, the designating label was all that was actually required. As a result of categorizing the music culture into consumable ethnic genres, Americans found a way to deal with the perceived threat diversity caused to the new nation searching for its own national culture and identity, as well as a way to help define the self in relation to others and the nation. By consuming musical difference, it became more familiar.

The ability of the music culture to exist as a space for ethnic, national, and racial contentiousness and familiarization was possible only because of music's central place in the lives of all early Americans. Music is one of the most democratic of all art forms and is thought to have been made by all human cultures regardless of time or place. No additional tools outside the human body are necessary to create music, making musical expression an available option to anyone. Regarding early American culture specifically, it appears that music infiltrated all aspects of people's lives. From domestic, political, religious, military, and social gatherings, few were complete moments of community without the use of some form of music. Without this loyalty to music as an art form, and without music existing as an expression available to everyone, its significance as a cultural space through which we can study incidental human interaction would not be possible.[18]

This situation, whereby consuming musical difference could increase familiarity, is similar to that from the early American stage. According to the theater historian Jeffrey H. Richards, in the early nineteenth century, ethnicity became a theatrical concept where "the labels Islamic or Irish or Indian or African have little to do with the living beings who claim those identities and more with previous and necessarily distorted representations on stage." Ethnicity was no longer attached only to real people but could become a caricature of itself. An ethnic "type" took on a life of its own, as it was constantly re-created on the stage. Because of this, "ethnic discourse allows the stage to speak of anxieties," especially "anxiety over heterogeneity in America." I suggest that, as in the theater, ethnicity took on a similar role as signifier in the music culture. Signifying difference in the music culture through defining difference from self, as the ethnic "types" of the stage did, could also help people deal with the stresses posed by diversity.[19]

This book examines the ways diversity threatened national unity, the resulting techniques used to mitigate such concerns, and the incidental ways individuals navigated within heterogeneity, through a case study of the region of the lower Mississippi River Valley. From the Louisiana Purchase until the outbreak of the Civil War, the inhabitants living in and between St. Louis, Missouri, and New Orleans, Louisiana, experienced frequent waves of newcomers. Into an already mixed population of Native Americans had arrived various Europeans, Africans, and their North American descendants before the United States gained political authority over the region. Throughout the early decades of the nineteenth century an influx of Americans and their slaves arrived from the East, as did refugees from the Caribbean, Native Americans fleeing disruptions elsewhere, and new and increasing numbers of Europeans, especially French, Germans, and Irish. Local residents, newcomers, and travelers consistently commented on this changing regional diversity. The perception of this region as being one of an especially diverse population during the years of increasing political control by the United States government has been well documented in both the historical narrative and modern scholarly accounts. One Philadelphia author summed up this concern with the region's peculiar diversity in his commentary on New Orleans, which he made soon after the Louisiana Purchase, as debates surrounding its incorporation flustered Congress:

> In all societies where a number of people from different countries have met together, every one will naturally persevere in those habits to which he has been accustomed in his own country; and though a promiscuous intercourse may induce many men to relax a little, yet it will be long before they form a general character. The residents here are English, Irish, Scots, American, French and Spanish. . . . The characteristics of these nations are nearly the same as in the mother-country, though somewhat altered by that natural progress of assimilation already hinted at. The climate too may have some influence.

Because this region was believed to be especially diverse during the decades of its increasing connection to the political entity of the United States, the issues of creating a unified national culture and the potential problems diversity could cause with the national experiment intersect in the writings about this place.[20]

Many of these accounts, both by historical actors and historians, have emphasized the diverse population of the lower Mississippi, and especially the city of New Orleans, as making the region unique, and as a way to contrast it with what were considered more homogeneous and more American experiences elsewhere. Despite this, however, most of the traits used to portray this region's distinctiveness were shared by many other places, as they too became more securely attached to the larger nation politically.[21] So, although the lower Mississippi River Valley embodied regional exceptionalism, its experience was simultaneously a quintessentially American one. For example, many other places that eventually became part of the United States in the post-Revolution years lacked an English colonial past, housed a varied and changing population prior to and during political incorporation into the United States, and experienced large migrating American (both free and slave) and immigrant waves. In these ways, the experiences of the population of the lower Mississippi River Valley between 1800 and 1860, in fact, reveal some fundamental experiences shared with other American places, such as how to deal with a changing and diverse population, while navigating the evolving relationship between the region and the nation. An example from San Antonio highlights one particular shared experience between the lower Mississippi River Valley and another place becoming politically American around the same era.

In 1849, as part of a forceful attack against Mexican culture, the San Antonio City Council outlawed the fandango. The fandango was a type of dance but also the term for the celebration surrounding the dance. Fandangos were family outings, places for courtship, but also scenes of vice and murder, prompting Mayor James M. Devine to declare the outlawing of fandangos to be the most important action taken by the city in that year. It was the first ordinance in a long line of others clearly attacking Mexican culture, and an important component in understanding later ethnic violence in the region and the Cart War that followed. In this example, like others this book will explore from the lower Mississippi, concerns surrounding the process and degree of regional attachment to the nation, especially in areas of great diversity and insecure national affiliation, could find expression within the music culture. Although this study does not attempt any comparison between the lower Mississippi and any other region, it assumes that many traits put forth to prove regional distinctiveness were actually shared with other places as they too became part of the United States.[22] The regional residents' methods for coping with changing ethnic and racial diversity, as examined in this book, reveal more about what made this place distinctively American, rather than peculiarly regional. Ironically, then, the language

contemporary commentators used to delineate particular ethnic components within the regional music culture, in an attempt to emphasize local
distinctiveness, is the perfect lens through which to examine nationwide
concerns with diversity, even if the changing diversity in other regions
was of a different composition. Using this region as a case study sheds
light on the regional experience of a national culture in formation.

This book also attempts to speak to the particulars within one strand
of cultural development within a limited geographic region in order to
make some larger generalizations about the process of culture within the
early United States. One way observers from the earliest colonial era to
the present day have tried to understand and explain the development
of uniquely American regionalisms has been with the concept of creolization. Creolization, to scholars today, refers to the process of creating
something new out of previously distinct entities. It is often applied in
cultural studies when distinct people encountered each other, often in a
new environment, and reacted to this difference by changing their own
assumptions, expressions, or practices to fit the new surroundings they
found themselves in. Detailing the particulars of the process of creolization is the way historians and others who use this theoretical framework
show how the various old worlds became something new in the Americas.
According to early American historian Richard Cullen Rath, creolization works by "forming a 'native' identity in a situation where there is no
natal society." Children who are born into such a society, then "take an
unstable polyglot cultural inheritance and create stable creole identities
from it." This book attempts to contribute to the details of creolization
in the Americas through the study of one particular cultural strategy—
the creation and consumption of ethnic music genres—through which
something new, although not necessarily something unified or unifying,
was created out of previously old ways.[23]

The term "creole" itself has had a contentious and changing history.
Originally the word seems to have been used to comment on the degeneracy that living beings experienced as they left their old world and
began to inhabit a new world in the Americas. I use the term "creole" to
mean native to the region, with qualifiers attached as necessary, because
this seems to be how early nineteenth-century Louisianians used this
term, as well as the definition modern scholars employ. Eventually, some
people in the region began to self-identify as Creole—a self-conscious
group whose members considered themselves to have a shared history
and culture that made them unique. The term "creole," whether used
by scholars or historical writers, necessarily creates a dichotomy tied to

place; by defining or describing a person or thing to be the local of a region, this assumes that this same person or thing would have been different had they become local to somewhere else. As a result then, I am attempting to place this cultural study in the framework of what made the lower Mississippi River Valley different and new: How did creolization proceed in the lower Mississippi River Valley during the early nineteenth century? This different and new could be in comparison to the places the new local inhabitants previously called home or in contrast to other American regions.[24]

The growing nation, as seen through a study of the music culture of the lower Mississippi River Valley, came to terms with its changing population by continuously questioning and redefining assumptions of what exactly American culture was and should be. Interactions with unfamiliar people and their ways had the potential to create a sense of nationhood, through the shared experience of making sense of and tempering that which was previously unfamiliar and potentially dangerous. Because this region was especially diverse and because music culture can be used as a lens through which to understand contemporary perceptions of ethnicity, race, and nationality the music culture of the lower Mississippi River Valley is an especially productive subject to examine. *Sounds American* looks at one particular place, the lower Mississippi River Valley, and one particular aspect, the music culture, to uncover how deeply embedded concerns of ethnic and racial diversity were to the American experience during the early nineteenth century.

Because music could signify ethnicity, ethnic tensions as well as encounters could be expressed in the music culture. In one particular example, the War of the Quadrilles, the overarching and divisive issues of political control and cultural ways collided on the ballroom floors of New Orleans during the transfer of Louisiana to the United States. Such tensions within the local music culture reveal the power of music to represent ethnic and national identity to the varied regional population. But the War of the Quadrilles and its echoes, which reverberated throughout the era, also remind us of the potential the music culture embodied. The regional music culture could also serve as a conduit through which the foreigner might be made familiar, no matter who was defining the other as such. Such potent musical identity extended outside of the ballrooms and into theaters, churches, benevolent societies, militia companies, music stores, print culture, and other public spaces. Here, music remained attached through language and performance to an ethnic, national, or racial group.

Although ethnically and racially specific gatherings served a particular purpose to members of the in-group, they served an important function to the group's nonmembers as well. These ethnically defined public music performances, combined with the overrepresentation of the foreign-born and racial outsiders within the regional music culture, reinforced the connection between music and a particular cultural tradition.[25] As one's encounter with music was commonly conducted by someone with an ethnic marker attached to them, or through a commodity classified with an ethnic or racial label, music increasingly held the potential to signify race and ethnicity to the regional population. Although a music way might retain the attachment of an ethnic taxonomy, this did not mean it continued to be a possession solely of the group whose name remained affixed, or even to have emerged from their distinctive cultural tradition. Instead, repeated public performance, commodification, and labeling created ethnic genres available for consumption by all.

Because so many music ways existed in the region, ethnic labels became descriptive delineators rather than boundary markers. These genres could serve as integrating mechanisms for outsiders to any given musical tradition, or as mediators between a particular music way and the larger national culture. In order for this to occur successfully, ethnic genres had to adequately, although not necessarily accurately, portray ethnic authenticity to the consumer. And, the musical expression had to occur either publicly or in print in order for witnesses to imbibe this difference. The way the regional population bounded its music culture into discrete ethnic, racial, and national entities, reveals a concern with diversity, and an attempt to make sense of the unfamiliar in its midst. The appeal of ethnically and racially labeled music ways came from people's ability to transform the strange into the familiar, even if done unconsciously and without breaking down all barriers of difference. By consuming the dissimilar, the unknown became part of one's repertoire of understanding. This process of naming others simultaneously created a self-identity and unconsciously succeeded in doing what the American nationalist commentators had been calling to accomplish—creating an American culture out of the shared experience with diversity.[26]

1 /   Insecurity and Nationalism: The Call to Create a Unified American Music Culture

Great is the power of music over a people! As for us in America, we have long enough followed obedient and child-like in the track of the Old World. We have received her tenors and her buffos, her operatic troupes and her vocalists of all grades and complexions; listened to and applauded the songs made for a different state of society.
WALT WHITMAN, "ART-SINGING AND HEART-SINGING"

Insecurity pervaded the new American nation. According to late eighteenth- and early nineteenth-century cultural commentators, America's lack of a unified national culture potentially threatened the success of the republican experiment. As a result, many American writers called explicitly for the identification, creation, and support of a national culture to unify, solidify, and legitimize the young republic. The diverse ethnic and racial groups within the United States, with their attached cultural forms, posed an especially potent threat to the unity cultural critics assumed necessary to a successful national culture. To alleviate this danger, writers explicitly called for an American culture by defining what it was not, and consistently labeled cultural forms with an attached national, ethnic, or racial marker. Because these commentators specifically considered music ways as intimately connected to a particular group, the music culture provides a particularly useful lens through which to study the perceived threat diversity posed to a national culture in formation. Through their calls to create an American national music culture, commentators reveal their assumption that a unique and unified American national culture was integral to the success of the nation. Implicit within their language exists the danger diversity posed to this task, as seen in their hyperawareness of ethnic and racial difference within the music culture. Also implied is the belief that a cultural group can be represented or signified through a particular musical way, as the writers neatly compartmentalized each musical form into a space clearly labeled as not-American. A deep reading of American music commentators from the early nineteenth century also reveals their certainty that a precise relationship existed between a people and its music.

The intellectual elite of the early republic remained focused on preserving the political, economic, and social stability needed to retain independence within a disparate young nation. In an attempt to alleviate the anxiety caused by the nation's uncertain future, a general call resounded throughout the nation to reject European, especially British, culture in order to support and rationalize a politically independent America; yet the appreciation for and habit of European ways proved hard to break.[1] Those who had not experienced the Revolution themselves, the first generation of American-born United States citizens, increasingly demanded a unique American culture. Commentators from this generation labored to define the nation in the midst of unanticipated changes, which questioned and at times threatened their self-perception as a united people. Many Americans were eager to define themselves culturally as they witnessed the founders pass away, their polity divide, immigration increase, the incorporation of new people into their nation through annexation, and the birth of new nations throughout the world whose supposedly distinctive characteristics gave them cause for existence. American intellectuals attempted to fashion the new United States with the awareness that a nation's existence should center on a people with a shared character. Their attempts to adopt, reject, and modify assorted foreign cultures, both from outside the nation but also internally, reveal the difficulty of forging a unified cultural vision.[2]

Many scholars commonly use the concept of the "other" to better understand the "self" being defined when discussing the creation of an identity.[3] Throughout the early nineteenth century, the mere act of obsessively portraying and delineating "outsiders" suggests in a broad sense the degree to which heterogeneity wracked the national subconscious and infiltrated the way some Americans struggled to define the nation. Because this "other" can attract as well as repel, European cultures became dangerously appealing to Americans at the very moment they were in theoretical need of rejecting what was foreign. American commentators after the Revolution consistently identified themselves in negation to both real and imagined European influence.[4]

The cultural founders not only defined themselves against European traditions but also against other races, ethnicities, nationalities, religions, and regions within the nation. According to theater historian Jeffrey H. Richards, American theater culture, similar to American music culture, "struggled with the bold outlines and curious details of national, cultural, and ethnic representation to American audiences." While "early American theatre certainly registered anxiety and amusement over heterogeneity," the ethnic discourse allowed the stage to speak of these anxieties. The way these thinkers, writers, and musicians went about attempting to define their nation is in some ways more telling of their conception of America than the conclusions they drew. As they proceeded through their cultural quest to identify a unity within diversity, they consistently worked to recognize and label these diversities.[5] By doing so, commentators could better decide what was American by eliminating what was not. This often depended on a highly racialized, or "ethnicized," discourse that oscillated between assigning a savage or hypercivilized "otherness" to the nation's nonmembers. These critics defined "American" by contrasts and in doing so more clearly revealed their vision for a national identity. To paraphrase Toni Morrison, they knew they were free because they were not enslaved and civilized because they were not savage.[6] Their quest to define ethnic cultural forms also allowed them to know what could be American, if for no other reason than it was nothing else.

American intellectuals explored their nation's own cultural distinctiveness within their understanding of an ethnically ordered world. These critics reveal much about their perception of the nation, culture, and ethnicity through their calls for a unique American national culture, and more specifically a national music culture. American musical commentators during the early to mid-nineteenth century saw music as clearly connected to a people of a place, and they variously perceived its transmission as being passed through the blood, connected to environment, or inherited via education. In doing so, they never questioned the attachment of a specific music way to a distinct cultural tradition. With this understanding in mind, the influx of foreigners (slave and free), the incorporation of new territories into the nation (often full of "non-Americans"), and questions concerning regional distinctiveness in a supposedly unified nation, caused great insecurity among the hegemonic cultural elite of primarily Boston, New York, and Philadelphia during the early republic. Their various explanations as to why America lagged behind European nations in the arts led them to call for methods to ensure the future existence as well as glory of the United States. As will be seen in later chapters, Americans variously ignored and selectively adopted these prescribed methods and found their own, albeit usually less self-conscious, ways of making sense of the diverse populations among which they were members. An examination of the intellectual elites' visions for creating a distinctive national culture, and specifically a national music culture, reveals the uncertainty occasioned by the increasing diversity within the nation as these thinkers organized their world into ethnic and racial categories.

In a 1778 letter, Thomas Jefferson complained, "Music . . . is the favorite passion of my soul, and fortune has cast my lot in a country where it is in a state of deplorable barbarism." In what might seem to be a surprising demonstration of aristocratic snobbery by the father of American republicanism, he proposed importing from Italy "a band of two French horns, two clarinets, two hautboys, and a bassoon." He suspected one could do this "without enlarging their domestic expenses," considering that in a country like Italy "music is cultivated and practiced by every class of men," and one "might induce them to come here on reasonable wages." Since Jefferson already retained as servants "a gardener, a weaver, a cabinet-maker, and a stone cutter," such expense for musicians seemed quite reasonable, given his love for music.[7] Jefferson's consideration of keeping an Italian band at Monticello demonstrates the colonial elite's opinions of local musicianship even when their vision to improve this situation, as in this instance, never became a reality.

Jefferson considered importing European culture to amend his meager musical options a logical choice, at a time when the colonies were fighting to free themselves from the excesses of monarchy. He wanted access to a certain kind of music not then available in the United States, so he considered importing it. Virtually none of Jefferson's contemporaries doubted that the new nation lacked a distinctive music or culture at its inception. Educated people in revolutionary America were well aware that their arts and tastes were not distinctly their own, that they were mostly from London. Revolutionaries such as Jefferson, reminds the historian Gordon Wood, "were not obsessed, as were later generations, with the unique character of America." American culture would outshine Europe one day, the founders believed, not for its rejection of, but by building on, its British and European heritage. Yale University president Ezra Stiles even believed that in America, "all the arts may be transported from Europe and Asia and flourish . . . with an augmented luster." The only possible cause for concern arose from the belief that the arts, in the words of Benjamin Rush, would best "flourish chiefly in wealthy and luxurious countries," where church and state funding promoted elaborate mechanisms to serve elite aesthetics. Hence, cultivation of the arts in America might undermine the republican national experiment if continued in such a way. The revolutionary generation alleviated this fear by emphasizing those forms, such as neoclassicism, which claimed republican simplicity. For the generation following the Revolution, however, an option in national culture development unforeseen by the founders emerged. Fresh voices called for the nation to follow an alternate course. These commentators believed building an American culture founded on European greatness to be a futile endeavor. As Gordon Wood described it, "By 1820 Americans . . . had experienced a social and cultural transformation as great as any in American history, a transformation marked by the search for an American identity."[8] This quest took as many forms as there were seekers, although two main visions shone the brightest.

A version of the cultural ideology as expressed by the revolutionaries, where America would build on European greatness, continued throughout the early republic and antebellum eras; but soon after the Revolution, an alternate vision for the future of American national culture developed. Exponents of this new ideology drew a different conclusion from their perception of American cultural barrenness: if this experiment was to succeed, the nation needed its own *distinct* culture. Noah Webster, writing ten years after Jefferson's indictment, chided Americans for "mimicking the follies of other nations and basking in the sunshine of foreign glory. . . . Americans unshackle your minds and act like independent beings." He continued, "You have an empire to raise . . . and a national character to establish." These tensions as expressed in Jefferson's appreciation of European culture and Webster's call for a distinctive American culture continued to influence the path of American cultural development well after the nation's political existence was secured.[9]

Cultural commentators worked to create a national culture during and after the Revolution for a variety of reasons. Most obviously and perhaps most importantly, they believed a nation required a corresponding culture. Because the United States was created to fight the British, the nationalism of the early republic was based on the common revolutionary heritage and adherence to the constitution. Hence, it was extremely fragile since it did not preclude any other regional, ethnic, class, economic, or political identities. Inspired by a sense of inferiority, fear their national experiment might fail, the need to unify previously distinct colonies, and a divisive political culture, the new nation's members searched for what they perceived to be distinctive American traits and forms that could be encouraged as a way to solidify the nation.[10]

This quest for an American cultural identity continued well into the mid-nineteenth century when the anxieties associated with the infant republic's success became less pressing. The consistent cultural diversity within America threatened the assumption that national unity would ever happen naturally. How, then, could they create unity out of diversity? Reaction to this precarious national identity took many forms, including attempts to construct an American language, educational system, and history.[11] Although virtually all cultural commentators' belief in the need for a unified American culture never wavered, they agreed on little else. Critics echoed Jefferson and Webster in various forms and degrees throughout the decades of the early national and antebellum eras. Whereas Jefferson saw no problem with wanting to import Italian musicians for Monticello to solve the deplorable state of American music culture, the next generation of critics offered new solutions.

The first generation of Americans sounded the call for a national culture with new vigor. With the passing of the revolutionaries, Americans needed to reimagine themselves in the light of their new role as inheritors of the republican experiment. The nation was incomplete, they usually concluded. It was a work in progress; it was something to be achieved. These Americans, especially those born after the Revolution, felt a responsibility to give the fledgling country its national culture. It became their mission to give meaning to the events of the Revolution, events they had not witnessed. A spokesperson for the Virginia Library Society pondered the question many were considering: "Will such a heterogeneous body ever firmly . . . coalesce?" The New England minister Lyman Beecher echoed such concerns, noting that "the integrity of the Union demands special exertions to produce in the nation a more homogeneous character, and bind us together by firmer bonds." The first generation of Americans had a clearly defined problem. "The intensely felt need to create a union from the disparate groups that formed their country" drove their actions and infiltrated their perceptions of their nation, especially in regards to the abstract "other" who was responsible for the diversity.[12] Their coming to terms with how to create unity out of diversity resulted in a heightened recognition of the diversity surrounding them. This usually took the form of a call to reject other cultures. Yet in some instances, and to some people, an overwhelming appeal of foreign ways remained.

The common perception of Europeans toward Americans, especially regarding "whether they have any national character at all; and the common impression . . . that they have not," also drove the American quest to create a national culture. Despite what they might say, European opinions mattered to American thinkers.[13] When travelers came to America in search of the country's "national character," they often fell prey to the belief that an American would exist the same way in the United States that a Frenchman did in France. Charles Matthews, an English comedian who toured the United States in the early 1820s, complained of the difficulty of getting at the American character because "all the menial situations are filled by negroes, and Irish and Scotch. This constitutes the great difficulty in picking up anecdote, character, or anything that would be called peculiarity. . . . If I enter into a conversation with a coachman, he is Irish; if a fellow brings me a note, he is Scotch. If I call a porter, he is a negro."[14] To Matthews, being Irish, Scottish, or black eliminated one from the potential of being American and thus exhibiting American character. This situation bothered some, but other American commentators recognized that ethnic and racial diversity were key components of their national identity. William Jenks, a New England biblical scholar writing in the first years of the nineteenth century, considered American character to be "such a chaotick [sic] state of character, such a mixture of Dutch phlegm, the sanguine complexion of the Englishman, French choler and vanity, Irish rapidity, German sensibility and patient industry, Negro indifference, and Indian indolence."[15] To Jenks, ethnicity had corresponding traits, and the American character would be built on this varied foundation, for good or for ill.

This perceived lack of unified national character caused some Americans to look outside the nation for assistance in creating a national culture. By the 1820s, European travelers were very conscious of these American borrowings from other cultures and even the deliberate rejection of native products over foreign ones. The English writer Reverend Sydney Smith advised Americans to be proud of their English ancestry, since "in the four quarters of the globe, who reads an American book? Or goes to an American play? Or looks at an American picture or statue?" Alexis de Tocqueville echoed, "The literary genius of Great Britain still darts its rays into the recesses of the forests of the New World. . . . They paint with colors borrowed from foreign customs . . . before settling on the merits of one of their own writers they normally wait for England to approve his work." Henry Fearon, in his 1818 emigration guide *Sketches of America,* called this phenomenon a "voluntary national dependence." The "jealousy that is felt of foreign superiority," noted the British travel writer James Buckingham, caused the love/hate relationship with foreign arts.[16]

Americans themselves frequently held similar disparaging beliefs on the comparable lack of success of American cultural forms within the nation. Although even the optimistic encouragement of American cultural development often held latent criticisms, anxieties, and insecurities, American writers typically tempered the voracity of such complaints with the belief that they were not on par with Europe *as of yet*, but would certainly achieve this goal in the future. In an 1856 speech given at the dedication of a statue of Beethoven at the Boston Music Hall, William W. Story predicted that "perhaps, too, the time will come when it will be the boast of a European nation that they can prove that some of their blood is in us, and shows itself in our character." A toast published in the *Vicksburg Daily Sentinel* went as far as recommending "Emulation in the Arts and Sciences: The sure road to national prosperity," during an 1838 celebration of American independence.[17] One stanza from a poem printed in the *Knickerbocker*, a New York monthly magazine, exemplifies the pride in American potential tempered by a realistic acceptance of the nation's current limitations:

> Bright flower among the nations?
> Wild blossom, half disclosed,
> Yet fairer in thy opening bud,
> Than with full bloom exposed:
> The lorry of thy forests
> Can ancient realms outshine?
> The pride of Art let other boast,
> but Nature's best is thine![18]

Americans' perception of themselves as second-rate cultural producers infiltrated all forms of commentary during the early nineteenth century.

The Transcendentalist thinker Margaret Fuller echoed these sentiments in the mid-1840s when she wrote, "We look about in vain for traits as characteristic of what may be individually the character of the Nation, as we can find at a glance of Spain, England, France or Turkey. America is as yet but an European babe." Writing from Europe she continued, "Although we have an independent political existence, our position toward Europe, as to Literature and the Arts, is still that of a colony, and one feels the same joy here that is experienced by the colonist in returning to the parent home." Without condemnation, she accepted the inherited condition of American culture as natural. According to her, American visitors to Europe should not try to detach from their European past, yet they should also celebrate being born in the United States. On the "thinking American" returning home from abroad, she wrote, "He is anxious to gather and carry back with him all that will bear a new climate and new culture," and although "some will dwindle; others will attain a bloom and stature unknown before."[19] Her vision of incorporating worthy European ways into American culture seemed appropriate among many of her contemporaries as well.

Other thinkers were more cautious regarding the role of European cultural forms in America. Ralph Waldo Emerson speculated on the necessity of creating an American national culture in his *American Scholar Address* considered America's "Declaration of Cultural Independence." He stated, "Our day of dependence, our long apprenticeship to the learning of other lands, draws to a close. The millions that around us are rushing into life, cannot always be fed on the sere remains of foreign harvests. Events, actions arise, that must be sung, that will sing themselves. . . . This revolution is to be wrought by the gradual domestication of the idea of Culture." His essay *Nature* further called for a uniquely American culture. For these "new lands, new men, new thoughts," he summoned Americans to "demand our own works and laws and worship." Yet even he qualified his hopeful proclamations of America's future possible greatness by the recognition of the "moribund . . . arts in America." In Emerson's writing, the nod to European greatness never disappeared: "We are living in an age of revolution when the old and new stand side by side and are compared. The historic glories of the old (what America lacks) are compensated by the rich possibilities of the new era." His phrase "what America lacks" lurked within the critical commentary of American culture throughout the first half of the nineteenth century.[20]

Even Americans intent on creating their own culture found it difficult to completely disentangle themselves from Europe and stop measuring themselves by a European yardstick, especially with the constant influx of new immigrants. The early American writer Charles Jared Ingersoll explained, "A people so lately sprung from Europe, so closely connected with it, and so much younger in the annals of civilization, naturally adopts European customs." The continued contact between the new nation and Europe, he believed, meant that full cultural separation never occurred. The Boston minister Ezra S. Gannett reminded his flock that "the arrival of a steamship every fortnight at our doors, freighted with the influences which the Old World is no less eager to send than we are to receive, must increase the danger of our losing independence, as well as our neglecting to cultivate originality of character." When the first transatlantic steamboat arrived in the United States in 1838, the journalist N. P. Willis betrayed his skepticism that Americans could retain any of their distinctive identity with the perceived upcoming onslaught of exchange when he caustically remarked, "Farewell nationality!"[21] The constant contact between the two hemispheres prevented adequate isolation thought necessary for cultural separation.

The perceived lack of a national history also haunted the young nation during a time when a people's alleged antiquity proved national legitimacy. Through their comparison with Europe, American cultural commentators recognized the "ancient" European peasant folk cultures, used as rallying cries around national sentiments, to be lacking within their nation. Although American literary culture began to come of age in the late 1830s, with the likes of Poe, Emerson, Hawthorne, Thoreau, Whitman, Fuller, and Melville, as late as 1860 in his preface to *The Marble Faun*, Nathaniel Hawthorne complained, "No author, without a trial, can conceive of the difficulty of writing a Romance about a country where there is no shadow, no antiquity." Ironically poised on the eve of a conflict that would inspire much future "romance," even after eighty years of nationhood and three successful national wars, Hawthorne still saw no subjects adequately inspiring in their age. In an 1838 article titled "American Antiquities," a *Vicksburg Daily Sentinel* writer lamented, "Memory furnishes a key to almost every thing which belongs to the Eastern nations, but in America our history extends back but to yesterday." Because the imagining of a shared heritage seemed necessary to those striving for a national culture, a "fabrication of authenticity" often resulted, fulfilling the ideological need for purity and homogeneity of race and ethnicity. Although emerging nations commonly used this concept, it became especially pertinent among former colonies who perceived their comparative youth and borrowed culture as legitimate disadvantages.[22]

Americans continued to turn to Europe after their nation's birth, in a way familiar to scholars of postcolonialism, because early Americans had been schooled to appreciate European taste. "It is this colonial spirit which causes incessant struggles between an instinctive love of country and a habitual veneration for what is European," ventured one prescient American writer. Only through great effort did Americans move toward creating a national taste. Despite the findings of Lawrence Levine that the cultural elites, by the late nineteenth century, had "sacralized" certain culture forms, effectively removing them from the aesthetic reaches of the masses, this never appeared as their intention, at least before the Civil War. Rather, cultural commentators, no matter what their disposition toward European forms, unanimously proposed elevating the taste of the masses so they might better experience forms already within their hearing. The frustration arose when trying to create an American taste to patronize American artists while simultaneously trying to create the American artists.[23]

Attempts to create distinctively American cultural expressions took many forms. The artists of the Hudson River School endeavored to express the grandeur of America through their landscape painting in visual expressions of nationalism. These painters, like American literary nationalists, considered the wild forces of America's untamed environment to be the antithesis of Europe. Hence, their works, based on uniquely "uncivilized" American subjects, differed from the serene pastoral scenes in much contemporary European art. The novelists Washington Irving and then James Fenimore Cooper also tried to express themselves in a distinctly American way by evoking themes of the American wilderness. Similarly, Walt Whitman's poetry celebrated the uniquely American style of democracy and individualism. His *Leaves of Grass*, first published in 1855, culminated to some degree, the antebellum obsession with proving artistic legitimacy and expression in a distinctively American way. His preface to the first edition articulated the assumption that his poetry emerged distinctively from American society when he wrote, "The proof of a poet is that his country absorbs him as affectionately as he absorbs it."[24]

Knowledge of these early American artistic expressions of nationalism, as well as the surrounding cultural criticism and encouragement, did reach many Americans. Aesthetic theory in America mostly appeared in periodicals and newspapers, making it available for the "literate many" rather than the "learned few." Newspapers reprinted the frequent journal articles dealing with the relationship of aesthetics, culture, and the nation, and featured reviews of both national and local cultural events. One article even parodied the flamboyant language common in many reviews, implying that at least the language, if not the content, of cultural commentators had reached a general audience.[25] The potency of the critics' opinions increased as the cultural debates reached more Americans across the nation.

Of the cultural ways these writers critiqued and promoted, the need for a distinctively American music culture garnered much of their attention. Those who debated Walt Whitman's opinion that "hardly anything which comes to us from the music and songs of the Old World, is strictly good and fitting to our nation," varied widely over exactly what American music should sound like. Yet all agreed that the United States needed to either develop or discover a nationally specific music. To antebellum

Americans, national affiliation was more about self-identification rather than a chance of fate. As a result, they were able to debate openly the meaning of a people's music in relation to their essence as a people.[26]

Throughout their calls for an American music culture, critics reveal visions of music discretely tied to ethnicity and their own understanding of the nature of national identity by defining themselves against what they were not and that which seemed more obviously known.[27] It became easier to create an American music not French, German, or Chinese, if the traits of French, German, or Chinese music were clearly delineated. The way commentators went about explaining the music of the "other" to themselves, and how they called for and attempted to define their own music culture, reveals the degree to which the concept of ethnicity infiltrated their understanding of a unified American nation. This cultural organizing was important for them to do as they tried to forge unity out of diversity and create an American national music culture.

At the beginning of the nineteenth century, virtually no Americans would have considered the nation as having its own music culture, just as few would have considered that the nation had its own culture in a general sense of the word. The *Monthly Register and Review of the United States* advertised in an 1806 Louisiana newspaper that they would "give some of our pages to music . . . with occasional reviews taken from the most approved authorities, of the best new musical pieces which shall be published in Europe." They did not mention reviewing American music because few would have assumed any existed. This attitude continued throughout the antebellum era. "We are not yet a musical people, and the art labors under peculiar disadvantages from our institutions, habits, manners of living, and prejudices," reflected one Boston music editor. Another writer echoed, "It may sound strangely at first, but it is an indisputable truth, that music, as an art, does not exist in this country; that is among Americans."[28] Walt Whitman, during his work as a journalist in the late 1830s and 1840s, decried this situation, challenging Americans to step forward and make their own music. "We have long enough followed obedient and child-like in the track of the Old World," he wrote; "we have received her tenors and her buffos, her operatic troupes and her vocalists of all grades and complexions; listened to and applauded the songs made for a different state of society." In an attempt to describe how Americans might find their own national music, one reviewer speculated, "Wherever the passion for music is so inwrought into the character of a people, that all their most sacred and controlling sentiments are expressed in song, there and only there purely national music springs up."[29] The assumptions in such comments divulge the contemporary notions that a nation needed a distinct character essential to ensuring its legitimacy, and that music both reflected and encouraged this national character development. Such premises generated the debate over the creation of an American music culture that vacillated between acceptance and rejection of European music.

During the first half of the nineteenth century, commentators proposed many reasons why the United States lacked a musical culture. Some blamed the call to discard all things European immediately after the American Revolution for hindering the nation's musical development, as they had for retarding the progression of other American cultural forms. After the American Revolution, "there was a general disposition to dispense, as far as possible, with foreign fabrics and inventions," recalled the editor of the *Musical Magazine*. This had advantages for the republican experiment, he recognized, and "was very consonant with national pride and the love of independence in an infant republic"; but it also had its disadvantages. The rejection of foreign music was so strong, "it grew . . . almost to a mania which threatened the total vitiation of taste." Others concurred with such sentiments. In his 1822 dissertation, Thomas Hastings, the American composer and author of the first extensive treatise of musical taste prepared in the United States, described a need for "the revival of the art in this country" as if it had been lost but previously known. Was the Revolution responsible for this, he wondered? Some children of the revolutionary generation remembered the rejection of things European as having stifled American cultural development so much that one American editor went so far as to remark, in his article titled "National Music," that "we have no national music."[30] This seemed problematic not because of any lack of music but because the music within the nation always seemed to belong to someone else whom they considered not American.

The nation's diverse population also caused many to believe that the United States would struggle to find a national music. "It would be highly unreasonable to look for any music in our own country, which deserves to be called national," remarked the editor of the *American Quarterly Review*. "The population is heterogeneous, and ages must elapse, before the discriminating lines can be obliterated." Considering the contemporary understanding of national music being intricately connected to ethnicity, in a nation full of immigrants, African slaves, and annexed populations, creating a sound to reflect its varied character seemed an impossible task. Because "national music is the offspring of national feeling," American lack of cultural unity "has kept us back from attaining such a treasury of song as is possessed by many inferior nations."[31] It also seemed problematic to some that most music instructors continued to be foreigners who taught in the European tradition. "Who are your professors and proficients in any branch of the art? Germans and Italians," answered one dismayed editor, as late as 1856, reiterating Jefferson's complaint some seventy-five years later.[32]

Music critics considered America's lack of antiquity detrimental to the nation's ability to create a national music culture, just as Hawthorne had with American literature. The belief that "enthusiastic outpouring of song generally happens only in the infancy and rudeness of nations," the features of which "were derived from the deep sources of national character . . . repeated from age to age," precluded the ability of the young nation to have a national music culture on par with other people.[33] This perceived absence of what might be termed a folk music tradition in the United States left the nation at a musical disadvantage. Whereas "the German tribes had been early trained to music," the United States had no "tribal history," critics thought, although occasionally some composers turned to the Native Americans as inspiration for that reason. Even if the nation had an adequate history and natural inspiration to represent in music, Americans too often created "ditties, sportive, and for a time in use, but now absolutely forgotten." An *American Quarterly Review* critic mourned, "What relics have we of the old French War? Not one. In what cherished song are the mighty achievements of the revolution embalmed? . . . Do boatmen on our mighty streams solace their weary hours by oft-repeated strains of the olden times?" Rather, Americans tended to quickly "lose the rugged but penetrating characteristics of national melody."[34]

Although this ephemeral and puerile nature of American music culture dismayed many, it inspired creative responses in others. The Polyglott Club from the Public Latin High School in Baltimore translated and published a collection of popular songs into Greek and Latin, including "Woodman, Spare That Tree!," in an interesting attempt to alleviate this perceived disadvantage American music had when competing with older traditions.[35] By doing this, they ventured to situate an American musical tradition within the context of more ancient republics and create cultural legitimacy. Critics reminded even those American musicians claiming to be working at the same level as Europeans that their music would prove its authenticity only by withstanding the test of time. "We are a nation new in music; we have barely begun to sing," reminded renowned American music critic John Sullivan Dwight in his *Journal of Music* to a "native American" musician insulted at the editor's reception of an American-composed song as having "uncommon beauty (at least for a young American)."[36] Such backhanded compliments infused most acclaim any American musician could hope to receive.

Music critics frequently suggested that music from the United States lagged behind that of Europe due to the intense American interest in making money. According to Charles Jared Ingersoll, "Poetry, music, sculpture, and painting, may yet linger in their Italian haunts. But philosophy, the sciences, and the useful arts, must establish their empire in the modern republic of letters." "All classes are here devoted to business; all are engaged in some active occupation, of a plain, practical character," lamented one author in his reflection titled "Prospects for a National Music in America." "The American character . . . is as yet chained down by our acquisitiveness, yet we confidently hope that it can be raised to a just conception of the beautiful," mourned another. "Divided between money-making and politics on the one hand, and religion . . . we have somewhat as a *people* lost the art of free, spontaneous, genial, happy life," remarked Dwight, as he encouraged Americans to further appreciate music as had the Germans of New York during their recent *Sangerfest*. He continued, "Prosperity is the bugbear tyrant whom we serve as anxious bond-slaves. . . . Your native American 'live Yankee' wastes his life rivaling a steam-engine. . . . We are the slaves of our own feverish enterprise, and of a barren theory of life." American progress occurred at the expense of national culture. "Could anything be more un-American," he wondered, than "the hearty enjoyment of simple and innocent pleasures," which included in the instance of the *Sangerfest*, singing, athletics, and drinking.[37] Critics condemned such business-minded obsessions as stifling any artistic development the nation might have inspired.

Both scholars and contemporaries viewed the predilection to import foreign music and the insecurity engendered by American-made music as something English in origin. American thinking that native music could not compete with foreign music came from their English heritage. According to one scholar, the idea that "music is not an industry that flourishes naturally in our climate; that, therefore those who want it and can afford it must have it from abroad," had been prevalent among the English since at least the eighteenth century. A good example of this is seen when the 1793 British embassy to China, in an effort to demonstrate the best of Britain, took along German musicians to play the ceremonial music.[38] Some American contemporaries extolled a similar view. One music critic remarked, "The kind of music we have termed *traditionary*, the rude, but strongly-marked airs of a romantic state of life, or the outpouring of universal enthusiasm, will never be known in America. . . . We have received nothing of this kind from England." Others speculated that America's primarily English inheritance doomed the nation with an inability to have a national music. While trying to discover "why is there no national music of England," one author wondered about his own nation: "Are we to have a national music, or are we, with all our wealth, luxury, and refinements, to be as destitute of music as England?" "In England, life is business," he continued, again comparing America's dismal musical culture to an inherited English trait, and music "is an exotic. . . . If England has little music of her own, still less has America. We are the heirs of England; if she had possessed a musical literature, it would have been equally our own. If her traditionary songs had been handed down from the days of Boadicea and Caractacus, they would now be heard along the Rocky Mountains."[39] Such remarks show, according to these commentators, not only why American music might have been lacking, and which heritages were considered available for nationalistic development, but also clearly testify to an understanding of music's implicit connection with nationality and ethnicity.

American cultural critics perceived that they did not have their own musical culture because of the rift with England during the Revolution, as well as the nation's heterogeneity, youth, predilection toward the "useful arts," and English heritage. Inherent in all these complaints was an assumed comparison with other national and ethnic ways. Critics spoke of foreign regions, if not nations, as having homogenous populations with ancient histories, appropriate mechanisms to support the art, as well as an innate predilection to appreciate music and perform it well—all things they believed the United States lacked. Would Americans have been so concerned with having their own national music culture if every other people they encountered did not have a music described as recognizable to their place and based on their shared character as a people? Or, did the constant identification of music with specific cultural traditions instigate among Americans a push to create not only a recognizable music culture but also a national character, two aspects viewed by contemporaries as part and parcel of the same thing? Although difficult to distinguish its origins, the early American understanding of "national character" included a group's musical ways. An author writing in the *North American Review* highlights this connection. On examining "the reasons why the arts have not hitherto found a genial nursery in America . . . the writer is naturally drawn into a consideration of our national character."[40] Early nineteenth-century American cultural commentators knew music as innately part of nation's "character," an amorphous categorization that variously included a combination of what today might be labeled ethnic, racial, cultural, and environmentally inspired traits. This frequently perceived lack of national character and its accompanying lack of music culture encouraged the exploration of the character of people considered non-American and a comparison with these foreign music cultures. Such contrast served as a way to bring into sharper focus the potential for the United States to develop or recognize its own cultural unity, a cultural unity integral for national advancement and a unity that could be exhibited through music ways.

The belief that foreigners were more musical, whether due to environment, education, or innate "national character," facilitated a push to educate the American populace musically, usually articulated through a comparison with European people. "In all the common district schools in Germany singing and music are taught, and every child is as much expected to read and write and perform music, as to read and write and recite any other lesson. . . . The reading of musical notation is learned even in the snow-covered huts of Iceland," noted one commentator.[41] Another reaffirmed his sentiments, "I believe that with the same opportunities America would rival Italy or Germany in music." An editor for *Dwight's Journal of Music* revealed his understanding of a music culture's ties to ethnicity in his commentary on musical education in America. While it is "common to ascribe the passion for music among the Germans to its being taught them in childhood . . . such teaching is the *effect* rather than the cause of the musical taste so generally prevalent."[42] Although music may have been teachable, this author believed, a natural predilection among some people prior to the teaching gave certain groups a musical advantage, a trait Americans perceived they lacked.

Out of the despair in the American music culture and because it was debatable if music was "a gift of nature, or rather a result of cultivation," came the proposed method of amending the nation's cultural barrenness by educating to elevate taste. This music critic believed that "the American voice is as good as either the German or the English. . . .We want two things: the general cultivation of taste, and the proper development of our musical capacities." An editor for the *North American Review* speculated in 1840, "We have nothing like national music, because we have nothing like national taste. We have not even decided a preference for any particular style. . . . We do not decide in favor of Italian music over that of Germany, or of French over that of Scotland. . . . [T]he preference is not decided enough in favor of any class or style of music, to indicate that there is here, as in France, Spain, Italy, Germany, Wales, Ireland, and Scotland, a distinctly marked national taste."[43]

According to Thomas Hastings, such glorification of the foreign further dissipated the music culture in America by allowing "illiterate pretenders too often [to] pass for men of real talents," thus encouraging a decline in taste. Being Italian or German gave instant prestige to any musician working in the United States, regardless of ability or qualifications. Touring European entertainers often retained an increased legitimacy merely for being foreign; they automatically drew larger audiences and, at times, even inflated critical acclaim. Hastings based his condemnations of this situation on the belief that taste is acquirable and that the musicians' job should be to help cultivate taste among the general population. Being duped into thinking a low-quality performance was outstanding not only made the audience seem foolish but also prevented the development of good taste among American audiences. Walt Whitman, among others, echoed Hastings's complaint. "It is astonishing how the public in America, can swallow superannuated third-rate artists from the Old World," reflected Whitman. "We have run after the pomp of European music long enough. . . . [M]ost, if blindfolded, couldn't distinguish a good amateur from French and Italian opera imports."[44] This condemnation of elevating foreign music while denigrating American musical taste shows the intricately connected contemporary understanding of ethnicity and its relationship to a cultural way.

The constant comparison with European music infiltrated a wide variety of commentary on American music. In a discussion of the practice of beating out the time during public performances, a *Musical Magazine* editor criticized American musicians by reminding that in Europe, "the practice of beating has been superseded by that of mental calculation. It may be a long while, before American musicians attain such powers." It could not have helped the national self-confidence when periodicals and newspapers consistently supported the belief regarding music that "almost all foreigners are proficients."[45] The level of musical sophistication embarrassed one writer in *Dwight's Journal of Music*, who accused American audiences of being unrefined listeners when he wrote, "A German or Italian audience always applauds in the *right place;* and [an] American as constantly in the *wrong* one." Another summed up the cause of the problem succinctly, "In Germany, everybody sings; in America, nobody. . . . [T]here is scarcely an obscure village of the Tyrol, that cannot send us a little band of singers that put all our own to shame." As late as 1856, a writer for the *North American Review* still decried, "There is something incongruous and queer in the combination of the words,—an American musician!"[46] Such denunciations from the pens of Americans toward their fellow countrymen meant to inspire cultural development, albeit often via condemnation, appeared frequently throughout the first half of the nineteenth century.

Even those who chided the mimicry of Europe and actively supported the development of a unique American music culture could not help but make a comparison between the two places, often unintentionally slighting American musical efforts. The editors of the songbook *Virginia Warbler* "thought best to include a liberal share of the strains of our native bards, who to say the least, do not fall much below their TransAtlantic contemporaries." The editor, in the first issue of the *Family Minstrel: A Music and Literary Journal,* tried to walk the line between those who rejected and those who embraced creating American music in the European tradition. He stated that "his object is, to elevate and establish, free from foreign blandishment and frippery (while he acknowledges his dependence on certain extraneous aid), the character of American Music."[47]

When calling to educate American youth in music, most commentators turned to European examples as precedent. If the United States were to have its own music culture, they believed, the nation needed to educate its youth as done in Europe. One Connecticut editor wondered "why music is not taught in our common schools as in Germany?" Often, even those musicians who stressed the unique nature and high quality of American music did little more than imitate European masters, according to some. Since many American composers were immigrants, studied abroad, or had been educated by European instructors in America, this was unremarkable. Only rarely did this competition with Europe not mean following their path. Few early nineteenth-century American composers gave thought to the issue of expressing a national culture; and those who did, never imagined it would develop outside the tradition of European Romanticism in which they had been trained. As the tone used by the writers in such periodicals exemplifies, "In comparing ourselves with Italy, Germany and other nations of Europe we have been led to reflect on our deficiencies in the cultivation of musick [*sic*]."[48] By emphasizing such deficiencies, and by paying attention only to the path they envisioned American music would proceed along, these critics missed the lively music culture developing in the nation beneath their very ears.

There existed no single vision of what this American national musical culture might sound like, only a frequently articulated belief that one was needed. Could a Bohemian immigrant who found inspiration in "the wilds of America, where the minstrelsy of nature, the songsters of the air, next to other virtuosos of the woods," as in the case of Anthony Philip Heinrich, be considered an American composer?[49] What if his *Opera Prima* included a minuet version of "Hail! Columbia" and a waltz version of "Yankee Doodle," as well as a quintet for piano and strings called "The Yankee Doodleiad"? The Norwegian violinist Ole Bull wrote compositions, "which may be claimed as American, in so far as they have this country for their birth-place, and owe their existence to the action of its scenes on the mind of the Artist," opined Margaret Fuller.[50] Ole Bull, who emigrated to the United States and helped found a community for his fellow countrymen while working to advance native American talent, took over the Academy of Music in New York in 1855 and offered a one-thousand-dollar prize for a native American opera, based on American subjects. Previously in 1813 the Philadelphia journal the *Port Folio* sponsored a contest with two one-hundred-dollar prizes for the best naval song, "in which the value of our institutions, the blessings of our condition, the peculiarities of our manners and the triumphs of our arms, could be familiarized to our ordinary amusements." Ole Bull's announcement for his competition stated, "The national history of America is rich in themes both for the poet and the musician; and it is to be hoped that this offer will bring to light the musical talent now latent in the country, which only needs a favorable opportunity for its development." Clearly, such sponsors pushed to build momentum toward an American national music. Yet, though Bull invested much time and talent into developing music in America, since many described his music as expressing distinctively Norwegian characteristics, could he be considered an American musician or playing American music, if he threw in some Yankee Doodle motifs during his concerts?[51] His contemporaries would resoundingly have answered, no. American music critics saw the United States as lacking the ethno-specific peasant folk cultures from which non-American composers, like Bull, drew inspiration for their regional, ethnic, or national sound.

This was just one of the many challenges facing those in search of a distinctive national music. Music in the United States, "to become national, must be received by the people at large," not for the wealthiest classes alone, the way it had in Europe, thought one music editor in 1840. "In America, music must be in a considerable degree popular.

That is, it must be addressed essentially to the people," as would befit a democratic republic. In 1845, Walt Whitman, on hearing the Cheneys, a family of musicians from Vermont, wrote admiringly, "For the first time we heard something in the way of American music." He appreciated that they "infuse nothing but sound American feeling in their songs." In his commentary on the New Hampshire group, the Hutchinson Family Singers, Whitman further developed his ideas, "They are nationalizing our sentiment and making us feel that Americans need not look abroad for noble deeds to celebrate, or inspired bards to commend them to the popular heart. This is precisely what we want—national melodies and if it may be . . . native performers," who are "the musical embodiment of the American character."[52] To Whitman, these performances could be considered American, because they expressed distinctively American traits through music. This rare acknowledgment of music performed in America as deserving the descriptor "national" contrasts with the recognition that many musical commentators would not consider some music made in the United States, by American-born people, on "American" themes fit to be considered national. These critics had very specific ideas of how an American national music culture should and should not sound.

During the 1850s, music critics John Sullivan Dwight and Henry Fry raised their voices in the debate that had been raging in America since its birth as a nation. Both men vocally inveighed against the lack of an American music culture, while vehemently encouraging its creation, but differed remarkably on the path to follow. Their differences reflect not just their understanding of music's relation to the nation and ethnicity, but also two separate visions within America, at times labeled Transcendentalism and Young Americanism. As music editor of Horace Greeley's *New York Tribune*, Henry Fry encouraged the development of a uniquely American musical tradition from American composers inspired by the distinctive nature of this new nation. "Until American composers shall discard their foreign liveries and found an American school," he preached, "we shall continue to be provincial in art." Fry's nemesis in this debate voiced his ideas in his own publication, *Dwight's Journal of Music*. Dwight believed such an agenda for the use of music was a prostitution of its purely spiritual nature to universally uplift all humanity. "Art soars above all narrow nationalities," Dwight declared. Music could best enlighten Americans through artists such as Handel, Mozart, and Beethoven, who had perfected expressing universal human feelings via music. These men could inspire the listener to the transcendent, he believed, not owing to their expression of a national feeling, but because of their overarching human sentiment, that extended beyond the mere human creation of the nation.[53]

Dwight's and Fry's differing philosophies of music and its relationship to culture informed their ideas on how American music should develop. Dwight believed in a universality of musical taste and that the use of American music as national music should occur only if it could perform at the transcendent level. Otherwise, encouraging American music culture would do more harm than good by allowing taste to devolve to the level of American artistic creation and eliminate any future chance of performing to the higher standards. Dwight hoped for "not an 'American system' in music, but an American new era of musical Art; a manifestation of musical genius, which would be distinguished not by narrow nationality but by the universality." He continued, "The idea of national genius, as entertained by many, is a fallacy. . . . [N]either climate, geographical lines nor naturalization papers can so modify it as to give it a distinct character in each land, or in each nation of the earth." Fry, in contrast, saw music as an expression of changing historical forces. The characters and events of each new nation would take a distinctively new form through its music, and such music "would describe the external realities of their culture." Both of these views, though not always explicitly, incorporated an understanding of music as innately attached to a people.[54]

Early nineteenth-century Americans so clearly attached a music way to a people that the perceived lack of a distinctive and unified American character fueled encouragement of a unique American music in the hopes of realizing their singular identity. Understanding this connection between music and a people's character divulges not only how American music culture was encouraged to develop but also more about perceptions of ethnicity. Various interpretations of the nature of music saw music as tied to blood, a product of the environment, a learned skill, or aspects of all three. An American music critic, possibly Fry, writing for the *National Gazette* under the name Honestus in the late 1830s, expressed this connection between a people's character and their sound. He believed that "the national music which might distinguish our country would probably accord with the sensible character of the people. It would have the piquancy of the French without its frivolity; the strength and solidity of the German without its pedantry; and the grace and passion of the Italians without its repetitions and mannerisms." Although these characteristics attached to nationalities and ethnicities as expressed in music may not have been those intended by the cultural propagators, they were nonetheless traits envisioned by some Americans as connected with various people of the world. As the theater scholar Jeffrey H. Richards notes regarding the early American stage, "Amidst a swirl of nationalities and ethnic types . . . American audiences would have seen identities so recognizable as to be unquestioned."[55] So, too, would they have heard recognizable identities.

Most frequently, the title of a work with an ethnic or national label signaled this connection between a people and their music. A belief in the distinctive characteristics of the sound of a place, enough to be recognizable as such by the American populace, emerged in most commentary labeling a song or dance as "national music." Printed music and commentary commonly spoke of songs as "national airs." A nation had songs peculiarly attached to the place and commonly sung by the people of that place. "Almost all nations, perhaps all, have national airs, by which the love of country is deepened and a national feeling is created and maintained," believed the Reverend John Todd of Philadelphia in 1840. There were "Spanish Airs," "Canadian Songs," "Irish Ballads," and "Tyrolese War Songs," among countless others. The Hungarian Orchestra preparing to tour the United States in 1852 was described as a band of "Gypsy's and most of the music they play is national . . . and full of such characteristic effects as much belonging to Hungarian music."[56] Each national style became something of a genre to the American audiences who consistently recognized that ethnic traits corresponded to a particular music when expressed through such descriptive language. Americans used this technique as a way to organize their diverse world into usable categories. By recognizing what clearly was not American, Americanness could be more easily noticed.

Not only a work's title but also its sound distinguished national music traditions. A distinct people must necessarily have a distinct sound style. "There are tones and modulations which can be produced by none but a Swiss throat," wrote an anonymous author in the *American Quarterly Review* in 1835. In an example closer to home, the traveler Christian Schultz revealed his understanding of music's relationship with a people when describing New Orleans. He wrote, "In attending to the amusements of the whites, the yellows, and the blacks, I had almost forgotten to mention the reds, who may likewise be said to have their own national music and dancing." Evidently, national music, according to Schultz, could include the conception of race. An article on Chinese and Scottish sounds from the *Family Minstrel* described music as a "species . . . natural to a people." The tie between a music and a people ran so deep in American perception that when commentators attempted to articulate a little-known style, they often included a comparison with a better-known ethnic music for a more accurate description. "All the specimens of Chinese melody which he had been able to collect . . . bore a strong resemblance to the old Scotch tunes," reported this writer in 1835. The author attempted to explain this correlation either through a common musical lineage (possibly Greek) or as being "natural to a people of simple manners" and old customs. He did not go into detail as to why other Greek-influenced "simple" and "old" nations might not exhibit similar musical styles. Another article compared Chinese music less favorably to "the Spanish seguidilla, as it is heard screeched by the muleteers in the mountain paths of Andalusia; only that while the muleteer screeches, the Chinaman howls."[57] Although neither description tells much about the music of China, Scotland, or Spain, they both strongly reveal the perception of a music way being naturally and inextricably connected to a people.

A deeper examination of the way American journalism discussed Chinese music gives further insight into the perceived connection between music and a people. "The national music of China . . . is so intimately blended with the state of society and the genius of the people," wrote one music editor. "The same sweetness and elegance, stereotypes now, but originally a deep root in their life as a race, may be seen in their poetry and music," instructed Margaret Fuller. When she first heard this music at the Chinese Museum in Boston she was "tempted to laugh, when something deeper forbade. Like their poetry, the music is of the narrowest monotony, a kind of rosary, a repetition of phrases, and, in its enthusiasm and conventional excitement, like nothing else in the heavens or on earth." This same link was implied in the notion that a certain people's sound was more meaningful to one of their own. "The beautiful and pathetic song of *Lochaber,* is known to, and admired by all who have an ear for music or a soul for poetry; but heard by a highlander in a distant land, and amid other scenes, the effect is similar to that produced on the Swiss by their national air, the *Ranz des Vaches*—it inspires a sad and earnest longing to return to the place of their nativity," described one Louisiana editor.[58] Whether an author misunderstood or appreciated a musical style unique to his or her ears, the bond between music and the character of a unique group remained.

Even when commentators attributed the natural environment to influencing a music way, they still suggested a connection with an ethnicity. A unique climate, as implied by contemporary writers, created the national character over long and undefined spans of time, which in effect created the national style. For example, a *New York Tribune* article reprinted in the *Mississippi Free Trader* lauded the Norwegian violinist Ole Bull for his "Northern imagination" and the Italian violinist Camillo Sivori for "all the warmth and delicacy and depth of the sunny poesy of the South." According to another writer, "The apathy natural to the Chinese" and "the influence of their climate" resulted in the unchanging simplicity of their music.[59] Dwight endorsed the opinion that "in Italy good voices are more the rule than in countries further north," yet even "in the most disagreeable climates of Europe—save Russia—some of the greatest voices have been produced." He made this argument to drive home the point that "it is nonsense to suppose that in the clear fine atmosphere of America, there must necessarily be a defect in the physical organization necessary to the great design." According to those working from the belief that "climate and scenery have . . . [an] . . . effect upon national character," Americans should soon be inspired by their native environs to create their own musical tradition. Since the United States encompassed the same varieties in climate "from the shores of the Bosphorous to the Orkney Islands," the American nation had as great a chance as those of Europe to effect a national music. "American music, if it ever exists in the true sense of the word, must be as varied as copious, and as comprehensive, as the character of a people growing up under such widely differing influences," especially that of climate, reflected one writer.[60] Others refined this understanding, positing that "although climate and scenery may affect the character of a national music, they can neither cause nor prevent its growth. In a clear and elastic atmosphere and a genial climate, the voice is generally more flexible and clear than in a cold and damp region. This would perhaps have an effect upon the music of such a country during its gradual formation."[61] In both cases, the authors understood the music of a people as an essential part of their "national character" that emanated from climatic aspects of their environment.

Others described how natural scenery exerted an influence on the character of a nation's music. As one commentator explained, "It is difficult to imagine the same music to be the growth of the sunny plains of Lombardy, and of the awful scenery of the Alps, or the wild shores of the northern seas. Whatever influences are exerted upon national character by these differences must become apparent in music." The airs of the Swiss peasant "lose their peculiar charm unless heard among the mountains. . . . They must be listened to in the very places for which they were made; among Alpine rocks, at the door of the chalet, or amidst the herd on the lake-side; with their own native accompaniments, the brawling of the torrent, and the noise of pines swaying by the wind, which serve as a perpetual bass."[62] The natural atmosphere that inspired a music style gave it unique characteristics, according to such authors, which eventually came to define the people of any given place.

This comprehension of music as a component of ethnicity, which developed in a way unique to a people due to environment and passed down through the generations via blood and tradition, emerged from American writings on music during the first half of the nineteenth century. This suggests that ethnic assumptions were deeply embedded within an American comprehension of the world, and motivated their vision for the future of the nation. The attitudes exposed in this chapter reveal the complex and varied views Americans had regarding the connection between a people and their corresponding cultural traits. These attitudes are important since they influenced how Americans thought about diversity within their own nation and the cultural path down which the nation might develop, as they tried to ensure a unified nation both despite and because of its diverse population.

2 / The Threat of Diversity: The Lower
Mississippi River Valley as a Case Study

We are now within twenty miles of the city of Frenchmen and garlic soups,
steamboats and yellow fever, negroes and quadroons, hells and convents,
soldiers and slaves, and things, and people of every language and kindred,
nation and tribe upon the face of the earth.

JOSEPH HOLT INGRAHAM, *THE SOUTH-WEST, BY A YANKEE*

The region of the lower Mississippi River Valley is a particularly fruitful
place to use as a case study to examine the interrelated issues of ethnic
and racial diversity and insecure national attachment within the new
nation. Between 1800 and 1860, this region moved from a contested borderland, to American territory, and finally into statehood, as it gradually became more securely part of the United States. Simultaneous to
the region's increasing ties to the American nation, the lower Mississippi River Valley experienced frequent and varied waves of newcomers
into its already mixed population. These two characteristics make the
region a useful space to examine the convergence of the issues of diversity's threat to national unity and skepticism about the republic's ability
to thoroughly absorb new regions into the nation. Both contemporary
commentators and historians have noted acute diversity as a distinctive
regional characteristic as a way to contrast the lower Mississippi River
Valley with other more "American" places. Instead of continuing to remove this region from the national narrative based on its unique demographics and history, the following chapters are built on the assumption that encountering and making sense of diversity were experiences
shared by many regions as they became part of the nation. This chapter,
a study of both the region's perceived diversity and actual demographics,
illuminates its unique, dynamic, and tessellated population, not to remove it from the national experience, but to emphasize the region's superior ability to exemplify the very common nineteenth-century American

experience of dealing with diversity in regions becoming more securely part of the nation.

The lower Mississippi River Valley's unique relationship with the nation emerged as it did, according to one scholar, because "nowhere else did settlers so conspicuously claim that local and regional peculiarities could coexist with national attachments." The relationship between the local inhabitants and the federal government evolved as the nation's hold over this area became more secure and its demographics shifted. Although the bond between this region and the nation remained unique, other places attached to the American nation partook of aspects of the lower Mississippi River Valley's regional experience. Many places that eventually became part of the United States had similar experiences, most notably, the rapid infusion of diverse populations into frontier settings, which at the time were insecurely attached to the United States. The striking differences between these newly incorporated places and those that had experienced national formation during the Revolution forced a consideration of new definitions of nationhood. Through the shared experiences of these regions in which local concerns gradually merged with national ones, the nation was redefined. Throughout this process, the lower Mississippi River Valley remained a dynamic society. New people arrived, bringing in their familiar ways, constantly responding to the environment, local inhabitants, and other newcomers they encountered.[1] Contacts between all groups in the region are best understood not as a dichotomy, where some were absorbed into or resisted others, but rather "as a process of creation and invention," where the very nature of existing among those unlike oneself forced a reevaluation of familiar ways.[2]

As discussed in this book, the lower Mississippi Valley is defined as the region bordering the river from St. Louis to the Gulf of Mexico. The area between St. Louis, where the Mississippi and Missouri rivers join, and Cairo, Illinois, where the Mississippi and Ohio merge, could be considered either part of the northern or southern leg of the river. Hence, this area is considered much more incidentally than the region south of Cairo. No unified regional identity existed during the early republic and antebellum eras; in fact, other than the importance the river played in the lives of these inhabitants, many here shared little in common. Hence, this region is both artificially and arbitrarily created out of a place that is geographically, economically, politically, and culturally diverse.[3]

The lower Mississippi River Valley gradually became part of the

American nation during the late eighteenth and early nineteenth centuries. The bulk of it came under United States jurisdiction in a few steps, although interpretations over boundaries differed among the Americans, Spanish, and diverse Native Americans. The Pinckney Treaty in 1795 transferred the Natchez region, later the Mississippi Territory, from Spain to the United States with the 31st latitude as the southern boundary and the Mississippi River as the western boundary of American control. By 1815, Native American cessions to the United States had quadrupled the size of the Mississippi Territory. The east side of the river south of the 31st parallel remained Spanish West Florida until 1810. In that year, after a successful rebellion by the inhabitants, the United States took possession of it as part of the Louisiana Purchase, although not officially ceded by Spain until the Adams-Onís Treaty in 1819. The Louisiana Purchase transferred all the lands on the west bank of the Mississippi plus the Isle of Orleans from France to the United States on December 20, 1803. In 1807, the United States surveyed the land around what is today Cairo, Illinois, and in 1818 the Kaskaskia relinquished their claims to this part of southern Illinois. The United States formally admitted these areas bordering the river into the union, beginning with Louisiana in 1812, Mississippi in 1817, Illinois in 1818, Missouri in 1820, and Arkansas in 1835. Although Kentucky and Tennessee had become states in 1792 and 1796 respectively, neither had the Mississippi as their western border, until the Chickasaw ceded what are now the western parts of these states in 1818. Though statehood implied security of the region's place within the union, making this place American was much more than annexation or even statehood, as both scholars and contemporaries understood. The perceived diversity of the region kept many from considering that it would ever fully join with the nation, no matter what the treaties and boundaries might imply.[4]

Between 1803 and 1860, many waves of new inhabitants swelled the already mixed local population. Choctaw and other Native American groups, the colonial French and Spanish and their African and creole slaves, the Acadians, a few native-born Americans, and other Europeans lived in the lower Mississippi River Valley when the French transferred Louisiana to the United States on December 20, 1803. Then, the enslaved, free black and white refugees from Saint Domingue, Native Americans fleeing disruptions elsewhere, and Americans flooded in from the East. Forced migration also frequently caused the demographic changes to the lower portion of the Louisiana territory after American takeover. The removal of Native Americans and the transportation of African

American slaves from other states, as "white Americans forcefully re-worked the demographics of the lower Mississippi valley," has led one historian to describe this process as "a demographic inundation leading to complete political and cultural change."[5] By 1850, even larger num-bers of immigrating Irish, Germans, and other Europeans had arrived. A consideration of both the perceived and actual changing population of the lower Mississippi River Valley reveals a shared experience of cultural encounter in the lives of those at this fringe of the American nation; all these people shared the necessity of navigating among those different from themselves.

The diversity of the population of the lower Mississippi Valley caught the eye of most travelers to the region. Migrants coming from Virginia, Pennsylvania, Ohio, and Kentucky met on the river with new immi-grants, slaves headed to a new home, and the diverse boatmen plying their trade. The disparate origins of the already settled population from various European, Caribbean, African, and American homes, as well as those of mixed heritage, such as quadroon women and Métis, became common characters in these travel narratives, whose authors used them to describe the region to outsiders. In such descriptions, authors spoke of the population in what we would today call ethnic or racial terms as a way of portraying the region to their reading audience. Although not al-ways accurate in the lineages they attributed to the region's inhabitants, their *perception* of an overwhelmingly diverse regional population is of most interest to the historian. An analysis of this perception reveals the region's heterogeneous population as a symptom of its insecure attach-ment to the nation in the minds of contemporary observers.

According to historian Daniel Usner, the "peculiar and exotic charac-teristics of the French-then-Spanish colony, as represented in historical texts, met a variety of intellectual and cultural needs across nineteenth-century America." One of these greatest "needs," was acclimating oneself to being surrounded by a diverse and constantly changing population, oftentimes in a new and unfamiliar environment. Although emphasized by writers as a unique regional situation, those within this region, as well as those in many other regions of the growing nation, shared the experience of living surrounded by those unlike themselves. Existing amid diversity was increasingly a part of the American national expe-rience. Stressing the connection between the region's diversity and its history as a non-English former colony met another of these "needs." This contrasted the region with the supposed homogeneity of the part of the nation with an English colonial history, from whose unified and linear development the nation allegedly emerged. Focusing on the ethnic, racial, and national "otherness" of the lower Mississippi River Valley helped bring into sharper focus a definition of "America," the ultimate aim of many commentators. Like the cultural commentators of the previous chapter, these observers struggled to reconcile such a heterogeneous population with a nation in formation, based on their assumption that a country should house a people with a shared character. Both the language contemporary writers used and the subjects they chose to comment on reveal a concern with regional residents' place of origin and all the trappings that accompanied this codification. To them, heterogeneity became a key component of a regional definition, in contrast to, rather than as a characteristic of, the nation.[6]

Most writers trying to describe the lower Mississippi River Valley emphasized its diversity as a regional trait as they organized the population into discrete categories based on ethnic characteristics. One of these, Robert Baird, noted in his 1832 immigrants' guide, "The Population of the Valley of the Mississippi is exceedingly heterogeneous, if we regard the great variety of nations of which it is composed. There is not a country of Europe which has not furnished some portion of its population." Others, like the historian John Monette, paraphrasing the Reverend Timothy Flint's travel account from 1832, gave more precise reasons for their perceptions:

> The people of the Mississippi valley are constituted from all nations, characters, languages, and conditions of men. Not a nation of Europe, not a class in all those nations, except royalty, which has not its full representation here; not a state in the Union which has not sent out its colonies to people more western regions; not a sect or denomination of Christians who have not their churches and their ministers here. The subjects of despotic monarchies, and the citizens of the freest republics in the world commingle here, and unite to form one people, unique in feeling, character, and genius. The Puritan of the North, the planter of the South, the German and the Iberian, the Briton and the Gaul, and even the sable sons of Africa and the northern Swede, all are here.

Here, Monette goes beyond attributing national variety to the distinctiveness of the region; however, an underlying connection between a people and their place of origin outside the region reinforces the perception that the region's distinctiveness should be attributed to its diversity. "Even now, in Louisiana, alone of all the American states, do we find, contemporary with each other, the manners of the old world and those of the new," wrote a reviewer of Charles Gayarré's *Historie de la Louisiane* in 1846. He continued, "Frenchmen, Spaniards, and Anglo-American, all find their peculiar institutions stamped upon the national manners, nor had the period, that has elapsed since Louisiana became a part of the great Republic, changed, or coalesced the habits, manners or laws of these stranger nations."[7] Commentaries such as these solidified the perception of diversity as a regional characteristic in the minds of their audiences and reveal some contemporary conceptualizations of ways to categorize the population.

As writers described the region's urban areas as having particularly tessellated populations, their readership would then especially correlate diversity with these towns and cities. In early nineteenth-century Natchez, "Visitors described in detail a ubiquitous presence of Choctaws in the city's ethnically heterogeneous populace," to contrast its difference with more familiar eastern places. The Englishman Fortescue Cuming described his first impression of Baton Rouge as home to "a number of genteel men, Frenchmen, Spaniards, English and Americans." In his travels along the lower Mississippi River during 1807, Christian Schultz mapped the newly acquired American river towns by their ethnic composition as a way to emphasize the peculiar regional diversity to his readers.

> The upper settlements of St. Louis, Carondelet, St. Genevieve, and New Bourbon, are composed of French, and since the cession a few Americans have settled at St. Louis and St. Genevieve. The Mines are mostly settled by Americans, with a few French. Cape Girardeau, near the river, consists mostly of Americans; but at a little distance back are some considerable German settlements; at New Madrid, French and Americans; at Little Prairie, French and Canadians; at Chickasaw Bluffs, Americans; at Walnut Hills, French and Americans; at Natchez, mostly Americans, and a few French and Spaniards; at Point Coupee, French and Arcadians; at Baton Rouge, mostly Americans, with a few French and Spaniards. . . . The settlements immediately below Baton Rouge consist of emigrants from Nova-Scotia, and their descendants. The next are two German settlements, intermixed with a few French. The Atacapas and Opelousas settlements west of New Orleans, consist of French, German and Americans. The city of New Orleans consists of French, about one fourth Americans, and foreigners; Terre aux Boefs, Spanish and a few French.

Clearly, to Schultz, place of origin distinguished both people and their towns from each other. The New England minister, writer, and missionary Timothy Flint also described the population of Natchitoches, Louisiana, on the Red River, as Spanish, French, and American, "with a considerable mixture of Indian blood," while wandering its ancient graveyard "where Spanish, French, Americans, Indians, Catholics and Protestants lie in mingled confusion."[8] Such accounts reveal not only what the writers thought about these river towns but also what those exposed to this published commentary would come to expect of this region.

The multiple perceived identities individuals might retain, or have thrust upon them, reveal these writers' desire to delineate with precision the populations they came across as a way to emphasize this region's distinctive diversity in order to contrast it with other more familiar parts of the nation. An encounter by Thomas Ashe in 1806, while traveling along the Mississippi just south of Ste. Genevieve exposes something of these identities outsiders found confusing. Ashe spent the night at the house of a man he termed an "Acadian," whom he described as "a Scotchman by birth, a Frenchman by education, a Spaniard by adoption, and an American *par force*. His name originally was Gordon, but having served in the army of Spain . . . has been known as Don Gordano." Fortescue Cuming also noted the multiple and confused identities of the region's population when he described his Baton Rouge acquaintance Mr. Egan as "an Irish-French-Spaniard."[9] Both Mr. Egan and Don Gordano exemplify the difficulty writers encountered when trying to untwine what we would term the ethnic or national identity within the region. Individuals might have so many connections that labeling became absurd.

Although the lower Mississippi River Valley consistently inspired remarks about its heterogeneous character, New Orleans, the largest urban center in the region, initiated some of the most detailed descriptions of the varied populace. The way in which outsiders commented on the diversity of New Orleans, a major international seaport, suggests much about their conceptions of ethnicity and the degree to which diversity infiltrated their assumptions. Tourists, travelers, and commentators divided the population in a variety of ways, including by complexion and language, but most frequently by what we would call ethnicity. Their terms of categorization implied that birthplace or homeland gave a person innate characteristics, which might include physiognomy and language, but also a variety of assumed and distinguishing behavioral traits. When Berquin-Duvallon succinctly remarked in 1802 that there was "no place in the globe, where the human species may be seen in greater diversity than in New Orleans," he was participating in a trend other writers continued to echo.[10]

Visitors commonly used descriptions of language to group people as they wrote about the diversity of New Orleans. "The mixture of voices spoke every language," exclaimed a French traveler. "There was the *by God* of the Yankee, the *per la madona* of the Italian, the *carambe* of the Spaniard, the *Diou bibant* of the Gascon, the guttural *God dam* [sic] of the Irishman. . . . In all a living Babel." During his tour of North America, Paul Wilhelm, the duke of Württemberg, noted, "The ear of the stranger hears every conceivable language of the educated and uneducated world." The Choctaw even referred to New Orleans as Balbancha, "a place of foreign languages."[11] Not only sound but also color caught the imagination of visitors, who used it as a means to portray diversity, and emphasize the city's distinctiveness. The English tourist Adam Hodgson remarked, "The population is of every complexion, from the most beautiful white and red, through all the various shades of brown and yellow, to jet black. Indeed perhaps no city in the world exhibits a more miscellaneous collection of inhabitants." The Yankee traveler Joseph Holt Ingraham noted, "New Orleans represent[s] every other city and nation upon earth. I know of none where is congregated so great a variety of the human species, of every language and colour."[12] Perceptions of aural and visual difference constantly infused descriptions of this early nineteenth-century city.

Despite such descriptors of language and skin tone, more often writers combined them with or subordinated them to particulars relating to place of origin when portraying the people of New Orleans. "Not only natives of the well known European and Asiatic countries are here to be met with but occasionally Persians, Turks, Lascars, Maltese, Indian sailors from South America and the Islands of the sea, Hottentots, Laplanders, and, for aught I know to the contrary, Symmezonians," continued Ingraham, somewhat sarcastically. As early as 1802 such distinctions had been noted by Bernard-Duvallon when he wrote, "It is too a tessellated pavement; here a Creole, there an Englishman; here a Frenchman, there a Spaniard; here a German, there an Italian. It is a tower of Babel." Decades later, writers even perceived and then circulated the account of the city's 1836 partition into three municipalities as based on the distinctive origins of each section's inhabitants. They referred to one district as American, another as French/Creole, and the third as immigrant. Although these labels were not entirely accurate, their perception by outsiders remained. "I doubt if there is a city in the world, where the resident population has been so divided in its origin, or where there is such a variety in the tastes, habits, manners, and moral codes of the citizens," declared Frederick Law Olmsted on his 1856 visit.[13] By choosing to emphasize the particular diversity of both New Orleans and the lower Mississippi River Valley as abnormal, these writers placed diversity within America in opposition to the assumed need for a homogeneous national character they and their readers shared. Thus, both readers and writers considered the region as questionably attachable to the nation. Such highly designatory language was a way these writers made sense of the diversity they encountered.

Often, commentators combined the perceived international foreignness with the foreignness of American nationals in the city as a way to accentuate its diversity. "In New Orleans, men from every State of the Union; from every country in North and South America; from every nation of Europe, and many from Asia and Africa, are to be found," wrote James Creecy of 1830s New Orleans. Another echoed, "Americans from every state, from Maine to Georgia; English, French, Spanish, Creoles, Indians and African," all retained a visual presence in the city. Even the New Orleans City Directory tried to explain the local population as a combination of international and national distinctiveness when it related, "The population is much mixed, consisting of foreign and native French; Americans born in the state and from every state in the union; a few Spaniards; and foreigners from almost every nation; consequently the society is much diversified, and there is no general character. . . . [I]n short it is a world in miniature." Place of origin might also be used to explain distinctiveness without necessarily implying ethnicity. A New Orleans guidebook from 1845 divided the town's population into four parts: the Creoles, of whom most were of French and Spanish extraction, those arriving from other states, the "nondescript watermen," and, finally, the migratory residents, likely a reference to the immigrants arriving in droves at the time. This author's choice of categories implies an understanding where previous habitation, or lack thereof, constituted an appropriate way to group the population.[14]

Many commentators on New Orleans's heterogeneity set their descriptions on the levee, an appropriate connection considering the centrality the Mississippi River played in urging populations to the region. The levee was not only the earthen barrier between the city and the river, it was also a hive of activity; it was a place of work, a site of debarkation and a leisure space. Although an important background to view the diversity of the city, as immigrants, local and foreign merchants, various free and enslaved dock workers, and sailors from around the globe, all met and mingled there, it is important to emphasize that the river the levee held back was responsible for bringing outsiders into the area. Without the Mississippi River providing access to the interior of the continent, serving as a facilitator for trade and a conduit for the people entering and moving about the area, the region's demographics would surely have taken a different form.[15]

When speaking of the levee, commentators used auditory, visual, and proto-ethnic descriptors to distinguish its masses, who "are among the representatives from all the unlucky families which, at the building of Babel, were dispersed over the earth." The actor George Vandenhoff spent time in New Orleans "enjoying the 'varieties' of the multiform, multi-colored, multi-lingual, multi-ludal city, which is [the] *levée* on the banks of the Mississippi." The architect Benjamin Henry Latrobe's first impression of the New Orleans levee was of "a most incessant, loud, rapid, and various gabble of tongues of all tones that were ever heard at Babel." The English traveler Charles Murray echoed, "The population passing in the streets, especially on 'the Levée,' and others adjoining the river, is the most amusing motley assemblage that can be exhibited by any town on earth. The prevailing language seems to be that of Babel—Spanish, Portuguese, French, English, mixed with a few wretched remains of Choctaw, and other Indian tribes; and all these are spoken in the loudest, broadest, and strangest dialects." Another of these commentators of the levee, the young traveler Henry Whipple described:

> Such a motley crowd one seldom sees. . . . Every variety of char-
> acter can here be seen from the curious Yankee like myself to the
> busy restless speculator . . . hoosiers, pukes, buckeyes, crackers,
> greenies, busters and other varieties of civilization are here exhib-
> ited in all the eccentricities of their individual character. . . . Every
> nation appears to be represented in this mart of business, from the
> hardy Scotch & Swede of the north to the tawny Maltese of a warm-
> er clime, each jabbering away in his native tongue like so many
> monkeys.

Even a man as familiar with the river as Samuel Clemens found the 1857 New Orleans levee striking. He considered, "I thought I had seen all kinds of markets before—but that was a great mistake. . . . Out on the pavement were groups of Italians, French, Dutch, Irish, Spaniards, Indians, Chinese, Americans, English, and the lord knows how many more different kinds of people."[16] In the minds of these chronicling sojourners, the levee's practical function remained secondary to its setting for people watching and cultural comment. Like in their descriptions of the city as a whole, the words writers used to illustrate the people at the levee implied that language, place of origin, and heritage distinguished one group from another. In doing so, these writers emphasized the levee's distinctiveness through the cultural categorization of its multitudes. From the local levee to the regional whole, visitors consistently interpreted and related this place as having a supremely mixed population.

The frequency with which such diversity impressed newcomers implies the degree to which this region differed from other regions in their prior experience. Even the worldly architect Benjamin Latrobe "felt myself in some degree again a cockney, for it was impossible not to stare at a sight wholly new even to one who has traveled much in Europe and America." Although their use of ethnic delineators might appear as separating markers, writers did not so much mean to emphasize fragmentation of the population as to accentuate the degree of mixing that such a situation facilitated. The extent of accommodation all groups exhibited in their shared existence together surprised visitors, as they commented frequently on mixed public venues and relationships. As Berquin-Duvallon noted, although "various are the dialects . . . if one general language prevails it is the language of interest."[17] Rarely, however, did these writers mention a trait when describing the region without attaching it to a corresponding people whom they made sure to note originated elsewhere. Even the Creoles were ascribed a distinct character because of some residual, although not total, "Frenchness." Hence, the regional distinctiveness, according to these commentators, appeared to arise from the ethnic diversity of the population. Writers typically presented this diversity in contrast to more homogeneous and more "American" regions elsewhere, using it as a way to emphasize the lower Mississippi River Valley's distinct and uncertain relationship with the nation as they searched to uncover what it meant to be American.

This vision of supreme regional diversity, as described by these commentators was grounded in reality. An examination of the region's demographics, based mostly on the secondary literature, reveals a population whose places of origin did span the globe and was not merely the fanciful imagery of inventive authors. A consideration of the actual diverse and dynamic population of the lower Mississippi River Valley reveals a shared experience of encounter with difference in the lives of the region's shifting populace. In order to discover how these residents navigated through difference in the following chapters, we must first discover precisely who these varied members of the mixed populace were.

Simultaneous with its ties with the nation being strengthened, the region's already diverse colonial population absorbed multiple waves of various newcomers. Although total and precise population numbers are difficult to achieve because of the continually shifting boundaries and incomplete census records, the records that do exist give the impression of lively diversity.[18] Even without making comparisons to other American regions, port cities, or especially cosmopolitan settings, a sense emerges that no matter where a person had come from prior to his or her life along the river, he or she would be awash in a multitude of others from someplace else. Between 1804, when the United States acquired the west bank of the river in the Louisiana Purchase, and the coming of the Civil War, the lower Mississippi River Valley experienced constant and repeated population movements mostly into, although also through and out of, the region. An examination of these waves reveals an unstable regional population in constant flux that would have to learn to exist among changing diversity while becoming part of a new nation.

Even before the United States government had officially gained control over both banks of the lower Mississippi, the region had already experienced multiple population shifts. Various Europeans arrived to colonize the area, bringing with them an enslaved African labor force to work land previously utilized by Native American inhabitants. The many tribes who had inhabited the region in the early eighteenth century, including, from south to north, the Chitimachas, Atakapas, Houmas, Opelousas, Tunicas, Natchez, Choctaw, Caddos, Chickasaws, and Quapaws, among other smaller groups, had experienced a "calamitous decline," due to disease and migration out of the region in reaction to growing colonial population. It was not until the 1780s, however, that the colonial European inhabitants first outnumbered the Native Americans of the lower Mississippi.[19]

Concurrently, throughout the eighteenth century, the number of French entering the region increased. Soldiers, officers, and administrators serving the French crown and stationed in the colony turned civilian after their terms of service. They shared space with deported French criminals, and voluntary German, Swiss, and Alsatian immigrants. Five waves of Acadian exiles arrived in Louisiana between 1765 and 1785 totaling about 3,000 people from various East Coast British colonies and France. They settled along the Mississippi River, Bayou Lafourche, and the lands west of the Atchafalaya Basin. Those fleeing the French Revolution after 1789 followed, beginning the trickle that would later become a deluge of refugees from the Saint Domingue Revolution. Although Spain administered the region from 1763 to 1803, Spanish settlers never contributed to the population to the level the administration had hoped. Outside of colonial administrators and some soldiers, few Spanish settlers came, although administrators recognized the importance of populating the region and pursued tactical policies with that aim, even if the settlers were not Spanish. British American colonists arrived to settle during Spanish rule, especially in West Florida, while the east bank of the river north of New Orleans became home to colonial British loyalists during the American Revolution. These inhabitants only had to take an oath of allegiance to remain in the province.[20]

Slaves consistently outnumbered the free population in French colonial Louisiana. Enslaved Africans were by far the largest demographic group who came into Spanish Louisiana, possibly making the proportion of African-born among this region's slave population the highest of any North American region during the 1760s and 1770s. If implications from Gwendolyn Midlo Hall's Point Coupee test study can be extrapolated over a larger area, this would make Africans 60 percent of the population in parts of 1770 Louisiana, even more than Philip Morgan found for 1760 South Carolina with a 49 percent African-born population. During Spanish rule, slaves made up about 55 percent of the total population of lower Louisiana. Of the nearly 6,000 West Africans who arrived in Louisiana between 1719 and 1763, two-thirds were from Senegambia, the vast majority Bambara. In Hall's recent study of the Pointe Coupee region in Spanish Louisiana, although the 2,632 slaves represented more than fifty different African nations, most came from relatively few and/ or closely related nations, especially Senegambia.[21] The enslaved African workforce, the colonizing Europeans, and the Native Americans whose land was being colonized were far from homogenous. Each of the three groups included within it those of differing ethnicity, language, religion, political, and economic interests.

Within such a general description of the population prior to American rule remain some demographically hidden people. A few examples of those of mixed ancestry reveal the varied types of intermixtures that had already occurred in the region. Although Scottish financier and promoter John Law's 1720s colonization scheme did bring some Germans to Louisiana (estimates for the number of Germans who actually arrived vary from three hundred to two thousand), the already established and then incoming Louisiana French incorporated this minority group through intermarriage because of few additional German-speaking immigrants and many French-speaking ones. These Germans finally "disappeared" completely with the translation or transliteration of their names into French. Further north, visitors to the Arkansas Post expressed surprise at "the remarkable symbiosis" between the Native American and white residents, whose overwhelmingly mixed heritage population spoke a French/Quapaw patois. Others reported that French Canadian immigrants had been "Indianized," during their Arkansas lives. In the course of one well-documented six-year span at the end of Spanish rule in Arkansas, French men had married women mostly of the Quapaw, but also Osage, Paduca, Kansas, Abenaki, Loup, and Cherokee. In New Orleans and the Gulf South an entire self-identified group, whose nineteenth-century descendants called themselves Creoles of Color, mostly solidified around their mixed race ancestry, French language, and Catholicism, ensuring their "middle ground" status in an increasingly biracially defined society after American takeover. According to John Blassingame, as late as 1860, 77 percent of New Orleans's free blacks were of mixed ancestry, while 74 percent of slaves were not.[22] These few examples reveal not only the fluidity of boundaries between supposedly discrete groups but also some of the flaws in the historical language of categorization. Despite this, it is clear that prior to the nineteenth century the region was already home to a particularly diverse and changing population.

By the time of American takeover, the regional population had already become a patchwork of racial, ethnic, and national groups, including many of multiple ancestries. Some of these people profited much more than others from the changing political, economic, and social atmospheres of the eighteenth century, yet all lived within a demographically heterogeneous world. The half-century following the United States's acquisition of Louisiana saw even more drastic shifts in the already fluctuating demographics of the region.

All remaining Native American groups became increasingly marginalized as both their trade goods and alliances became less useful to the new American administration. When New Orleans's American leaders hosted formal visits for Native Americans, "residents perceived them with increasing amusement and fascination," exemplifying their changed status in the region. Between New Orleans and New Madrid an attempted census after the Louisiana Purchase "lists remnants of Indian nations and Indian villages ... [on] both banks of the Mississippi," including many "wandering families," making the accuracy of the census figures doubtful, but emphasizing the refugee status of many Native American people in the region at the time. Between 1795 and 1817, during the territorial period of Mississippi, local tribes who had constituted a great majority of the population lost their status as nations in dealings with the American government. They became overwhelming minorities in territories increasingly occupied and governed by non-Natives. The dissension following this shift led to large-scale removals and combined with the sheer number of incoming non-Native people to overshadow the Native American population. Although their political presence waned, Native Americans never disappeared from the region. Those who remained to peddle their hunted, gathered, or handmade goods on a small scale, either in towns or to individual plantations, more often consisted of extended family units or the remainder of tribes like the Seminoles, Creek, and Choctaw that had declined, merged or migrated through and out of the region.[23] The continued although changing presence of Native people within the lower Mississippi River Valley reveals one aspect of the fluctuating regional demographics, and one that could be used to emphasize the region as place apart from the rest of the nation. However, many other regions also experienced drastic changes in Native American demographics as well, as they too became more securely attached to the United States.

Just as remarkable diversity existed within Louisiana's francophone population at transfer, the incoming French-speaking immigrants who arrived after 1803 also varied greatly. Because they arrived during years of uncertain although increasing attachment between the region and the nation, this group was often used to emphasize the region's distinctiveness from the "American" experience and accentuate its questionable loyalty to the United States. The first large in-migration after American takeover involved refugees from the Saint Domingue Revolution, who, prior to 1809, often entered the region after sojourns in other Caribbean or American locales. Between 1793 and 1809, at least 11,000 Saint Domingue refugees migrated into Louisiana, over 9,000 in 1809 alone, most settling in or near New Orleans. Their sudden arrival doubled the population of the city and more than doubled its free black population. Just under one third of these refugees were white, another third free people of color and over one third enslaved. This migration, in the words of one scholar, gave a distinctiveness to the region of the lower Mississippi making it "less southern" than other parts of the South; it reinforced the Gallic culture already present, including contributing to a large free black community, and bolstered the many slaves intent on asserting their own claims to freedom. This influx also increased tensions between the French- and English-speaking populations. The latter had heartily begun trying to strengthen the bonds between the lower Mississippi and the United States and hence interpreted the new refugee population as a major setback to their prior gains.[24]

The Saint Domingue refugees endangered the unity Americans perceived necessary to secure this region with the larger nation both politically and culturally. The refugees reinforced the local inhabitants' need to discover ways to live among a dynamic and diverse population, while the region became increasingly attached to the United States. Even though the refugees' varied race, status, and class suggested a fractured entity, they shared an identity, or "symbolic ethnicity," because of their common homeland and refugee experience. The Saint Domingue refugees did not arrive in a completely alien landscape, however, since they joined a community where their language, religion, and some other customs were known, allowing them to slowly dissolve "into the Louisiana Gallic fabric," all the while retaining a distinct identity. Unlike the later Irish and German immigrations, the Saint Domingue immigrants reinforced the unique racial structure and French-derived culture of the region at a time when the American administration threatened its existence.[25] The Saint Domingue refugees forced a reevaluation of the path the region would take as it became part of the nation by reinforcing the perception of distinctive regional diversity and intensifying the local population's encounter with difference.

These refugees were only one component of the changing regional francophone population. Other waves of immigration from Europe, known as the "foreign French," continued to arrive during the antebellum era for a variety of reasons. The consistent political upheavals in France encouraged not only political refugees, but more often peasants suffering the economic instabilities, especially food shortages, occasioned by such frequent political restructuring. Over 8,200 people, who identified themselves as "natives of" France, arrived at the Port of New Orleans between 1820 and 1839. Another 11,500 arrived between 1840 and 1848, and 8,800 between 1849 and 1852, making New Orleans second only to New York as a port of entry for French immigrants between 1820 and 1860. Many of the later immigrants may have come from Alsace or Lorraine due to the high frequency of German surnames, although region of origin is infrequently recorded in the manifests.[26] Despite the large influence the "foreign French" had on the demographics of the region, they hardly compared to the huge influxes of Irish and Germans who arrived during the 1840s and 1850s.

Unlike the Saint Domingue and French immigrants who encouraged a continuation of already existing Gallic culture in the region, the massive number of non-French European arrivals forced a consideration of issues that other parts of the United States simultaneously experienced. Thus, although the Irish and German immigrants did help form a unique regional demographic situation within the lower Mississippi River Valley, their important local presence should be seen in the context of larger national trends. With this influx, the regional population and newcomers alike found themselves among new neighbors whose ways seemed unfamiliar. As with the case of the Saint Domingue refugees and foreign French, both locals and new arrivals would have to find methods for navigating among difference.

Even though a wide variety of non-French European immigrants had entered the region prior to 1840, the drastic speed and numbers of arriving Germans and Irish during the following two decades shaped regional demographics most dramatically. Their presence, both through their cultural contributions and because of their vast and quick appearance, forced the prior population to come to terms with their new neighbors quickly. The shared experience between this region and others of intense immigration forced the lower Mississippi River Valley to become more strongly connected with the North, West, and other southern urban areas also dealing with the incorporation of these new members into both their locale and the nation.

Although typically considered a phenomenon of the North and West rather than the southern states during the mid-nineteenth century, foreign immigration into the urban centers of the lower Mississippi River Valley shared more in common demographically with New York, Boston, Philadelphia, and Cincinnati than with the rest of the region or the rest of the South. Historians have found the massive imbalance between northern versus southern states' immigrant population ratios around midcentury difficult to ignore, considering that in 1860 fewer than one in fifteen free southerners were foreign-born, compared with the northern states' one in five; however, "the peculiar pattern of European migration and settlement in the slave states gave immigrants importance far beyond their numbers," as they settled mostly in cities and towns. Because of the role of the river as an artery of commerce during the antebellum years, the lower Mississippi experienced especially high levels of urban growth compared to other southern areas. New Orleans was the South's (and for a time in the 1830s, the nation's) leading export center. Even though New Orleans's regional dominance may have inhibited the possible growth of other urban river towns, they too continued to grow, with increasingly immigrant populations, as collection points for products from the interior. In 1850, only New York City welcomed more immigrants through its port than did New Orleans.[27]

The comparative percentage of various immigrating groups into New Orleans remained virtually identical to immigrants entering at New York and into the nation as a whole, connecting the region to a national experience in this way as well. For the city of New Orleans, this wave of immigration "makes the traditional American versus creole approach to its history not invalid, surely, but certainly in need of considerable explication."[28] Ironically, the diverse foreign population that many commentators had so clearly considered a regional peculiarity, and emphasized as a way to contrast the lower Mississippi River Valley with other American places, was a very American circumstance.

Between 1840 and 1860, most foreigners who came to the South directly from Europe entered at New Orleans. The over 50,000 immigrant arrivals to New Orleans in the 1830s, tripled to 161,657 in the 1840s, and peaked with 250,000 additional immigrants between 1850 and 1855.[29] Although some new immigrants moved up the river to farm or find industrial work in northern cities, many remained in southern towns working as "shopkeepers, tradesmen, artisans, and certain specialized laborers," where they found excellent opportunities. Another common route brought immigrants who had entered through northern ports southward via the Ohio and Mississippi Rivers where they might stop for several years at a time before moving further downstream. Of the four million foreigners who lived in the United States in 1860 only half a million resided in the slave states. They were not distributed with any degree of uniformity throughout the South, however, which would have rendered them much less visible. Rather the vast majority was "pocketed in the larger river and coastal towns where they comprised a considerable portion of the free population."[30] For example, the foreign-born made up 25 percent of the 1850 Vicksburg population, but the surrounding area was only 6 percent foreign-born.[31] Since relatively few foreigners interested in agriculture came to the southern states, the majority of the foreign population lived in cities and towns. Their concentration in places like 1860 Memphis, where immigrants made up almost a third of its 40,000 free inhabitants, was comparable to Philadelphia and Boston.[32] In this way, the impact of immigration at these centers of concentration produced a significant alteration in local demographics. The foreign-born made up half of the free population of 1850 New Orleans, almost a third of Natchez, and a quarter of Vicksburg. In 1860, both the Natchez and Vicksburg adults of foreign birth were almost as numerous as adults of native birth.[33] This intense European immigration into the urban areas of the lower Mississippi River Valley precipitated the shared experience of encounter with difference among natives and newcomers alike, which would eventually lead to the creation of strategies for making sense of the diversity all these groups confronted.

Prior to 1850, the first year the United States census recorded place of birth, numerical approximations are difficult to compile for each immigrating ethnic group, although a picture of a mixed and growing population can be inferred. Estimates on the origins of the population of Natchez suggest that in the first two decades of the nineteenth century immigrants made up half the population with the vast majority coming from the British Isles.[34] Between 1800 and 1850, 126,000 Germans entered the port of New Orleans. By the mid-1830s, 7,000 Germans lived in New Orleans, while fifteen years later this reached 11,425. Although some entered at New Orleans with plans to move west or up the Mississippi, many remained in the region or returned to it after failed agriculture attempts elsewhere.[35]

Beginning in 1850, records of the inhabitants' birthplaces are much easier to come by. In this year, Irish constituted one in five New Orleans residents and one-third of the foreign-born Natchez population, as well as 23 percent of 1860 Memphis.[36] Almost half of the South's 1850 Irish population lived in Louisiana, making up almost 10 percent of the state's population, while only two other southern states had even 1 percent of their white population born in Ireland. Potentially one of the reasons for this was that from the 1830s through 1850s, northern Irish newspapers advertised the great opportunities in Louisiana and New Orleans for new immigrants. New Orleans's Irish population reached 20,200 in 1850, or 20 percent of the city's white population and 24,398, or 17 percent, in 1860.[37] In 1850, New Orleans's population totaled 116,375, with the foreign-born, in addition to the Irish, numbering 11,425 German, 7,522 French, and 2,670 English and Scottish.[38] German-born Louisiana residents numbered 17,500 in 1850, which grew to 25,000 in 1860, mostly concentrated in and around New Orleans.[39] In 1850, only 17,262 residents of Orleans Parish were non-Louisiana-born Americans, compared to 51,227 foreign-born and 50,965 Louisianans born in the state.[40] The foreign-born made up 24 percent of the total 1850 Louisiana population, representing more than thirty different countries. Of all Louisiana residents in 1850 who had not been born in the state, over half were foreign-born, making the incoming Americans fewer than either native Louisianans or foreigners. The lower percentage of incoming Americans compared to foreigners makes the state population of Louisiana unique within the region. Twenty-four percent, or 66,413 of Louisiana's 1850 population were foreign-born compared with 22 percent, or 60,447 American-born from outside the state.[41]

The high concentration of European immigrants in Louisiana and the Mississippi River towns can give a false impression of the regional population in its entirety because the foreign-born were quite concentrated in these specific areas. When considering the whole population of the states bordering the lower Mississippi River, whites of American birth greatly outnumbered all foreign-born in 1850. Outside of Louisiana, whose foreign-born population was an exception to this trend, the other states in the region had far more American-born than foreign-born residents by this time. Those born outside of the state made up over half of all white Mississippians. They arrived in the region from somewhere else in the nation, especially North and South Carolina, Tennessee, Alabama, and Georgia. The foreign-born, on the other hand, constituted a mere 2 percent of the state population. Arkansas makes an even greater contrast with over 60 percent of the total 1850 free population having been born out of state and only 1 percent of foreign birth. Virtually all incoming white Americans to this state arrived from another slave state. Because these reports do not indicate the birthplaces of the slave populations, these numbers deal strictly with the free population.[42] Such numbers suggest that the lower Mississippi River Valley was increasingly home to Americans who had already experienced the nation in a very different setting. Through their presence, expectations and assumptions of nationhood entered the region that would have differed from those of both new immigrants and the local-born populace, based on the emigrating Americans' past experiences within the nation.

These statistics delineating the lower Mississippi River Valley's changing European and white American populations imply that all who inhabited this place would have likely reflected on how best to maneuver among those unlike themselves, while living in a place increasingly attached to the American nation. Although the demographic situation could be, and has been, used as a way to highlight the region's inability to become thoroughly integrated into the nation, such intense demographic changes were not confined to this particular region. Instead, reading this regional demographic shift as exemplary of the larger national experience resituates the lower Mississippi River Valley back into the national narrative and allows the problematic American relationship between diversity and nationalism to be considered.

Encounters with diversity were not confined to the increasingly racialized white segment of the regional population during the first half of the nineteenth century. The enslaved black inhabitants also confronted and maneuvered through difference in their lives, oftentimes in a new environment as well. Although remaining a distinctive group in the region, because of the racial codification and enslaved status forced on them (free blacks will be dealt with later), the region's enslaved population also lived among a changing and diverse population. The distinctive regional slave population, which included those from various parts of the United States, the Caribbean, and Africa, became another circumstance for commentators to accentuate when contrasting the region with the nation in their attempt to distance the lower Mississippi River Valley from the national experience. Although the enslaved population in the region did consist of people with especially diverse origins, exhibiting this region's superior ability to answer questions about diversity's relationship with national consolidation, the enslaved in other American places also experienced dislocation into new environments as they were forced into unfamiliar communities. The following discussion of the enslaved in the lower Mississippi River Valley shows how the black population was equally as heterogeneous and dynamic as the region's white population.

After the United States officially ended the foreign slave trade in 1808, a declining number of people were brought to the lower Mississippi directly from Africa or the Caribbean. Rather, most had been removed from their former American homes east of the Mississippi, either migrating with their owners or sold by them into the region.[43] Although, when the Saint Domingue refugees arrived in New Orleans with about 3,200 of their slaves in 1809, Governor Claiborne gave in to pressure and allowed them to disembark. Eventually the federal Congress granted Claiborne's exception into law. While most slaves entered the region via the domestic slave trade during the nineteenth century, the foreign slave trade did continue illegally.[44] The combination of the discontent of planters toward the prohibition and the difficulty of policing the Louisiana coast has led scholars to believe a significant number of slaves from Africa, Cuba, and the Caribbean continued to enter through Louisiana, although the numbers are not known with any degree of certainty. Estimates on the total number of slaves smuggled into the United States between 1808 and 1860 range from 500 to 270,000. Both the pirate Jean Lafitte and the slave-trading Bowie brothers continued to import African slaves even after the ban, usually taken from raids on Spanish ships, prompting the reports of "Fresh imported Guinea negroes" in New Orleans newspapers as late as 1818.

Although made illegal with the creation of the Mississippi Territory in 1789, frontier planters ignored the law ending the foreign slave trade into the region and continued to import slaves from foreign ports. This law reflects the American government's fear of a slave revolt on the order of Saint Domingue's. Planter demands in the region, however, led to the reopening of the African slave trade for a decade before the nationwide ban. On the other side of the river, an 1804 ordinance for the Territory of Orleans banned the importation of any slave into the territory who had not been born in the United States or imported prior to 1798. That Louisiana planters never abandoned their desire for African and Caribbean slaves and protested this law, while continuing to purchase them covertly, is evidenced by the fact that as late as 1858 a bill passed the state House of Representatives but not the Senate, which would have permitted Louisiana to import slaves from Brazil, Cuba, and Africa. The following year a committee of the Louisiana House of Representatives recommended reopening the African slave trade on the grounds that the federal law prohibiting it was unconstitutional.[45] New Orleans remained "one of America's most recognized centers for the post-1808 foreign slave trade." The 1870 census listed Louisiana as home to the highest number of African-born persons out of all the states.[46]

Although slave importation into the region from outside of the United States likely never completely ceased, the incoming enslaved African Americans clearly overshadowed the earlier African and Afro-Caribbean newcomers by midcentury. One estimate suggests 18,000 new Africans arrived in Louisiana and Mississippi between 1790 and 1810, while only 5,000 came from the Chesapeake states, whereas the following decade saw 77,000 slaves from the Chesapeake states enter Mississippi, Alabama, Louisiana, Arkansas, and Missouri and only 5,000 from Africa.[47] Another estimate suggests that between 1800 and 1860 traders and masters brought over 234,000 slaves into the state of Mississippi from other American regions while another 94,700 entered Louisiana and 82,300 were taken to Arkansas. The slave population of the lower Mississippi consistently grew more via the importation of slaves from other parts of the United States between 1800 and 1860 than from any other source. Most of these enslaved men and women left their former homes in Virginia, Maryland, and the Carolinas.[48]

By such means, the slave population of the lower Mississippi River Valley swelled for the first thirty years of the nineteenth century and then exploded during the next. These enslaved blacks entered the region with a different history, "rooted in different blends of African traditions" and a history of encounters with different free peoples than had local-born slaves or those brought to the region before or during the early years of American rule. These men, women, and children had prior experience within the American racial system, spoke mostly English and practiced versions of Protestant faiths, all different from many slaves who had entered the lower Mississippi River Valley earlier.[49] This situation also connected the region to other American areas through the shared experience of dealing with an expanding slave labor system and the common experience of forced dislocation of those enslaved.

This forced migration of African American slaves added another layer to the particular diversity of the regional population. In 1804, the Americans divided Lower Louisiana, called the Territory of Orleans, from Upper Louisiana, or the Territory of Louisiana, whose name was later changed to Missouri Territory when Louisiana became a state in 1812. The thirty-three degree latitude line divided the two, the current boundary between Louisiana and Arkansas. The enslaved population made up about 55 percent of the total population of Lower Louisiana at American takeover, and the census of the Territory of Orleans for 1806 reported 25,493 whites, 3,550 free colored, and 22,701 slaves.[50] The 1810 census reported 34,660 slaves in the Territory of Orleans, or 45 percent of the total population; 17,088, or 42 percent of the Territory of Mississippi; and 3,011, or 14 percent of the Territory of Louisiana.[51] Two decades later, according to the 1830 census, Mississippi slaves totaled 65,659, or 48 percent of the state population; Louisianans held 109,588 slaves, or 51 percent of the state population; and the 4,576 slaves in the Arkansas Territory made up 15 percent of its population. Slaves constituted 17 percent of the population of the river counties of Missouri and Kentucky, totaling 2,558 and 870 people respectively, and 35 percent of the population of Tennessee, totaling 4,473.[52] Over the next twenty years, a huge number of new African American slaves were brought to the region. The total slave population in the states of Mississippi and Louisiana, the Territory of Arkansas, and the river counties of Tennessee, Kentucky, and Missouri in 1830 was 187,724; by 1850 this number had more than tripled to 644,641. Until the 1840s the Arkansas slave population was never above

20 percent; however, the river counties always had a much higher percentage than the interior. Arkansas's Chicot County was over 70 percent enslaved in 1840, and three of the five river counties had slave majorities by 1860.[53] The enslaved population of each state according to the 1850 census reported Mississippi housing 309,878 slaves, or 51 percent of the total population; Louisiana 244,809, or 47 percent; and Arkansas, 47,100, or 22 percent.[54] The slave population in the river counties of southern Missouri totaled 18,442, or 48 percent; Arkansas, 9,770, or 49 percent; Tennessee, 22,843, or 39 percent; and Kentucky, 2,626, or 18 percent.[55] These river counties had a much higher percentage of enslaved to free in Missouri, whose state population was only 13 percent slave; Arkansas, whose slaves totaled 22 percent of the population; and in Tennessee, where they totaled 24 percent. Only Kentucky's river counties were nearly the same as the state average.[56]

The city of New Orleans presents a slightly different picture through a delineation of its racial demographics, most notably in its triracial social structure, revealing another layer to the particularly regional pattern of diversity. In 1805, the city was 43 percent white, 19 percent free people of color, and 38 percent enslaved, while 30 percent of the city's population was of mixed race, and 33 percent of its nonwhite population free.[57] The year 1810 saw the largest percentage of nonwhite people in New Orleans at 63 percent, with 45 percent of these free and 54 percent enslaved. In 1820, the city's population was half white and half black; in 1830, 56 percent black; in 1840, 42 percent black; and in 1850, 24 percent. By 1860, the number of immigrants had so swelled the population that slaves and free people of color made up merely 15 percent of a city where just thirty years prior they had been the racial majority. Between 1810 and 1840 New Orleans's free black population made up around 45 percent of the total nonwhite population, until 1850 when they constituted 37 percent.[58]

Despite the impact the Saint Domingue migration made on the status of free blacks in New Orleans, Louisiana, and the Gulf Coast, as discussed earlier, few lived outside of this area. Those who did experienced increasing restrictions on their movements and decisions. Even in New Orleans, free blacks' prior rights gradually deteriorated after American takeover, although some evidence indicates that those who lived in the "virtually autonomous creole municipal districts" lived with relatively lax racial law enforcement until the 1850s.[59] This decade brought not only consolidation of the three separate municipalities of the city but also new legal restrictions from the state and city governments. After new 1850s legislation no free black could keep a coffeehouse, sell liquor, shoot fireworks, play cards, hold a ball with slaves, or assemble in any way. Docked free black ship workers had to register, and in 1859, remain in jail while in port. No free black from out of state could enter Louisiana, although they could choose their own master and become slaves for life. New Orleans free blacks totaled 15,072 in 1840, 9,905 in 1850, and 9,105 ten years later. Migration out of the country, to France, Liberia, Haiti, Mexico and Canada, and a new law against manumission, resulted in their numerical decline. Free people of color represented 29 percent of New Orleans's population in 1810, 23 percent in 1820, 25 percent in 1830, 18 percent in 1840, but only 8 percent in 1850. This proportional decline is due to the intense arrival of European immigrants.[60]

Free blacks in New Orleans and Louisiana were not only Louisiana natives but also came from other parts of the country, despite laws in place to keep any new free blacks from entering the state. Such a situation meant that the Louisiana free black community, like the enslaved, was more heterogeneous than it might at first seem. Other parts of the region more successfully expelled or prevented free blacks from entering their states. The 1850 census reports 930 free blacks in Mississippi and 608 in Arkansas, but 17,462 in Louisiana. This disparity increased during the following decade with only 753 free blacks in Mississippi, 114 in Arkansas, and 18,647 in Louisiana.[61] Outside of Louisiana, free blacks remained a minuscule portion of the regional population where African heritage defined one's status as enslaved.

Like the voluntary migration of immigrants and white Americans, the forced migration of black American-born slaves into the lower Mississippi also connected the region with a larger shared national experience. After the "middle ground eroded and the frontier exchange economy gave way," an economy based increasingly on plantation-grown cotton took its place in many parts of the region. Slaves filled this new economy's need for labor. In this relocation, all slaves from the East experienced a major disruption, leaving not only a familiar place and community, but often their families, as they moved westward.[62] Other borderland and frontier places along the edges of the American nation simultaneously experienced the development of a slave economy, legal code, and society with a biracial structure. Regional decisions and debates in the lower Mississippi River Valley shared much with those of other places experiencing similar dynamics, such as California, Texas, and Missouri, as East Coast planters headed west looking for fresh land, propelling new territories to statehood as regional slavery became the focus of national concern.[63]

The colonial and frontier conditions of the lower Mississippi River Valley nourished the development of a new and constantly evolving creole culture from those brought to the region by the diverse African, Native American, European, and American inhabitants. It was a process of continuous reinvention, as populations redefined themselves within new situations and in reaction to others. This resulted in, according to one scholar, "an especially rich ethnic stew as white Americans, their black slaves, and European immigrants settled among an already variegated population of Spanish and French Creoles, Métis, and Indians."[64] For this reason, a demographic analysis like this one can provide temporary, if incomplete, glimpses into this multiform and transitory society.

Commentators considered the lower Mississippi River Valley unique in its diversity. Most of their perceptions, as well as its actual demographic history, stemmed from the region's position as a major gateway into the interior of the continent. Whereas some argued that its French and Spanish colonial history made the region different from other American places, many areas that became part of the nation had shared this lack of British colonial rule, making this regional experience more common within the nation than many assumed. Although unique in the precise elements of its demographic history, other parts of the growing nation shared the experience of diverse population movements through or to the territories. This resulted in an evolving creole culture in the lower Mississippi that was neither identical to other local ways nor completely divorced from other places. Native Americans left and were removed from areas increasingly coveted by Americans in a wide variety of locales that became United States territory during the early republic and antebellum eras. Those slaves forced to accompany their owners or sold into new homes, shared the experience of dislocation and changed work regimes in their new environment. Ports throughout the nation continued to see transitory populations as well as mass influxes of Germans and Irish in the 1840s and 1850s. In these ways, and through the shared experience of existing among the diversity surrounding them as will be examined in the following chapters, the population of the lower Mississippi River Valley participated in very American experiences.

Using the lower Mississippi River Valley as a case study, then, sheds light on a national culture being created out of the shared experience of diversity, by seeing these regional experiences as national characteristics, instead of using them to provide contrast with more "American" regions elsewhere.[65] The changing heterogeneity of the regional population, as presented through this demographic survey of the lower Mississippi

River Valley during an era of its increasing attachment to the United States, suggests that this region is an excellent arena for inquiring into the shared American experience of encountering diversity and simultaneously experiencing a unifying nation. It is also the perfect place to study diversity's potential threat to the unified national culture assumed necessary for American security and legitimacy.

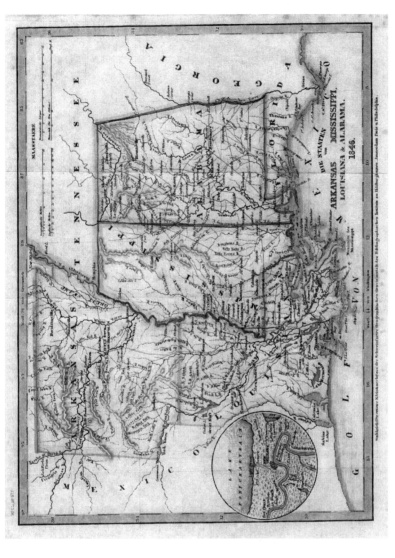

FIGURE 1. Map of Arkansas, Mississippi, Louisiana, and Alabama. 1846. The Historic New Orleans Collection, accession no. 1980.233 i, ii.

FIGURE 2. "The Southern Marseillaise." 1862. Item #: Conf. Music #376. Historic American Sheet Music. Rare Books, Manuscript and Special Collections Library. Duke University.

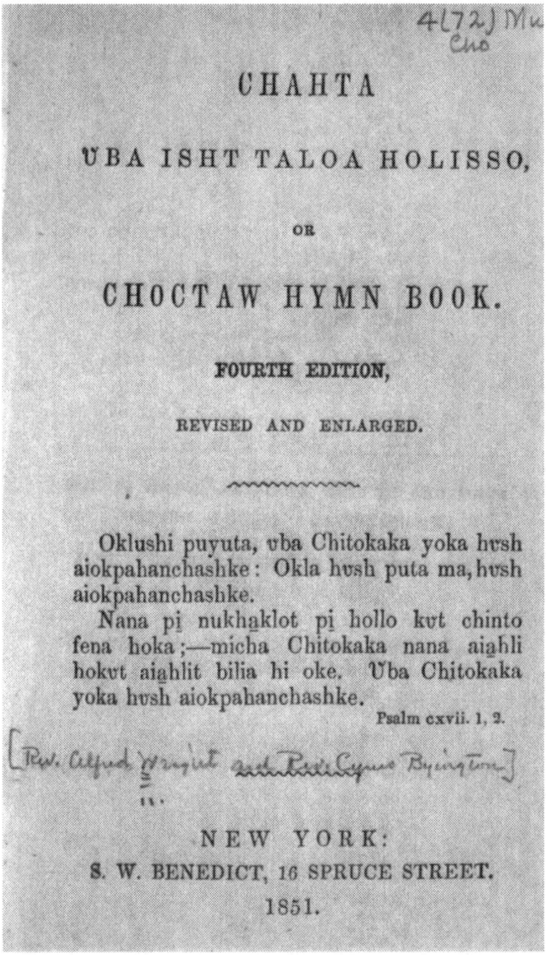

4[72] Mu
Cho

CHAHTA

UBA ISHT TALOA HOLISSO,

OR

CHOCTAW HYMN BOOK.

FOURTH EDITION,

REVISED AND ENLARGED.

Oklushi puyuta, vba Chitokaka yoka hvsh
aiokpahanchashke: Okla hvsh puta ma, hvsh
aiokpahanchashke.
Nana pi nukhaklot pi hollo kvt chinto
fena hoka;—micha Chitokaka nana aiahli
hokvt aiahlit bilia hi oke. Uba Chitokaka
yoka hvsh aiokpahanchashke.

Psalm cxvii. 1, 2.

[Rev. Alfred Wright ... Byington]

NEW YORK:
S. W. BENEDICT, 16 SPRUCE STREET.
1851.

FIGURE 3. *Chahta vba isht taloa holisso,* or *Choctaw Hymn Book.* 1851. The Huntington Free Library Native American Collection. Courtesy of Cornell University Library, Making of America Digital Collection.

THE VOLKSFEST, OR GERMAN MAY FESTIVAL, AT NEW ORLEANS. See page 298.

FIGURE 4. The Volksfest at New Orleans, 1859. The Historic New Orleans Collection, accession no. 1955.22.2.

FIGURE 5. "Ethiopian Quadrilles." N.d. From the collections of the Center for Popular Music, Middle Tennessee State University.

FIGURE 6. The Greek Romaika, danced by Mademoiselle Celeste. ca. 1837. Cia Fornaroli Collection. Jerome Robbins Dance Division, The New York Public Library for the Performing Arts, Astor, Lenox and Tilden Foundations.

FIGURE 7. Mademoiselle Celeste as the Wild Arab Boy. 1834. Cia Fornaroli Collection. Jerome Robbins Dance Division, The New York Public Library for the Performing Arts, Astor, Lenox and Tilden Foundations.

FIGURE 8. The Rainer Family in "The Miller's Maid." 1841. From the collections of the Center for Popular Music, Middle Tennessee State University.

3 / The War of the Quadrilles: Ethnic Loyalty and American Patriotism

We have been Spaniards thirty years and the Spaniards never have forced
us to dance the Fandango. We do not wish to dance either the reel or the jig.
LOUISIANA CREOLE BALL-GOER

The lower Mississippi River Valley between 1800 and 1860 remained tenuously if increasingly attached to the United States, while home to a markedly diverse and dynamic population. During this era, many commentators, working to create a unified national culture, called to strengthen the ties with regions previously unattached to the nation. Because of this, and because music ways in early America were believed to be linked to ethnic, racial, or national groups, a study of the regional music culture, both its perceptions and its expressions, reveals how the mixed population interacted during the process of being annexed to the nation. As this attachment between the lower Mississippi River Valley and the United States strengthened, the national culture that East Coast commentators were calling for seemed less relevant in a place of great diversity that remained on the fringe of the country. Rather, the regional music culture remained a site where fractious ethnic loyalties and national patriotism both coexisted and merged. The way people wrote and spoke about the music culture in the region reveals an understanding of the world divisible into clearly identifiable and distinct groups of people, each with its own peculiar musical ways. Yet, the regional music culture also remained a place of introduction, where previously unfamiliar people encountered the ways of other residents, as well as their new nation, helping to make what was foreign to them better understood. In the process, the regional population, both old and new, became more familiar with the nation and their fellow residents, as they created a more accessible, flexible, and usable American culture.

While the young American republic struggled to define itself, its geographic and demographic expansion into the lower Mississippi River Valley forced a reevaluation of the assumed meaning of its nationhood. Possible concepts of nationhood here seemed endless, because of the uncertain status of this region and its changing relationship with the nation during the early nineteenth century.[1] In newly annexed areas of great diversity such as this one, a sense of nationhood was created through interactions with unfamiliar people and their ways. Ethnic distinctiveness, combined with the decisive attachment contemporaries assumed between music and ethnicity, and the fact that music, like culture, is both a reflection and shaper of identity, allows the music culture of the lower Mississippi River Valley to become a useful lens through which to examine the path this region took as it became American. A study of the music culture of the lower Mississippi River Valley as it became increasingly a secure part of the United States reveals that the way people dealt with diversity in a nation yearning for the security of unity shaped American culture during the early republic and antebellum eras.

The necessity of actively connecting the lower Mississippi to the United States culturally seemed especially important due to its perception as a "modern Babel."[2] Based on accounts of visitors, as seen in the previous chapter, this perception reinforced the divide between the local population and the rest of the country, dashing all hopes of easily incorporating such a notorious "Babel" into the national culture—at least from the perspective of nonlocal inhabitants.[3] The great diversity of people, combined with its distant location from the center of power, prior colonial background, and distinctive immigration experiences forced new methods for dealing with national integration. According to Reid Mitchell, what most set New Orleans apart from other American cities was not its cultural diversity or range of ethnicities, although these accounted for much of its uniqueness, but that Anglo-Americans were its immigrants. Hence, "the usual models of immigrant adaptation and assimilation do not sit comfortably on either the newcomers or the Creoles. . . . To a certain extent, Americans 'Americanized' New Orleans and its Creoles. To a certain extent, New Orleans 'creolized' the Americans." However, emphasizing the exotic and peculiar history of the region separates it sharply from other parts of the United States's history even though it should be seen as a part of this whole. By examining this region as a "multicultural settlement process," rather than through an imperial perspective, one sees the degree of intercultural interaction as American nationals attempted to solidify this region as part of the nation. Much of the local population saw themselves as simultaneously American and specifically ethnic, while outsiders attempted to integrate in their own minds the ethnic character of the region with its place in an American national culture. Representatives of the American government within the region confronted a situation very different than had those new administrators working to build a nation following the American Revolution. These men were concerned with how to make people American who had not experienced the Revolution yet whose home was becoming annexed to the nation.[4]

Keeping in mind the regional diversity as detailed in Chapter 2 and the contemporary connection between ethnicity and music as shown in Chapter 1, it is not surprising that ethnic tensions found expression within the region's music culture. This becomes especially important when considering the multiple meanings attached by the locals to their music culture, including its symbolic meaning as an ethnic or national marker. In this way, music reflected identity. The ethnomusical assumptions as expressed by the music critics of the East became much less theoretical when applied in very practical ways to the policies of nation building along the lower Mississippi. Despite divisive instances, the region's music cultures were not completely fraught with discord. They also served as means of introducing the ever-changing local populations to each other and their new country.[5] In contrast, the use of music perceived as authentically ethnic in situations of national significance, such as elections and patriotic celebrations, helped all Americans make sense of the "others" in their midst, whomever they might consider this to be, potentially widening their vision of the nation's membership. In this way music helped shape identity. At times, incorporating aspects of a nationalizing American music culture into already extant practices happened smoothly. Expressions of national identity through patriotic songs and celebrations combined with a partisan political music culture to provide locals with a national music experience, new to some but familiar to others, although evidence of apathy toward such displays remained common. Successful expressions of national music culture did not attempt to override familiar ways; rather they complemented existing methods of expressing identities, substituting new loyalties rather than methods of expressing loyalties. A republican hero's nationality mattered little to honor him with a ball, nor did the country of an inept politician to lambaste him in song. Despite some initial ballroom controversy in 1804 at the time of transfer, according to Henry Kmen, the foremost scholar of early New Orleans music, "the public balls of New Orleans played an extremely important part in overcoming national differences. . . . By learning to play together, the polyglot peoples of this unique American city took an early and giant stride toward necessary understanding."[6] A study of the lower Mississippi River Valley's music culture reveals instances of divisive ethnic loyalty but also unifying nationalistic sentiments, manifesting an American culture struggling to come to terms with the meaning of nationhood in this region. Only after confrontation could conciliation begin.

Although retaining ethnic musical distinctiveness between transfer and the Civil War, a national music culture developed within the region, attempting to transcend ethnic loyalties and solidify the region's place within and connection to the American nation. According to the historian David Waldstreicher, it is necessary to examine such American nationalistic expressions in relation to other identities, beliefs, and practices, since local, regional, and national identities could exist simultaneously without contradicting each other.[7] Increasing numbers of Americans moved into the area bringing along their preferences for national songs and a music culture infused with public commemorations of national events. They also introduced a national political culture, which often used music to achieve its partisan aims. Yet, neither the nationalizing American music culture, nor any of the multiple ethnic music cultures won out over the other. Rather, a multitude of music cultures existed simultaneously. Because music could represent both national and ethnic identities, when ethnic and national music ways did merge, the people and the nation began to join as well. This process of competing music cultures is best understood with a study of American national and French Creole music cultures in New Orleans.[8]

Virtually everyone who wrote about the French and French Creoles and Anglo-Americans in the Mississippi Valley remarked on the stark contrast between their two colliding worldviews and the implications this had for the new nation's identity. The "competing ways of imagining the nation were contested and entangled" in this region. The French frontier became a symbol of the path not taken during antebellum America's empire building. Visitors commonly noticed the antipathy between these two groups. Based on the conversation of Creoles, one traveler, the duke of Saxe-Weimar-Eisenach, concluded that "they do not regard the Americans as their countrymen." And according to another visitor, the soldier William Gilpin, "The French language and a *French air* predominate tho' signs present themselves every where how rapidly the Anglo-Saxon is pushing aside the Frenchmen and eating him up." This presentation of two monolithic and opposing regional experiences of Anglo versus French ways has infused much writing of the region's cultural history.[9]

The relationship between these two music cultures shows the powerful ethnic and national meaning inherent in music ways and how in a setting where the only real certainty was insecurity and change, cultural accommodation, competition, tension, and even violence all remained viable options to settle cultural differences. As both outside administrators and locals alike attempted to shape the path down which this region joined the union, it became evident early on that wholesale importation of American musical ways would not be wholeheartedly accepted by the Creole population, and that local practices lacked relevancy to the new emigrants. What the dance historian Maureen Needham has termed "The War of the Quadrilles," proved to the local population and national officials that cultural ways could and would be negotiated.[10] The fights between American and French-speaking contingents on the ballroom floors of New Orleans at the time of transfer remained potent memories during its first decade as a territory, and similar, though less violent, musical antagonisms echoed throughout the rest of the antebellum period. The annexation of this place by the United States merely initiated a process of national attachment that was much more complicated than anticipated.[11] Tensions between instances of unifying nationalism and divisive ethnic identity found expression through the region's musical culture.

On January 8, 1804, just two weeks after the United States took control of the Louisiana Territory, the first of a number of disturbances occurred between the locals and the newcomers at a public ball in New Orleans. As a French and English quadrille formed simultaneously on the dance floor, an argument ensued over which the band should play. When an American raised his walking stick at a fiddler, "bedlam ensued." The new American governor William Claiborne, who was present at the affair, managed to calm the crowd. Dancing resumed with a French quadrille. Soon, an American again interrupted, calling for an English quadrille. Then, someone cried out, "If the women have a drop of French blood in their veins, they will not dance." The women abandoned the hall, ending the ball.[12] Although this was the version of the evening presented by the former French governor Pierre Clement de Laussat, Claiborne himself verified the urgency of the events in his letter to Secretary of State James

Madison two days later. "A *Fracas* also took place at a Public Ball on Thursday last which altho' it rose from trifling causes has occasioned some warmth. It originated in a contest between some young Americans and Frenchmen, whether the American or French Dances should have a preference. I believe this affair is at an end, but being desirous at the present juncture of communicating every circumstance which might have a political tendency, I have deemed it worthy of mentioning."[13] Unfortunately for Claiborne, this incident was only the beginning of many disagreements between the new Americans and the locals that would be articulated in ethnic terms and expressed through the music culture.

To prevent future conflicts, city officials, including Mayor Boré, requested an increased police force at the balls and the publishing of a prescribed dance order. Governor Claiborne complied by posting an officer and fifteen men at the ballroom door.[14] These new regulations seem to have had the opposite effect of that which was desired, and mayhem once again ensued on the night of the new rules. The ball began following the new legal dance order of two rounds of French quadrilles, followed by one round of English quadrilles, and then one round of waltzes.[15] "The ball began in a generally bad atmosphere," recalled Laussat, which may have led to its quick descent into confusion as further arguing developed over following the posted dance order. The inability of the two groups to communicate in the same language, many speaking only French or English, further prevented the chance for compromise. Thirty Americans and Frenchmen commenced fighting, and the guards began making arrests. When the fighting died down and everyone realized that almost all the women had left, the American "General Wilkinson intoned the 'Held [Hail], Columbia,' accompanied by the music of his staff, then 'God save the King,' then huzzas. The French, on their side, sang '*Enfants de la Patrie, Peuple français, peuple de frères,*' and shouted '*Vive la Republique!*' It was an infernal brawl." After this cabaret scene, Claiborne and Wilkinson, stationed in New Orleans to help oversee the transfer of Louisiana, escorted by the Americans and the band, returned to their homes.[16]

This "war of esteem" finally ended when the "influential and rightminded Americans" invited the French to a reconciliation banquet, who, after much coaxing, accepted. Laussat blamed poor American leadership, especially by Claiborne, for the frays. The governor's perceived hard-line style of forcing the French to accept American ways, including a variety of issues outside the ballrooms, did little to endear him to the local population. But Claiborne had recognized the necessity of continuing and even participating in the public balls, despite their being the site of frequent violent cultural clashes and rumors that he intended to end them. "On my arrival at New Orleans, I found the people very Solicitous to maintain their Public Ball establishment, and to convince them that the American Government felt no dispositien [sic] to break in upon their amusements (as had been reported by some mischievous persons) General Wilkinson and myself occasionally attended these assemblies," he wrote to James Madison after the second ballroom squabble. He continued, "I fear you will suppose that I am wanting in respect in calling your attention to the Balls of New Orleans, but I do assure you Sir, that they occupy much of the Public mind and from them have proceeded the greatest embarrassments which have heretofore attended my administration."[17] The music culture here retained such potent ethnic meaning among the native and incoming populations that it occupied the new political administration.

Others besides Secretary of State Madison expressed interest in the local cultural conflicts surrounding Louisiana's transfer to the United States. The War of the Quadrilles appeared in a detailed report in Philadelphia, New York, Boston, and Washington newspapers, bringing the lower Mississippi and its musical confrontations into the national press. These articles blamed the "misunderstandings" at least partially on the French officer's reply of "'We want the Walse [sic]' . . . being made in French, not being understood by the Americans, but, on the contrary, being interpreted into a menace, increased the disorder." Hence, according to these reports, it was not the difference in dance preference per se, but rather the inability to communicate about these preferences, which caused the problem. The continued presence of French soldiers also fueled speculation on the degree of control American forces actually held in the region. The editor of the New York Herald speculated on "what the national consequences of this quarrel will be." Would the French peacefully evacuate the territory, or would there be a "war of expulsion"?[18] The local dialogue regarding the incorporation of the region into the nation found expression on the stage of the New Orleans ballrooms where overarching divisive issues of language, political control, and cultural ways merged.

The American administrators found it difficult to imagine how such violent reactions could stem from the "trivial" issue of ballroom dances. In these episodes, they saw political intrigues running much deeper than a simple fight over dance styles. According to Wilkinson and Claiborne, in a letter from February 1804 to James Madison, "A Difference of rather a serious Nature, has sprung up, Apparently from a very trivial Source, between the American and French Citizens (in which hitherto, the Creoles or Natives of the Province, have taken no Open Part, though we suppose them to favor decidedly the French Interest)." Such a reference to their dances as trivial certainly would have angered both the native and foreign French, and reveals the American administrators' unfamiliarity with local customs. The episode assumed a political meaning to the American administration, representing French fear over their loss of power in the area. The letter to Madison continued to explain the American administration's perception of the French distaste for the dances Americans preferred. Rather than any connection to a dance style, according to Claiborne and Wilkinson, the French distaste stemmed from the local name of "*Contra Danse, Anglais*, against which (as great Importance is often Attached to mere Words) the Officers and Citizens of France, Strangers & not permanent Residents here, have manifested a decided Disapprobation, and pretended, that the Taste of the Americans, for this Danse [*sic*], indicated a partiality, to the English, their Enemies: Of Consequene [*sic*], they undertook, not in a very open way at first, to prevent the Americans from practicing this Danse [*sic*], at the Public Ball Room, which Occasioned a trifling Disturbance there."[19] In aligning the Americans with the English, suspected Claiborne, the French soldiers attempted to reinforce the Creoles' loyalty to France and vilify the Americans.

Claiborne and Wilkinson insisted that the intrigues of the "foreign French," especially "French Officers & troublesome young Men from Bordeaux," not the local population, fueled the disturbances. By doing so, they tried to define the native Louisianans, over whom the United States government would be ruling, as well behaved and amenable to the new government, while the foreign French, many whom should soon be leaving with the French military withdrawal, as the unruly party. The deposition of one American witness to the scene by a tribunal investigating the events supports this claim. He testified that "several Frenchmen, in order to justify their conduct, observed that the Americans wished to force the dancing of English dances, and that the people of the Country would never Consent to it . . . which is so far from the truth, that when they are proposed the whole Company seem willing to join, even the dance which was interrupted, was so much crowded that it could scarcely be effected, which was composed of less Americans than Creole French. . . . Not one Creole seemed to Contenance [*sic*] those unruly men." Their conscious attempt to downplay any role the native Louisianans may have had in the incident shows the administration's awareness of the multiple "French" identities in the region, and the volatility of accusing the wrong group. That the disturbance occurred during the week when the French troops were to evacuate the city proved to the American administration the necessity of expediting this process. New Orleans Mayor Boré blamed political intrigues of a different nature on the disturbances. The "spirit of disturbance and discord . . . [has] been favored or even aggravated by those who had the duty to suppress them. Hot heads, persons eager for influence, at any price, have contributed much to them: they daily contribute towards misleading the depositories of power and cause them to take false steps."[20] Yet, whatever contingent held responsibility for the ballroom brawls and the media crusade that followed, many found Claiborne's cultural sensitivity, if not his culture, lacking.

Despite Claiborne's best intentions, his handling of the ballroom frays at the beginning of American takeover became a legacy attached to his administration and a symbol of the American newcomers' disregard for local ways. For years after the incidents, when criticizing him, the local press reminded their readers of how he had handled the ballroom affairs. Locals politicized the cultural blunders, making them illustrative of all that was wrong with the American administration. A newspaper article by a French speaker, written in response to a defender of Claiborne, reminded readers that until Claiborne, "descending from his lofty station, committed the engregious [sic] blunder of meddling in the Country Dances at a public Ball, and showed so little energy or judgment in the contest that afterwards took place about them, and thereby made a national affair of a Country Dance, there were no quarrels; because, until, by his example in creating one there were no parties; . . . the blame of these misfortunes are imputable solely to the Governor." This writer insisted that the people of Louisiana rejoiced on Claiborne's arrival, but when "he vilified and abused them, representing them as ignorant, turbulent and incapable of appreciating the blessings of a free government . . . he saw no inconvenience likely to arise from the delay of providing for the organization of government in Louisiana while absolute authority was lodged in his own hands." Louisianans saw "their rights annihilated, their laws, languages, manners and customs trampled on."[21] Claiborne's handling of the ballroom affairs assumed a heightened political significance because his administrative decisions represented the new federal government to the local population. Claiborne's actions, as an American government official, were how locals experienced the nation. As locals pushed for immediate statehood in 1804, Claiborne recommended a more gradual incorporation, and the ethnic-infused War of the Quadrilles took on a newly politicized meaning.

The public renewed their complaints against Claiborne's manners in January of 1805 after he committed a disrespectful mistake of etiquette and kept his hat on during a theater performance, an act believed by some to be premeditated. This episode triggered memories of his past faux pas and became symbolic of all that was wrong with American rule. One editor alleged, "A decent respect is due to the manners and customs of a free people. . . . The most cruel Roman tyrant, never ventured to infringe the amusements of the people, much less to control and abuse them. . . . Nay even the Negroes on board their prison ships, are allowed their active amusements, and their keepers will join them while they clank their chains to the drum or the song." This writer blamed the governor for attempting to "introduce dances with which we were unacquainted, which resulted in a battle, and broke up the public amusements for the whole season. We were in hopes that such improprieties would have ceased with the winter, and that the Governor would have ended their evil consequences. But no! The same blunders still continue. . . . Does he fancy it a privilege and to his office, or that he is among Indians or YAHOOS? In either case he is mistaken. It is not an official privilege; he is among a polite and polished people."[22] Such complaints against Claiborne's cultural blunders combined both political and cultural issues into larger diatribes against him. Blending political and cultural grievances reveals the potency the mistakes of the dance hall must have held with the reading public for such a technique to be effectively persuasive in aligning the population against him.

Although forced changes to their dancing habits may have been enough to instill distaste in the local population toward the Americans, there were other underlying issues that found an outlet during these mixed public events, including language, law, and politics. Locals assumed that the new American rule would proceed directly based on the wording in the treaty of transfer, which the American government did not always interpret the same as the Creoles. The prejudices of Jefferson, Madison, Claiborne, and members of Congress disappointed those native Louisianans who assumed they could immediately apply for statehood after transfer.[23] Claiborne advised President Jefferson in February of 1804, "The greatest advocates for a Complete Representative Government in lower Louisiana, entertain serious doubts as to the Capacity of the people to govern themselves."[24] The potency of the issue of statehood appears in an oration delivered in French celebrating Louisiana's first

Fourth of July. The speaker reminded the audience that "we are all by birth or adoption children of the same country; remember that our interests are the same, that the same spirit should animate, and the same close union combine us. . . . [H]itherto it is true procrastinated beyond our expectations, but not, we trust irretrievably lost. . . . [We] . . . hope that the justice and wisdom of the legislators of our new country will accede to our ardent wishes by incorporating us into the Union, and admitting us to all the rights, immunities and advantages of citizens of the Unites States." Some Louisianans found irony in the fact that they were represented as unfit for self-government by "men who are now among them without knowing their ways, their manners, their customs, *their language?*"[25] New Orleans Mayor Boré complained to President Jefferson of Claiborne's new policy of using English when drawing up public acts. He advised, "Mr. President: it is indispensable that the deeds of Louisiana should know the French language, as well as the English language: if they had had this advantage, we should not have experienced the occurrences which have produced so bad a Feeling and the course of business would not languish and Would not be exposed to numberless embarrassments."[26] Having not yet experienced the nation of America but rather only understanding it in an ideological way, many French Creoles felt disappointed when their experiences with the nation seemed to contradict its ideals.

Although the American administration could not fathom it, the belief that uncouth American outsiders had invaded their dances genuinely offended some local French inhabitants. The French colonial love of dance and its importance to their ethnic identity was well known during the colonial era and early years of American rule. Without the Creole attachment to their own musical culture, the ballrooms could not have been made the setting for ethnic and national power struggles. The number of ballrooms in New Orleans alone illustrates this obsession. In 1805, there were fifteen public ballrooms, by 1815 almost thirty, and over twenty more sprung up during the next twenty years. Between 1836 and 1841 over thirty new spaces for dancing opened in the city. These numbers do not even take into consideration the private residences that hosted dances. Dancing supported the theaters by drawing audiences to shows, after which was a ball. Balls followed concerts, plays, operas, and variety acts. Henry Kmen speculates that this love of the dance developed since it was inexpensive and feasible in frontier regions; it could be enjoyed by all despite language barriers; and in the region's heritage as Latin-Catholic dancing carried no connotations of sinfulness. According to him, "The story of music in New Orleans must begin with dancing."[27]

Travel writers and historians alike have been surprised by the frequency and consistency of this mode of amusement among the late eighteenth- and early nineteenth-century inhabitants of the lower Mississippi River Valley. From neighborhood gatherings in small backwoods cabins, to grand affairs of state in New Orleans ballrooms, commentators used the Creole love of dancing to exemplify cultural traits unique to the mostly French colonists in the area. Such descriptive labeling, which connected fondness for dancing with "Frenchness," showed the ability of the music culture to signify ethnicity within the region as a way to differentiate this group from others who called the region home. By also using ethnic difference to highlight regional distinctiveness the ability of the lower Mississippi River Valley to become securely attached to the nation remained uncertain.

The first American Civil Commandant of Upper Louisiana at transfer, Major Amos Stoddard, noted that the French Creoles "are particularly attached to the exercise of dancing and carry it to an incredible excess. Neither the severity of the cold, nor the oppression of the heat, ever restrains them from this amusement, which usually commences early in the evening and is seldom suspended till late in the morning. They even attend the balls not infrequently for two or three days in succession, and without the least apparent fatigue. At this exercise the females, in particular, are extremely active, and those of the United States must submit to be called their inferiors." Stoddard's description implies an ethnic understanding of dance culture. The French excelled, and the Americans remained inferior. He continued, "It is not uncommon to see thirty or forty charming females in a ballroom, dressed with taste and even elegance, suited to the most fashionable society, when perhaps the males of their own families appear in their blanket coats and moccasins. It is rare to see in such an assembly more than four or five young men, whose appearance is even tolerable. This strange diversity is prevalent in the detached settlements of the country, and even in some of the villages."[28] Though lacking the resources of an urban ball-goer, such displays testify to the passion for dancing and the social activities surrounding these dances among the local population. It also shows the region's cultural distinctiveness according to the perspective of this American government official.

Outsiders disparaged these former French colonists, especially those at the Arkansas Post, as unmotivated and too fond of amusements, often specifically linking a love of dance to either their French or Native American heritage. In either case, commentators were situating the region as being distinctive culturally. When hunters returned to the post in the spring after their annual hunt, they passed their time "dancing, drinking, or doing nothing: similar in this respect to the savages with whom they live the greater part of the year, and whose tastes and manners they contract," related the Saint Domingue refugee François Marie Perin du Lac. A soldier at the post in 1807 noted that the inhabitants of this mostly French village were "remarkably fond of amusements, particularly of dancing, cards and billiards." To satisfy these cravings, "the inhabitants frequently have balls." James Miller, the first governor of the Arkansas Territory in 1820 found the society "very uncultivated." He recalled that the "population was originally French, and the Americans who come in fall into their practice," especially their fondness for balls and cards. Unlike Claiborne, he refused to attend the Saturday and Sunday night affairs, which "never disperse until daylight," although he did occasionally attend those on other nights of the week. The missionary Timothy Flint, while ministering to those in Arkansas he considered "principally French," was shocked when they came to hear his preaching "arrayed in their ball-dresses, and went directly from worship to the ball." The English botanist Thomas Nuttall who visited the fort in 1819 also believed that "the love of amusements here as in most of the French colonies, is carried to extravagance, particularly gambling, and dancing parties or balls." Further downstream, Nuttall again observed, this time of Louisiana planters, a group he took as being nearly all of "French or Spanish extraction": "Dancing and gambling appear to be their favourite amusements." Further up river, in Ste. Genevieve, Missouri, the traveler Christian Schultz noted, "One ball follows another so close in succession, that I have often wondered how the ladies were enabled to support themselves under this violent exercise, which is here carried to extremes."[29] According to these perspectives, being French in these isolated settlements meant being intimately attached to dancing.

Likewise, nearly every travel writer who visited New Orleans, the premier colonial French urban area, commented on the inhabitants' love of dancing, and typically connected this to something distinctly French. "The female Creoles being in general without education, can possess no taste for reading, music or drawing; but they are passionately fond of dancing. They will pass whole nights in succession at this exercise," remarked one visitor in 1802. He continued, "The local residents make pompous eulogies to foreigners and newcomers about their local balls with which they seem infatuated, comparing them to the brilliant Vauxhall or the Grand Galas of the Paris Operas." Another visitor, Thomas Ashe, described the chief amusements of the white women of New Orleans as attending balls, concerts, and private music parties in their homes. A Creole ball in New Orleans pleased the English tourist Charles Murray: "The *contre-danses* were well danced, and there was waltzing without swinging, and a gallopade without a romp. . . . I had seen nothing so like a ball since I left Europe," although he had attended dances in many "provincial towns in America." The architect Henry Benjamin Latrobe believed in 1819 that "the dancing of the ladies was what is to be expected of French women; that of the gentleman, what Lord Chesterfield would have called, too good for gentleman. I hope and believe that we Americans have qualities which make up for our deficiency in dancing, a deficiency which marked those young Americans that were upon the floor." Even the New Orleans City Directory advertised this ethnomusical trait when they noted that "there are several handsome ballrooms, where balls are frequent and well attended by the inhabitants, more particularly the French, who in general, are remarkably graceful performers, and much attached to so rational, healthy and improving an amusement." Except in the ballrooms, according to one American, you could live in New Orleans and not mix with French Creoles. As late as 1862, a settlers' guide still portrayed the old French settlers as a "jovial, frolicksome [sic] people, fond of music and dancing."[30] Without this intimate connection between the local French and their dance ways, the ballrooms could not have become a site of conflicting loyalties.

Although the War of the Quadrilles originally may have been more about competing French and American political power than dance styles, it entered local memory as an example of ethnocultural conflict. Bernard Marigny, a long-time New Orleans resident, recalled the episode years later as one of many American attempts at cultural domination of the locals, defined in ethnic terms. He wrote, "The Anglo-Saxons, who loved to amuse themselves but differently from the races of French origin, pretended that in Louisiana, having been bought by the United States, we should amuse ourselves in the American manner, and that the Virginia reel should replace the waltz, and the jig the cotillion. Creoles, informed of these ridiculous pretenses, went to the ball, as well as the French, naturalized by the fact of the cession of France to the United States. An infernal disorder arose; men were armed. This ball had been selected to test which would carry it over the other, the waltz or the reel." In the midst of the disruption, he recalled, a young woman jumped on a

bench and shouted, "We have been Spaniards thirty years and the Spaniards never have forced us to dance the Fandango. We do not wish to
dance either the reel or the jig." The War of the Quadrilles had taken
on new meaning by the 1840s, when Americans and European immigrants greatly outnumbered the French speakers, and the Creole "men,
by their indifference and apathy . . . [have] . . . lost much of the influence
that they should have in the country," regretted Marigny.[31] Yet this perception of the era of Louisiana's Spanish rule between 1764 and 1803 as
being culturally accommodating existed only once a comparison to the
American intrusion could be made.

In a case remarkably similar to the American and French dispute at
transfer, French and Spanish ballroom quarrels highlight the ethnic potency of music inherent in identity even before American rule. The Spanish governor's son, during a visit to the colony in 1793, asked to substitute
English country dances for French ones, a request "tolerated from deference for his distinguished rank." However, "This act of compliance was
misunderstood by the youthful Spaniard," and as soon as French dances
were formed, he repeated his request. The dancers, "inflamed at his want
of moderation, ordered the music to play on, exclaiming unanimously,
'Contre-danses Francaises!' The son of the governor soon found parti-
sans, who joined with him in the cry of 'Contre-danses Anglaises!' while
the dancers firm to their purpose, reiterated 'Contre-danses Francaises!'"
The Spaniard ordered the fiddlers to stop playing while the officer stationed at the door ordered his men to fix their bayonets and disperse the
dancers. The Frenchmen drew their swords, while the few Americans
present reportedly remained neutral and assisted "the fair ladies who
had fainted away." Physical violence was averted only when three young
Frenchmen, lately arrived from Europe, mounted the orchestra stand
and exhorted all to restore peace and harmony. The ball resumed with
French country dances, in the presence of the governor who had arrived
to calm the tumult.[32] This colonial ballroom fray reiterates the attachment between a music culture and the inhabitants' national identity even
before the American administration entered the scene.

This previous experience likely colored the French Louisianans' ballroom expectations, heightening the meaning of events surrounding
transfer to the Americans in 1803. The occurrence just described was
not, however, the only incident of the Spanish administration meddling
in the French Creole music culture. In 1793, when Spain declared war
against the new French Republic, "The sympathies of the colonists were
not concealed; at the theater the celebrated French hymn 'La Marseillaise'

was frantically asked from the orchestra." The singing of this and other Jacobin songs, including "Ca ira," prompted such fear in the Spanish governor of the colony, Francisco Luis Hector, baron de Carondelet, that "he outlawed anything resembling revolutionary music and martial dances at the theatre." Prior to this, in October 1792, the Spanish government had published "Regulations for the Theatre" in seven articles, including one stating, "The performance shall never be interrupted by shouting, whistling, or in any other manner. . . . [A]nyone who is not satisfied with the performance is free not to attend."[33] Carondelet found the lyrics to one song, written by a well-known local lady of French leaning, particularly offensive. The French words read:

> Quand nous serons Républicains,
> Nous punirons tous ces coquins.
> Cochon de lait le premier
> Sera guillotine.

> When we become republicans,
> we will punish all these scoundrels.
> Suckling pig the first
> shall be guillotined.[34]

The comparison between Carondelet and *Cochon de lait*, a suckling pig, as the first to be guillotined did not strike the governor as amusing.

The American governor Claiborne may have experienced a similar lyrical insult during a later time of ethnic and national tensions within the region in 1804. When thirty Frenchmen visited a fellow countryman imprisoned in New Orleans for instigating some ethnically charged fighting, they composed and sang a song whose verses remain unknown, but the chorus intoned *Périsse à jamais l'Anglais* (May the English ever perish). Although technically an insult to the English, Madison believed, as previously noted, that the French often considered the Americans suspiciously partial to English interests around the time of transfer and the Napoleonic wars. This event seemed significant enough for Claiborne to forward a copy of the incident and lyrics to Secretary of State James Madison.[35] No matter which administration appeared more willing to allow the French Creoles to retain their music culture, the Spanish or American, it is important to note the frequency with which the various inhabitants of the region considered the music culture a possible conduit for the expression of ethnic and national accommodation as well as conflict.

After the end of the first year of American rule, Claiborne reassured Madison, "I have never witnessed more good order than at present pervades this City; and as far as I can learn the whole Territory. I discover also with great pleasure the existence of a friendly understanding between the Modern and Ancient Louisianans. The Winter amusements have commenced for several Weeks; the two descriptions of Citizens meet frequently at the Theatre, Balls, and other places of Amusement, and pass their time in perfect harmony." A public celebration marking the first anniversary of transfer included, among other happenings, a "band of music . . . playing many patriotic airs," and, not surprisingly, a ball. Newspapers reported that "the company in the Ball room was numerous and respectable exhibiting throughout the evening a cheerful love of order and decorum, which delights and we are all anxious to see; the pleasure of the ball was not disturbed by a single murmer [sic]."[36]

Yet, such goodwill did not completely bury prior feelings, and the region's music culture continued to convey ethnic tensions. Episodes of ethnically derived musical conflict did not remain confined to the War of the Quadrilles. Its echoes reverberated throughout the lower Mississippi River Valley during the antebellum era, preventing the creation of a unified regional music culture and foiling efforts to connect this place musically with the nation. As more Americans and their musical expectations arrived in the lower Mississippi River Valley, divisions between styles perceived as American national music ways and those believed to be distinctly appropriate for expressions of other identities continued. The tensions within the local music culture reveal the power of music to represent ethnic and national identity to this varied population. Just as echoes of the War of the Quadrilles haunted Governor Claiborne's tenure, its legacy informed the relationship between the varied regional music ways and the incoming American national music culture. Musical differences continued to represent ethnic and national differences to the regional population.

Posting dance orders, as had been required beginning in 1804, continued long after the need for such measures might seem to have passed. The *New Orleans Bee* published regulations for a masquerade ball held at the Orleans Ballroom in 1828: "Managers alone have the charge to maintain good order, and to regulate the music. . . . Two French Cotillions and a Waltz, will be danced alternately: Reels may be called for by one of the managers." A ball held to celebrate George Washington's birthday that year included the same dance order, printed in both English and French. Theaters took similar precautions. Posting programs ahead of time allowed managers a greater degree of control over the events that might occur in their theater. The theaters of New Orleans had also been the scene of cultural conflict around the time of transfer. In November of 1804, less than a year after American takeover, the New Orleans City Council posted a list of articles to help maintain decorum at the theater. One in particular related to disturbances caused by national fervor. It stated, "If good order is to be maintained, the orchestra of the hall cannot be subject to fanciful demands to play this or that tune; the management binds itself to satisfy the public's demand by the rendition of national airs; no person by bringing up any request in this regard shall disturb either the orchestra or the audience without running the risk of being brought before the magistrate."[37] Evidently, musical displays of ethnic pride were not limited to the ballrooms but found outlet in other venues as well.

The practice of the audience shouting out preferences, especially patriotic songs, continued despite such regulatory attempts. It was common for theater audiences at the time to be vocal participants during performances, expressing their preferences for and dislike of songs with various noises and the occasional projectile. Frances Trollope described one Cincinnati performance: "The applause is expressed by cries and thumping with the feet, instead of clapping; and when a patriotic fit seizes them, and 'Yankee Doodle' was called for, every man seemed to think his reputation as a citizen depended on the noise he made." This style of audience participation was common in New Orleans and the lower Mississippi as well. In 1853, a New Orleans judge even declared that audiences had the right to hiss and stamp in the theater. Although this usually caused little more than a nuisance, it had the potential for inciting violence, depending on the audience. The most famous theater riot occurred in 1849 in New York at the Astor Place Opera House, where twenty-two people were killed and 150 injured. Although class antagonisms largely caused the Astor Place Riots, they also had an ethnic component. The New York native Americans utilized both class and ethnic discourse when they posted handbills throughout the city during the affair asking, "Working Men, Shall Americans or English rule this city?"[38]

A Fourth of July concert occasioned once again a reminder that issues of ethnic and national identity remained unsettled in the city of New Orleans. The elderly and nearly deaf French orchestra leader Louis Desforges had rehearsed with his company for several weeks an overture from the opera *La Dame Blanche*. When the night of the performance arrived, the Camp Street Theater "was filled to repletion with a crowd, the majority of whom were backwoodsmen from the Western country. . . . They had come to have fun and fun they were determined to have." As the symphony began, "All of a sudden, a call for 'Yankee Doodle' was heard from the galleries." Not hearing the interruption, Desforges continued conducting. "When the cry of 'Yankee Doodle' was taken up again, and began to resound from dome to pit. . . . crashes following crashes gave notice that the work of demolition of benches and chairs had commenced, amid angry shouts of 'Yankee Doodle.'" The theater manager came out, stopped the music and explained the situation to the deaf Desforges, who "stood up in a stupor, and only had time to gasp out, 'Yankee Dude!' Then, stung to the quick by the affront put on him by the populace, he shrieked out in quick, piping tones: 'You want Yankee Dude? Well, you no have Yankee Dude! Because why? Because no necessair.'" Although this encounter did not end in violence, but rather applause and laughter, this New Orleans audience heard neither a French opera nor "Yankee Doodle" on the stage that night.[39]

Public festivities could also be scenes of ethnic antagonisms expressed through music performance. At a New Orleans celebration on the anniversary of the destruction of the Bastille, a number of Frenchmen "hoisted the French flag and sang their favorite national Songs," which "excited the jealously of *the Americans* and it required some address to prevent their taking it down by violence." It was only on explaining that Americans abroad frequently celebrated the Fourth of July that "the day passed away without disturbance." Governor Claiborne believed these confrontations to be the result of "intrigues of certain late Emigrants from France and some of the Satellites of the Spanish Government . . . to foment differences between the native Americans and the native Louisianians; every incident is laid hold of, to widen the breach and to excite Jealousy and confusion." Fostering political insecurity might later aid either nation in regaining their former hold in the region, a possibility many, including Claiborne, feared. Claiborne also accused the *"rash, and very imprudent"* Americans, as well as the newspapers, for stirring up discontent among the various parties. Even the lack of violence at public celebrations might garner comment, emphasizing the assumed potential for disorder. "Thus terminated without any accident to impair its joys, another Anniversary of American Independence," reported one editor.[40] The potential for disruptions during public displays of national significance always seemed a possibility.

The very existence of a musical culture on the Sabbath heightened the awareness of distinctions between the Catholic French and Protestant

Americans, and was used as a way to mark regional peculiarity in contrast to other places. Visitors frequently commented on, and often condemned, the French Creole tradition of participating in amusements on this day. "The most offensive feature of French habits is the manner in which they spend Sundays," remarked Latrobe. To some especially pious visitors, this distinction pervaded their observations of the two groups' musical cultures, and usually proved to them the degeneracy of the French. According to Henry Whipple, the Sabbath was not respected in New Orleans because of the "large mass of foreigners located here whose notions of religion are very vague and indefinite and either run into the skepticism of the French infidel school or the bigotry of the papists." French theaters commonly posted playbills around town on Sunday morning to advertise that evening's performance. Once, as the minister Timothy Flint happily noted, "a paper of the same dimensions, and the same type, but in English, was everywhere posted directly under the French bill. It contained appropriate texts from the scriptures, began with these words; 'Remember the Sabbath and keep it holy,' and mentioning that there would be divine service that evening." An especially vociferous description of these two competing traditions comes from the musician Anton Reiff touring with an opera company from New York. He was shocked to find in New Orleans a "'Tableau Vivant' of the crucifixion! Which was *encored*!! In New York with all its wretchedness it would be hissed off the stage. And today I heard they are about producing a tragedy called the Messiah! I think I shall go and see it if only for the *Flavor* of the thing—only to think that this should be in enlightened America—it is absolutely dreadful."[41] As long as public music events occurred on the Sabbath, distinctiveness between groups as seen through their religious traditions and music cultures remained evident.

Reinforcing ethnic divisions by way of the regional music culture continued into future generations through an ethnically divided ballroom youth culture. Children's balls were common affairs and often held by a dancing instructor to showcase the young talent. More often than not, they preceded a ball for adults. As late as the 1830s, children's balls in New Orleans remained segregated, with the "French" youths, by this date largely French Creoles, dancing at one end of the ballroom and the Americans at the other. Their different physiognomy and hairstyles distinguished the two groups, according to one Yankee visitor. He was assured, however, this division existed not from any spirit of "rivalry, jealousy, or prejudice"; rather the "irremediable one of language" necessitated the arrangement. If they "were indiscriminately mingled, the result would be confusion like that of Babel, or a constrained stiffness and reserve, the natural consequence of the inability to converse—instead of that regularity and cheerful harmony which now reign throughout the crowded hall."[42] While the French and American children of New Orleans shared a space, albeit a divided one, adults often found it expedient to maintain separate venues.

The retention of separate facilities and events for the French and Americans ensured "safe" spots for a particular musical way, implying instances of musical segregation. As the population grew, having one general Carnival ball became impractical, according to the American resident George Morgan, and ethnic divisions entered Carnival celebrations. French-speakers attended the evening *fete* at the French coffeehouse, while a second ball at another location included a mixture of the city's groups. Such distinctions entered the theaters as well. The Orleans Theater advertised in 1822, "There are dramatic performances here almost every night throughout the year by full and respectable French and English companies, who play alternately." But even in spots typically frequented by the French or Americans, segregation was never complete, and mixture was the rule. The primarily French-language theaters had performances in English, and the primarily English-language theaters in French. Although venues might cater to mixed American and French Creole audiences, it did not necessarily mean the audiences felt comfortable mixing. The American Nathaniel Cox, writing from New Orleans in 1807 to a friend in Kentucky with a particular disregard for the French Creoles, reassured him that one could "live among those people without partaking of the customs and manners." He reported that the English Coffee House catered largely to Americans and English, and only in such establishments as the ballroom "where a mixture at all happens—And even at the ball room the American only become spectatory [sic] as much to see the French boys & girls dance as you would visit a theatre to see the actors perform. Few very few of the Americans partake of the French Cotillions—Fear not for my principles or any change of manner as it can't be effected unless I particularly wish it and voluntary assume it."[43] Just because Americans and French Creoles danced in the same ballrooms did not mean they partook of each other's dances, nor were they willing to participate in ways not familiar to them. Remaining "spectators" in such instances could allow one to experience the other at a safe and comfortable distance.

The competition between the local Anglo and French music cultures found expression in other interesting ways. In 1819, Anna Cox of New

Orleans vented her feelings toward the local French through her views of their theater. "M—Gray's elopement! And with that vagabond Pirate Canonge has afforded a great triumph to the French Theatre, for they could not bear to think the American company were so much more respectable than themselves. . . . I believe they have not a chaste woman among them," she remarked. When the American James Caldwell began constructing a new theater in 1835, a traveler reported, "The Anglo-Americans, striving to equal the attainments of the Creoles, have also built a beautiful theater." The new orchestra attached to this venue especially pleased the Americans, since "it would be a good rival to that at the French theater."[44] The American and French opera companies of New Orleans, led by their respective managers James Caldwell and John Davis, raced to see who could first produce the Giacomo Meyerbeer grand opera *Robert the Devil*, or *Robert le diable*. The Americans won. But, in order to secure a box office success, Caldwell included an act by Thomas Dartmouth Rice, the creator of the minstrel sensation Jim Crow. As Davis's theater faced financial ruin in 1824, many French Creoles appealed to ethnic loyalty as they attempted to defer the crisis. Frenchmen "who loved their country" and who hoped to conserve the "tongue and customs of our ancestors" should purchase subscriptions. When the Revolutionary War veteran the marquis de Lafayette visited New Orleans during his tour of the United States, he drew straws to see which theater he would attend first, the French or American, so as not to offend either group.[45] Such competition between the French and Americans exemplifies how music culture could manifest ethnic differences and suggests the broader resentments continuing to exist in the region between these two groups.

The climate in the ballrooms and theaters of New Orleans, at least to some degree, helped measure the security of American rule. The War of the Quadrilles came to be about more than the dances at a public ball, although, considering the French Creole regard for dancing, it was certainly about that as well. This episode became a symbol to the local French of the perceived corruption and incompetence of the American government in Louisiana, and to the Americans of the excess and frivolity of the French Creoles. Claiborne experienced the ire of locals due to his ballroom faux pas, which they attached to other complaints against him, such as his inability to speak French and his representing them as unfit for self-government, using the episode to further illustrate his incompetence. Only because of the potent ethnic meaning inherent in the music culture could such a technique effectively align the two groups vying for power. According to some Americans, ethnic displays within the Creole music culture appeared as an affront to their own nationality. American insecurity surrounding their hold over the region caused anxiety, which also found expression within this competitive musical environment. The lower Mississippi River Valley's attachment to the nation never entirely became secure in the minds of locals or outsiders. These destabilizing possibilities included rumors of a coup by the local French population, fear that the Spanish would retake Louisiana, the Burr Conspiracy (a separatist movement supposedly instigated by this former vice president), the English threat during the War of 1812, as well as the threat of slave rebellions.[46] To some, the ability to forge a unity between this place and the rest of the United States seemed preposterous due to its peculiar diversity, of which the francophone community was just one of many disuniting components. Aspects within the music culture proved ethnic distinctiveness to residents, which might then limit full acceptance of the region into the nation.

Yet simultaneously with such ethnic musical exhibitions within the lower Mississippi Valley, the escalating number of American newcomers increasingly cultivated a national musical culture in the region. Both the divisions within the populace as presented thus far, and the attempt at encouraging American national affiliation through the music culture in the region, which will be dealt with next, were predicated on the belief that a music way could signify ethnic or national identity. Loyalty was especially important to cultivate in this region where its reputation of a loose national attachment arose from its great diversity.[47] Although a national music culture emerged in this region, it little resembled that which the cultural commentators called for. Rather, the national music in the region fit the special needs of this particular place. In some instances, it developed distinctively from groups that straddled ethnic and national loyalties, while attempting to reconcile these two identities. In other instances, those whose American national ties remained their only affinity felt the need to publicly promote this allegiance among the regional population in order to strengthen the ties between the region and the nation and temper the potential threat diversity posed to national unity.

American elites within the region at times sponsored a nationalizing music culture while attempting to connect this place with the rest of the country. On the first anniversary of American independence after transfer, Governor Claiborne assured Madison of his intention to fund a national public celebration and enforce his authority in Louisiana. He wrote, "The 4th of July will be celebrated in this city with great Pomp. I think it may have a good Political tendency, and I shall therefore spare *neither trouble nor expense."* The celebration included a mass, orations in English and French, parades, and military exercises.[48] He previously had endorsed the first anniversary of Washington's birthday in the U.S.-controlled Louisiana Territory in a similar fashion, including an evening ball. This celebration proceeded under the "general orders of his Excellency Governor Claiborne," with "zeal and pride" giving "satisfactory evidence of the future disposition of the Louisianians toward the general government." The description of these events in the press shows the intentionally unifying nationalistic sentiments such affairs were meant to cultivate even when competition remained evident. Governor Claiborne expressed hope for "the future disposition of the Louisianians towards the general government. The *old* and *new* Americans of the Orleans Volunteers, proudly vied with each other" during the parade performances in honor of George Washington in 1806. After the event, one editor inscribed:

Tho' dead the name of *Washington* shall live,
and patriots true, will their praises give.
American and French, his praise proclaim,
and raise new trophies to his honor'd name.

Others echoed Claiborne's use of public spaces and the music culture performed in them to promote the nation throughout the vicinity. The "leading citizens" typically marched in, and likely organized and funded public parades commemorating national events.[49]

Further examples, however, show instances where the music culture expressed impromptu national sentiments, which grew more organically from the local population and less from elite encouragement. In the Arkansas backcountry, a farmer on the Forche le Favre gave "a grand entertainment—or frolic, as it is called" to commemorate Independence Day. By noon, a fiddle played for the dancing youth, while the women cooked and the men lounged. The German traveler Friedrich Gerstäcker, who "had never succeeded in acquiring the dances of my own country, much less the extraordinary movements of those of America," amused himself by watching the attendees arrive from all corners of the state on horseback. The women, he thought, "seemed they were going on a pilgrimage, instead of coming to a ball," considering the supplies they carried. After dinner, a speech honored the nation's birthday, and then the dancing began again inside the log house, while cards, athletic events, and storytelling commenced outdoors.[50] Further north on the river, another visitor recorded his Fourth of July experience: "We awakened about half an hour before sunrise, got the fiddle in tune; as soon as the music was up, all hands were out of bed and commenced hoeing down at a round rate; there was something truly comic about the performance which continued for some time until some began to pick splinters out of their feet." The young German immigrant Max Nuebling celebrated the Fourth of July in 1825 at St. Francisville, Louisiana, with a "parade of canoes on the Bayou." One Memphis citizen remembered the day being "animated by the fife and drum discoursing national music."[51] These celebrations of American independence connected this region with the nation by honoring days of national significance with music.

Whether these festivities developed naturally or were encouraged by the leadership, successful expressions of national identity took forms already popular among the local population. After American takeover, the already existing ballroom culture took on a new role of familiarizing the Creoles with their new nation by using dances to celebrate anniversaries of national significance. The balls allowed the local population to pursue a nationalizing unity in ways that made sense to them. Public balls commemorated national anniversaries including Washington's birthday and the Fourth of July.[52] New Orleanians celebrated Washington's birthday in 1817 with cannon fire in the morning and a ball in the evening. Newspapers printed advertisements for Washington Balls in New Orleans in both French and English. At an 1808 Natchez celebration of Washington's birthday, celebrants interspersed their toasts with songs such as "Hail, Columbia," "Washington's March," "Yankee Doodle," "The President's March," and other songs with equally patriotic titles. Residents also organized balls to welcome nationally important figures, including Andrew Jackson, Henry Clay, and the marquis de Lafayette. After Andrew Jackson increasingly assured the region's connection to the United States in January of 1815 at the Battle of New Orleans, residents could celebrate at "Jackson's Ball to be held on Washington's Birthday at the American Coffee House."[53] The 1825 ball given to honor Lafayette's visit to the city attracted over one thousand dancers.[54]

Local inhabitants also used balls to celebrate events of particularly potent local significance but that were also meaningful nationally, such as the anniversary of transfer and the Battle of New Orleans. The inhabitants of Baton Rouge celebrated the anniversary of the Battle of New Orleans with a ball in both 1845 and 1846. By commemorating this day, they were simultaneously remembering their regional distinctiveness and their locale's significance within the national memory. "The anniversary of the Battle of New Orleans, [is] a day that ought to be remembered by every American in general, and every Louisianian in particular," lectured one editor from this city. Those at a ball in Rapides commemorating Jefferson's birthday in 1805 heard a toast to "the recent change of government in our country—emerging from vassalage to freedom, may no national prejudices intercept our peace, or obstruct our happiness."[55] Such expressions of national loyalties connected those throughout the Mississippi Valley with each other and the nation, and could at times simultaneously reinforce regional and national identity.

Fetes marking Independence Day presented some of the most boisterous and most musical of all these national public festivities. Events on this day might include orations, banquets, parades, military maneuvers, toasts, balls, and songs. At times, celebrants pronounced the orations, toasts, and even the Declaration of Independence in both French and English.[56] As early as 1808, even before Mississippi had become a state, some Natchez residents celebrated the nation's independence with a dinner where, "a number of toasts were drank [sic], interspersed with songs," and then a ball.[57] Independence Day balls were very common and held all along the river throughout the era, as were banquets where "toasts were drank [sic], accompanied with appropriate songs and music." These "appropriate songs" included patriotic hymns such as "Hail, Columbia," "Washington's March," and "Yankee Doodle" but might also incorporate more surprising choices like "Bonaparte's March" and "Landlady in France." Toasts intoned ethnic, national, and even international loyalties, interspersed by "appropriate music." If, for example, Ireland, in its republican struggles, was toasted, it might be followed with an appropriately "Irish" song, usually one with "Ireland" in the title. When republican France was toasted, "The Marseilles" commonly followed. In a similar example from 1853 Los Angeles, songs considered appropriately patriotic for Independence Day celebrations depended on one's identity. Americans sang "Hail, Columbia" and the "Star-Spangled Banner"; the Frenchmen, "The Marseillaise"; and the Mexicans, the "Ponchada."[58]

The sounds of martial music announced celebratory occasions in many Mississippi River towns. Martial music played by military companies accompanied many public gatherings to instill a national significance to the day and helped to promote an atmosphere of national cultural consensus in these places. The New Orleans Legion and their band escorted the visiting John Calhoun to his lodgings, and four military divisions marching to music helped celebrate the anniversary of the Battle of Monterey. "At an early hour the Military Companies roused the citizens by their martial music" to celebrate independence in 1838 Vicks-burg.[59] New Orleans militia companies organized along ethnic lines, in-cluding companies of Irish, German, Spanish, Italian, and Swiss, among the dozen American and French groups, as well as one composed of "Free Men of Color." Bands accompanied these troops in their Sunday morn-ing maneuvers and paraded for celebrations of national significance such as the Fourth of July and Washington's birthday. These bands occasion-ally clashed in "windy wars," where "both playing different tunes at the same time" brought ethnic competitiveness to national festivities.[60]

Despite evidence that a public festive music culture connected this region with the nation through celebrations of national import, evidence also suggests apathy among the population toward these particularly American celebrations. "This is the first time in many years we have had no public demonstration of this day in the city," condemned a Vicksburg editor of July Fourth in 1841. "Not a drum was heard, nor a plume wav-ing in the streets, all dull and cheerless." An attempt to organize a Wash-ington's birthday ball in New Orleans in 1829 failed for want of subscrib-ers, despite daily advertisements in both French and English beginning a month in advance. A few years prior, another Washington Ball had a poor showing, especially considering that "in former days," tickets sold for ten dollars but were now "reduced to three dollars a ticket and hardly filled up at that price." Such indifference might be accounted for by the commercial affairs of the city, supposed one visitor, yet he suspected it could more likely be "traced to the incomprehensible want of attachment among the creoles to the United States."[61] When George Washington's birthday fell too close to Mardi Gras, the local trumped the national. Its bad timing in 1841, falling the day before Mardi Gras, hampered the patriotic celebrations. One editor lamented, "Our volunteer companies that attempted a turn-out on Monday last, presented a sorry appear-ance. . . . The *Mardi-gras Fantasticals* both horse and foot on the day following was a much more attractive affair, such a number of motley figures in masks and visors sufficient at most to call to remembrance *La Carnival de Venice*."[62]

Such indifference triggered condemnation by local figures of influ-ence. Newspaper editors bade locals to express more interest in these national events. The *Baton Rouge Gazette* chastised its readership dur-ing preparations for the 1844 Independence Day celebration stating, "It would be more to the credit of Baton Rouge if the citizens would make a general celebration than a partial one, as has been the case for some years past." Just three years prior, they had wondered, "Is it necessary to inform our friends and fellow citizens that the Fourth of July is at hand? What arrangements have been—or are to be made in Baton Rouge for its celebration?" The following year the complaints continued, "This glorious anniversary is fast approaching, and as usual, we see no movement made on the part of our citizens for its celebration." Although the militia and fire company marched in commemoration, this editor wondered, "Will these patriotic young men who compose them bear alone the glory of celebrating a day that ought to be held in reverence by every citizen of this republic? We hope not." A lackluster Washington's birthday celebration called for similar accountability: "Our citizens generally have made no demonstrations.... At times like these ... when the Union is shaken to its very center, and the fit and glorious fabric of our republican government is threatened with disunion," the public needed local solidarity with the nation.[63]

The anniversary of transfer seemed frequently forgotten as well. On the seventh anniversary of transfer in 1810, a New Orleans editor reflected, "The twentieth of December for two or three years was held as a national *fete*—with cannons, ringing of bells, and even demonstrations of joy were exhibited among all ranks and classes, particularly the Americans. Those festivals have become less and less for some years, and yesterday passed entirely unnoticed. We ... [illegible] the rulers of our land to account for the *national apathy*." The following year, "The anniversary of taking possession of Louisiana was celebrated yesterday with some spirit—it being the first time it has been noticed since the year 1807." Washington's birthday in 1811 occasioned reflection by the editors of both the *Orleans Gazette* and the *Louisiana Gazette* on the need to continue commemorating national leaders.[64]

A visit by Andrew Jackson to New Orleans in 1828 and the celebratory accompaniments effectively illustrate the degree of local apathy toward nationalizing events, especially if the event seemed to represent a partisan political culture.[65] The people of New Orleans showed far less interest than the festivity's organizing party might have hoped. Despite meticulous preparation for his visit, "nothing was wanting but that which a committee cannot give: That enthusiasm which is nothing less than the spontaneous tribute of the heart." The editorial continued:

> A programme can be made, certain ceremonies determined on, to increase the crowd; and by cunning maneuvers to march and countermarch the volunteer troops, who by the state law are obliged to march every 8th of January. Flags may be hoisted on the roofs of

taverns, and colours may be hung from the front of each window of the theater; gapers may be collected by an incessant beat of drum; by marching though the streets ensigns followed by children both white and black, and who for the trifling compensation of a few cents worth of squibs are taught to cry *hurra for Jackson*. But the joy of the people is not so easily obtained, it is more difficult to collect them where they care not to go. If anything like a crowd was seen, it was not so much for the General as the beautiful sights of 17 steamboats dressed off in colours, and firing cannon, that caused it to assemble. If some hundred persons were seen inside the church, it was on account of the music, good or bad, which never fails drawing that class of people called idlers.[66]

During the celebration there were even shouts of "Lafayette," a sentiment this editor explained as trumping the partisan politics Jackson represented and connecting the locals "with all the other states of the union," who heroized Lafayette's role in the American Revolution, not necessarily because of his French nationality. The third day after Jackson's arrival saw "a committee organizing in the morning for the purpose of getting up an *impromptu* ball." By four that afternoon, "for the purpose of more effectually *inflaming* public zeal," ticket prices were reduced by half, despite being advertised in both English and French. Yet at the ball, "the ordinary room was scarcely filled, while at the Lafayette ball, the ball-room, the theatre made level, and all the boxes were so completely crowded, that it was difficult to form a cotillion." According to this writer, only party men expressed interest in Jackson's visit, and he only published this description of well-known facts "to prevent deception from taking advantage of our silence." Jackson's reception in New Orleans suggests that despite the existence of a national festive culture in the region, it lacked significance among much of the population. It is also important to keep in mind, though, the enmity many Creoles held toward Jackson after he questioned their loyalty during the War of 1812; although after the successful defense of the city from the traditional French enemy, the British, many forgave his doubts.

However, party politics may also be partially to blame for this editor's perspective. Another editorial suggested that "the cause of so cold a reception," by the citizens of New Orleans was not due to their lack of gratitude toward the general, rather it was because of the "delicate position in which were placed the greater part of our citizens by certain persons obstinately persisting to give an appearance of party spirit" to the celebration. Although Jackson represented a partisan political culture, while Lafayette appeared above this as a national revolutionary hero, the frequent recourse to invoke the name of Lafayette, versus any of the other revolutionary heroes except George Washington, implies an ethnic pride the local Creoles held toward this Frenchman's role in creating their nation.[67]

Despite such evidence of apathy, as the festive, music, and print cultures coalesced, other instances from the regional music culture show an increasing connection between the lower Mississippi and the rest of the country.[68] Throughout the region and the nation, newspapers reprinted accounts of the festivals and music celebrating events of national import from other locales. The *Louisiana Advertiser* listed the various ways the residents of New York and Washington celebrated Independence Day in 1823, allowing locals to compare their own celebratory techniques with those of other parts of the country. Local media also reprinted political songs national in scope originating in cities outside the area. One Vicksburg newspaper derided Nicholas Biddle's Second Bank of the United States as a thief via printed song lyrics originating from *The Philadelphia Spirit of the Times,* connecting the Mississippi Valley to the politics of the nation through a shared politicized music culture. "Democratic papers are requested to copy this notice," advertised one announcement for a "Barbecue and Bran Dance" to be held at a political assembly in Clinton, Louisiana, and at least one, the *Mississippi Free Trader,* located in Natchez, complied.[69] Such combined force of the print, festive, and music cultures strengthened local ties to a common national politics, as well as those between the region and the nation.

Although a nationwide political culture as expressed through music could be a unifying force between the region and the nation, on occasion it could also be disruptive. "Festive innovations through which Americans of the early republic practiced a divisive politics and a unifying nationalism at the same time," occurred both regionally and nationally.[70] By participating in partisan politics with song and dance, inhabitants experienced a very American, albeit divisive, politically infused music culture. Although partisan campaign music divided the region into parties, it connected local residents to a national experience. Participation in such forms of nationalizing festive culture, even if they were part of a divisive political culture, baptized both immigrants and newly annexed Americans into the ways of American political culture via music. Such was the case when Signor Felippe Cioffi, a New Orleans musician, composed a new "Tippecanoe March" expressly for the local Whigs during the particularly musical election year of 1840. His piece was first played during the publicly partisan act of constructing a log cabin, the Whigs' usurped party symbol and "common man" connection. Celebrations of national significance that took partisan expression further initiated the region into the nation. Not only did participants support some abstract American nation, they consciously defined what the American nation should be. "Politicization gave nationalist rituals their most important meanings. Conflict produced 'the nation' as contestants tried to claim true American nationalism and the legacy of the Revolution," explains historian David Waldstreicher.[71] Through the divisive music culture of the political campaigns in the 1830s and 1840s, inhabitants participated in an American musical culture, which unwittingly strengthened local attachment to national ways.

Campaign song culture helped incorporate the lower Mississippi River Valley into the United States. Political songs did more than spread nationalist sentiments; they also constituted a national popular political culture. Just as national print languages helped create, not just reflect, national consciousnesses, so too did a national print music culture.[72] Newspapers frequently reprinted songs from both within and outside the region, connecting Natchez, Vicksburg, New Orleans, Baton Rouge, and other riverside towns with the national political culture through printed music and lyrics. The *Baton Rouge Gazette* printed pro-Whig songs during 1844 from newspapers as far away as Detroit, Brooklyn, Nashville, Natchez, Washington, D.C., Louisville, and Xenia, Ohio. The *Mississippi Free Trader* in Natchez printed songs from Baltimore, Boston, and Huntsville supporting the Democratic Party. The *Vicksburg Daily Sentinel* supported Polk and the Democrats with songs previously appearing in Boston, New York, Woodstock, Vermont, and Yazoo City, Mississippi.[73] The practice of a divisive political music culture expressed through a unifying print culture fused this region to the nation by allowing the local population to share in a nationwide and particularly nationalistic musical experience.

The 1844 campaigners for Whig candidate Henry Clay and Democrat James Polk considered political music an especially powerful force. An article printed in the *Baton Rouge Gazette* from "the Reverend Mr. Brownlow, of the Jonesborough Whig, in defending Whig songs from the attack made upon them by the Locos," likened the political music climate to the Bible story where David's harp drove the Devil from Saul. He speculated, "May not the music of the Whig songs drive the devil out of the Locofocos?" Concern arose within this campaign music culture when Henry Clay named Frelinghuysen his running mate. "The nomination of Mr. Frelinghuysen was a capital one," remarked one Whig, "but there was one difficulty—it could not be sung—it would rhyme with nothing." Luckily, an enterprising lyricist discovered that with a few tweaks Frelinghuysen actually could be made to rhyme with many words:

> Don't you see the people risin'
> For Harry Clay and Frelinghuysen?
> The Locos hate, as bad as poison,
> Our Harry Clay and Frelinghuysen
> But patriots all are sympathisin'
> With Harry Clay and Frelinghuysen.[74]

Locals remembered the Natchez Whig arrested for betting on the election as having "warbled the beautiful melodies of 'Tippecanoe and Tyler too' . . . morning noon and night . . . and with what gusto he sung the chorus to his favorite ditty while the bowers echoed: 'Little Van is a used up man.'" A New Orleans Democrat took his Whig neighbor to court for supposedly teaching her parrot to sing "Van, Van, Van—Van is a used-up man," but this case was dismissed. An 1848 *New Orleans Bee* article describing the Whig music culture in various cities showed how significant campaign songs had become to the political culture. "The appearance of Taylor Songs, which are enlivening the canvases and stirring up the clubs, gives serious alarm to the official paper," it reported from the Baltimore *American*. "We warn the South," wrote the Washington *Union*, "against this musical movement." A Whig club in Pennsylvania even had a "Committee of Singing."[75] These examples of national partisan politics being expressed in the regional music culture show that national loyalty existed simultaneously with the ethnic identities previously described in the music culture of the region.

Interestingly, many of these campaign ditties utilized songs ostensibly connected to an ethnicity but with new lyrics. "Scots Who Hae' With Wallace Bled," became a song heroizing Andrew Jackson, the son of Scots-Irish immigrants, while the "Mariners of England," did the same for Lewis Cass, "the Champion of the Seas." The *Baton Rouge Gazette* printing of the "Song of the Clay Club," set to the air "Sparkling and Bright," required an addendum explaining the term "gloaming" in its final stanza as "Scotch for night." A booklet of Fillmore and Donaldson campaign songs included several national patriotic hymns such as "Star-Spangled Banner," and "Hail, Columbia," but also "Jordan Am a Hard

Road to Travel," "Villikins and His Dinah," and "Paddies and No More." In some instances within this song booklet, the lyricist usurped "ethnic" tunes to express nativist feelings, such as,

We're a Native Band, on our Native Land;
then let our voices raise,
Till native birth and native worth;
receive their need and praise.
And shall a horde of 'foreign' lord;
what native blood hath gained?
No! Native Right by Native Might,
shall ever be maintained.

A similar song booklet called *Songs for the Campaign, Union and Peace*, included nativist lyrics to songs linked to a foreign people or place by their titles including, "Lützow's Wild Hunt," "Battle of the Boyne," "Rule Britannia," "Marseille's Hymn," "Villikins and His Dinah," "Canadian Boatsong," "Uncle Ned," and "Old Dan Tucker."[76] Likely, the lyricist chose these songs precisely because of their ethnic and racial connection in the minds of people in order to make the lyrics, which parodied the "foreignness" of each group, that much more humorous and effective within the nativist audience. In doing this, American politics confronted musically those considered ethnic others within the polity.

National songs shared space on the campaign trail with these popular songs made comic by nativist lyricists. Both Democrats and Whigs in the 1840s usurped the French "La Marseilles," adding to the many previous reincarnations this tune had experienced. Since the early parts of the French Revolution, Americans sang this song amid a variety of changing meaning. In the 1790s, the Democratic-Republicans, honoring the French Revolution, introduced the song within a partisan American political culture, featuring it in concerts throughout the country. "The Marseilles" became a symbol of opposition to both England and Federalism, and in support of republican government.[77]

In Louisiana, the song retained a French connotation, while simultaneously infiltrating American national music culture. The 1830–31 season at the English-language theater in New Orleans opened with the singing of the "Marseilles Hymn" and the display of the tricolored flag "in honor of the recent and glorious revolution in France." While the French Opera Company of New Orleans toured the North, news arrived that Parisians had overthrown the Bourbon King Charles X. Between their two evening shows, a French eyewitness recalled, "The orchestra struck up a national tune, the curtain rose, and the entire company wearing tricolor cockades and carrying tricolor flags appeared . . . singing 'la Marseillaise.'" At a Louisiana assembly celebrating the 1848 French Revolution, "the band struck up *la Marseillaise*, which was re-echoed by the voice of almost the entire company. The spirit-stirring strain of *Mourir Pour la Patrie* and *la Parisienne*, also contributed to awake all the Gallic enthusiasm of these fiery sons of France." Toasts followed to both the American and French nations. The *New Orleans Bee* even published a new set of lyrics honoring Lafayette as a "Disciple of our WASHINGTON." The song existed so securely as an American patriotic hymn by 1860 that Confederates revived it as "The Southern Marseilles" during the Civil War.[78]

"The Marseilles" and other "ethnic" or national songs had become conventional enough that most readers would know their melodies, and hence they could be employed for campaigning purposes. However, plenty of well-known patriotic songs securely tied to the American nation existed that could have been co-opted for use by these parties. Occasionally, "Yankee Doodle" or "Hail, Columbia" might be set to new partisan lyrics, but this was rare.[79] Such national songs may have seemed above application to partisan displays that frequently employed crude and insulting lyrics. Even though these ostensibly ethnic songs may not have had any actual "ethnic" components to them, their significance lies in their *perception* as authentically "ethnic" and thus, according to some, non-American. By singing these "ethnic" songs during such particularly national events as elections, the ever-changing American nation confronted and dealt with these "others," whoever they might be. Acknowledging the various groups in their midst, even if done covertly, widened the vision of the nation's membership, even if admittance did little to practically better their condition or remove the pejorative connotations attached to one group by another. This was one way the varied populace of the United States encountered and confronted the "others" in their midst. Because of such music's questionable ethnic authenticity, it likely did little to welcome members of these ethnic groups into the national fold. However, for those Americans using music believed to be authentically ethnic during nationally important situations, it had greater significance. This music helped them deal with the uncertain status of groups they deemed marginal. This was especially important in places of great diversity and insecure attachment to the United States, like the lower Mississippi River Valley. Because music could be used to represent ethnicity within the national partisan politics, by integrating "ethnic" music ways into the national music culture, ethnic others had the potential to merge with the nation, a nation that in other instances they had been defined against.

Not only campaign songs, but also patriotic music in general, encouraged a nationalizing experience within the regional music culture. Audiences expressed extreme loyalty to American national tunes during public performances. The finale of one of Ole Bull's New Orleans concerts ended with the audience shouting "their vociferous approbation, and there were mingled in the tumult cries of 'Hail, Columbia,' and 'Yankee Doodle.' He commenced with the '*Carnival of Venice*,' executing it in his most brilliant style, but gliding from there into our own national airs, or rather mingling them all. The shouts that were sent up as the house recognized their patriotic tunes were absolutely deafening." After "the celebrated musicians" Henri Hertz, a Parisian, and the Italian Camillo Sivori gave concerts in Baton Rouge, one reviewer wrote, "Their performances were no doubt grand and most difficult to acquire—but for real, down right heart touching music give us the 'Star-Spangled Banner,' played by a full regimental band."[80] Local audiences steered performers toward their favorite national hymns through these various ways.

Attempts to promote American nationalist music originated from music makers as well as the listening audience. The local composer Philip Laroque wrote a grand musical celebration of the American victory at the Battle of New Orleans called "Battle of the Eighth of January, 1815," for full orchestra, which depicted the battle musically. Its performance commemorated the battle for the following two anniversaries. Once the American public had made strong enough demands to hear "our national airs from the orchestra of the St. Charles," the New Orleans theater manager James Caldwell arranged for a contest for the best full orchestra arrangement of "Hail, Columbia," "Washington's March," and "Yankee Doodle." Felippe Cioffi, trombonist for the St. Charles orchestra, won first prize and M. Jean Baptiste Guiraud of the Orleans Theater took second, neither of whom were likely born in the United States. But, even this compositional competition provoked complaints among some who accused Caldwell of being "ashamed of having national airs without accompaniment in his fine theatre," although "millions of native born citizens were not ashamed to hear them. None but the foreign foe ever expressed shame at the sound of 'Yankee Doodle,' or 'Hail, Columbia,' tho' both were played upon a Jew's Harp!" Both Cioffi and Guiraud had introduced elements into their arrangements that this critic found repulsively un-American, a distinction he made by associating "fancy" with

European and "simple" with American. He continued, "Why not be ashamed of our Declaration of Independence? Why not introduce some French, Spanish, or Italian quotations in it? . . . Why not decorate everything that is plain and simple with some foreign insignia?"[81] In such an instance, this commentator specifically defined American music against the foreign "other."

Signor Cioffi continued writing music with American themes, although his motivation for doing so seems mixed. Although he may have composed national music as a way to prove his loyalty to the community or out of a sense of patriotism, there were also significant pecuniary rewards for successful composers in this genre. One might suppose profits motivated Cioffi when considering that he wrote songs for both the Whigs and Democrats in the 1840s, but he also served in the military just before the Mexican War as part of a regimental band. In 1843, the American Theater in New Orleans advertised the "First Night of the Grand Opera of ANDRE—founded on incidents during the Revolutionary War . . . by Signor Cioffi." The local press clarified the importance of this event: "The idea of a Native American Opera is something so new and unexpected that our musical amateurs and connoisseurs were not a little taken aback by the announcement of 'Andre.' . . . [W]e shall be glad to hear of any more such attempts by our young musicians.—Any such artistical skill that is brought to bear upon native and national subjects should command our best encouragement at all times." Ironically, this response to the eastern music critics' cries for a native American music culture, in this first expression through a grand opera, came not only from a marginalized region, but most likely from an immigrant, probably not at all what they expected.[82]

Mississippi River Valley residents enjoyed patriotic tunes privately as well as publicly. New Orleans alone had more than one thousand pianos by 1840 and more than eighty businesses sold sheet music or musical instruments. Thus, sheet music collections of patriotic songs became increasingly popular in the home, such as *Atwell's Collection of National Songs of America*, which included "Land of Washington," "Hail, Columbia," "Our Flag Is There, Huzza! Huzza!," "Star-Spangled Banner," and "Yankee Doodle."[83] A collection published in New York and New Orleans by Theodore Von La Hache called *The Musical Album for 1855* included "The Confederate Waltzes." First, the eastern and middle states, then the southern states, and finally the western states garnered musical incarnation, as each state received a one-page tribute in La Hache's instrumental piece. Patriotic music sounded in schools as well as homes.

Music instruction at the New Orleans Boys School included patriotic songs, and one *Daily Delta* article from 1850 even suggested replacing "secular prayers" with national music in the public schools. New Orleans music shops sold Felippe Cioffi's original and arranged patriotic airs. In 1839, he published a new arrangement of "Yankee Doodle," "Hail, Columbia," "Washington's March," and the "Star-Spangled Banner," as national waltzes in the style of Johann Strauss Sr. Local stores sold his campaign songs, "The Tippecanoe March" and "The President's March," and his "Texas Annexation March and Quick Step," written at the request of General Zachary Taylor.[84]

Patriotic displays with national music took on a local flavor, as regional residents expressed their American loyalty and ethnic identity through the musical culture. Concerts in New Orleans featured both patriotically French and American pieces sung in both languages. One 1808 concert featured arrangements by New Orleanian Philip Laroque, which included "General Moreau's Favorite March," dedicated to the exiled French republican then living in New Jersey. The program also contained an arrangement of "Hail, Columbia," by the local Louis Desforges, as well as his composition, "A Creole Waltz," dedicated to Major General Jacques Villeré, commander of the local militia, and an arietta called "Washington, or the Glory of American Heroes," sung in French.[85] The famous French dancing master Jean Baptiste Francisqui, who had fled the Saint Domingue rebellion in 1793 and toured East Coast cities until ending up in New Orleans, combined tribute to both the United States and France during his performances. One of his last recorded appearances included mostly French song and dance, except for his solos to the tunes "O Columbia, Happy Land" and "*Marché de President des Etats-Unis*." He had previously written American patriotic pantomimes, such as "American Independence; or the Fourth of July," while working in Charleston, South Carolina. Even Louis Desforges, prior to his "Yankee Dude" outburst, knew how to please his diverse audiences. In a concert celebrating the anniversary of Louisiana's transfer to the United States, he played to the loyalties of all parties present. Pieces performed included ones dedicated to General Eleazor Ripley, a veteran of the War of 1812, the Louisiana Creole governor Jacques Villeré, and a march dedicated to one of Napoleon's generals, Lefebvre-Desnouettes.[86] By expressing their combined loyalties through the music culture, Louisianans did what so many other new Americans had and continued to do; they integrated their previous identity into their understanding of what it meant to be American, forever changing the meaning of the nation as well as themselves.

As the American regime exerted increasingly firm control over the lower Mississippi River Valley politically, at least until 1860, ethnic tensions, although not necessarily ethnic identity, expressed through the musical culture, waned. Ethnic music ways did not disappear in the region, nor did an American national music culture consolidate and homogenize the region with the nation. Rather, local Americans likely felt less threatened by displays of ethnic music culture once their place within the region, and the region's place within the nation, became more secure. Hence, the American music culture along the river began to be less a reaction to the antagonism felt from local ethnic displays and more integrated with a national American music culture found throughout the country. As this region's place in the nation became more certain, Americans there became less defensive of their patriotism, especially as it seemed to seep into "ethnic" musical displays, resulting in fewer overt ethnomusical conflicts along the lines of the War of the Quadrilles. As the historian Peter Kastor explains, "On the fringe of a nation where nationality itself was under debate, in a world gripped by revolutions, Louisiana seemed replete with possibilities. . . . After precipitating the crisis of nationality, however, the Louisiana Purchase eventually reinforced the union. In the process it was Louisiana that helped Americanize the United States." Through choices of inclusion, exclusion, and accommodation in the music culture, the many "patriots by adoption" along the lower Mississippi River Valley defined and redefined American nationality.[87]

4 / "Other" Musicians: Ethnic Expression, Public Music, and Familiarizing the Foreign

Mary is taking music lessons from the ugliest German you ever did see, poor man I really feel sorry for him, his manners and appearance is very much against him though I believe he is a pretty good musician not quite as good as I could wish for.

ANN BUTLER, LOUISIANA PLANTATION MISTRESS

The music culture of the lower Mississippi River Valley revealed contentious diversity during the first half of the nineteenth century. Ethnic and racially specific organizations flourished in the region, which used music to strengthen and redefine their group identities. Suggesting changes that affected the country in general, this regional population searched for meaningful ways to make sense of the swiftly changing diversity around them. As a result, they tended to arrange their music culture into ethnic and racial categories. Because many of the cultural activities of benevolent societies, militia companies, singing clubs, church choirs, dances, and theaters were available for public consumption, the ethnomusical expressions of this place were open to a variety of interpretations. Through ethnically labeled public music displays, the inhabitants of and visitors to the region could safely encounter the "other." This process allowed for the potential of making the foreign more familiar, and thus less dangerous.

This connection between music and an ethnic or racial group within the region was strengthened by the fact that many of the professional purveyors of the music culture were either foreign-born or black. Because regional musicians, music teachers, dancing masters, instrument makers, sheet music sellers, and publishers were mostly nonwhite or non-American born, this reemphasized the ethnic and racial nature of their music to witnesses. This situation, in which those with attached ethnic or racial markers facilitated the public music in the region removed their music's availability to promote an American national culture in the region in the way cultural commentators envisioned music could. Because so much of the music made in the region was made by those perceived as not American, their music remained outside the potential for consideration as national. Yet, all the while, their frequent ethnically labeled public musical displays helped facilitate the very American cultural experience of familiarizing oneself with the foreign "other" by consuming its cultural product.

The musical activities of the Louisiana family of Judge Thomas Butler help illustrate the role of the foreign-born and ethnic labeling within the regional music culture. Judge Butler encouraged the art of music in his family. His children received instruction on flute, violin, piano, and dancing in their home, and continued their music education at school, his sons in northern colleges and his daughters in New Orleans boarding schools. These musical pupils bought vocal and instrumental sheet music, kept musical journals, attended operas and balls, participated in church music, and, most important, kept a record of these activities, revealing both an implicit and explicit connection in their minds between music and ethnicity. Although not a typical antebellum Louisiana family, the Butler plantation household reveals common attitudes toward music in the region and exposes the activities of the more emblematic purveyors of the region's music culture, thus allowing an exploration of the relationship between music and ethnicity.[1]

Those who brought music into the lives of the Butler family represent the typical "foreignness," at least from the perspective of this American planter family, of those working in the regional music industry. F. P. Gaertner, a German music teacher, regularly taught at the Butler's Cottage Plantation and other nearby homes. The family purchased music and instruments for these lessons from the shop of the Frenchman T. E. Benoit of New Orleans. Another French music store owner, Adolph Elie, taught the Butler girls music while they attended the New Orleans Female Academy. They also studied with the Spanish-born dancing master, Mr. Vegas, and the French danseuse Madame Angelina. In 1850, Mrs. Ann Butler, the judge's wife, wrote regarding her daughter, "Mary is taking music lessons from the ugliest German you ever did see, poor man I really feel sorry for him, his manners and appearance is very much against him though I believe he is a pretty good musician not quite as good as I could wish for." Even when the Butlers' flute broke, a Bavarian-born music store owner, Philip Werlein, repaired it.[2]

Not only did foreign-born musicians infiltrate the lives of this Louisiana plantation family in potentially unknowing ways, but in other ways they appeared quite aware of the "foreignness" of their musical choices, and even relished participating in a fashionably "ethnic" music culture. Interestingly, the musical notebooks of the Butler family from 1802, 1808, 1809, and 1829 gradually move from a preponderance of songs with titles implying American national concerns, such as "Washington's March," "Jefferson's March," "The Republicans," and "The Siege of Tripoli," to incorporating many more with foreign nations or ethnic groups in the titles, such as "A Portuguese Hymn," "Shamrock of Erin," "Tyrolese Waltz," and "Hungarian Air." The Butler daughters expressed particular interest in learning the Mazurka, La Cracovien, and La Cachucha, all recently imported dance styles at the height of fashion and connected by the descriptors "Polish" or "Spanish" to a particularly "foreign" cultural way to these American youth. One of these girls, Anna Butler, at her request for "a quantity of Spanish music," received the *Bijou Musical* "for the sake of the seven Spanish airs in it." However, the purchaser of this book requested that she also learn "the many beautiful Italian and French airs in the *Bijou*." Her sister Margaret's music notebook dated 1829 contained songs labeled as Irish, Scotch, Hungarian, French, and American. When "the Hungarians" gave a concert at a neighboring plantation, a Butler brother insisted on taking guitar lessons from one of them. Elise Ellis, a Butler cousin, proudly recounted her experiences at "the bona fide Creole Ball I attended, where I broke all the hearts of the French carpenters." In another letter, Ellis reported on a party at a nearby plantation where "there was a fine German band from the City, tho' the gentleman complained that the music was too much of a military style."[3]

Such commentary leads to a variety of questions about perceptions of ethnicity and its connection to music. Why did the various members of the Butler family attach ethnic delineators to the musical happenings they experienced? And what exactly did these labels mean to them? Did the Butler family particularly choose foreign-born musicians because of a perceived natural predilection they attributed to them or because a certain style of music they desired was likely to be presented by one of each group? Or, was it more practical? Were these were some of the only people willing to work to perform and promote music in the region? Whatever the Butler family's motives for making the musical choices they did, foreign-born musicians dominated all components of the region's public music culture during the antebellum era.

It is likely that one meaning of music to the Butler family, a skill necessary as part of a polished education, differed from those who brought music into their home. These musicians considered music, at least on some level, a means of making a living. It is also likely that to some, based on the frequency with which musical expression occurred within ethnically specific groups, music helped preserve or create an identity, or enabled the mechanism to exist in which one could participate in an aesthetic style most meaningful, appealing, and comfortable. For example, ethnically specific benevolent societies, singing clubs, church choirs, dances, or theater performances allowed participation in meaningful musical activities within a familiar community. The sheer variety of musical options available within a region with such a diverse population, such as the lower Mississippi River Valley, reinforced the trend to make music within a familiar setting to strengthen the connections of the in-group, who sought to define themselves against so many others whose musical options continued in their midst. Other instances of dealing with the diversity surrounding them, as will be described in the next chapter, were much less self-consciously expressed, and often unwittingly emerged in the way local residents spoke and wrote about the aural experiences surrounding them. First, though, the following section describes some of the ways people entering into the region from a specific outside location, or of outsider status, brought in or created unique music ways, which they attempted to actively, and often publicly, pursue within the region. This shows that local perceptions of an extremely diverse regional music climate, and one defined along ethnic and racial lines, was based on a situation grounded in reality. This does not pretend to be either a complete list of groups that took on or were assigned ethnic labels, or of the forms they used to express their identity through music. Rather, it is a sampling of some of the ways some groups expressed their attachment to and belonging to what they saw and defined as culturally specific organizations.

The preponderance of ethnically organized assemblages with musical components within the lower Mississippi River Valley implies that music could be used as a way for members of an in-group to express their identity. This does not necessarily mean that each group was hoping to continue an old tradition unchanged in new circumstances, although at times this may have been the case. In other instances, though, newcomers to the region actively chose to or unconsciously did alter their music ways and the musical assumptions they arrived with to suit their own needs in a new environment.[4] These examples also should not imply that because activities organized around ethnic or racial lines existed, that no exchange between groups occurred. In fact, rarely were any of these musical events closed; they were often public and experienced by mixed audiences. Because of this, witnesses to these ethnically and racially arranged public displays of music assigned their own meaning to the relationship of music and a people, and increasingly fixed an ethnic label, including the African-as-ethnic label, to a musical form they encountered. It is likely that precisely because so many and varied music ways existed in the region that ethnic labels became descriptive delineators rather than boundary markers. Through public performances, exposure to unfamiliar music ways meant that such categorizations became more akin to genres accessible for the experience by all rather than reserved purely for the in-group's expression or use. By witnessing ethnically labeled musical forms, the foreign became more familiar, and diversity, in this region of uncertain attachment to the nation, less disorienting.[5]

What follows are examples of ethno-specific music ways being controlled by the group that was responding to the pressures involved in making one's way in a new home or in a home rapidly changing by an influx of others. Then, the role of the foreign-born, slaves, and free blacks, and their predomination in the region's public and professional music culture far in excess of their numbers, will be considered. The public visibility of these musical people reinforced the culturally specific nature of music to all observers.

A multitude of ethnically and racially specific organizations and institutions emerged during the first half of the nineteenth century whose members expressed themselves through music. Groups that gathered for religious worship often used music as a way to express an identity that extended beyond church affiliation. As places of worship increasingly organized in the lower Mississippi River Valley, they often, though not always, did so along ethnic and racial lines. Contemporaries referred even to those with mixed congregations by the delineators of German, Irish, French, Black, African, or slave churches.[6] Although a common religion could join people together in mixed congregations, ethnic loyalties and culturally specific worship preferences could also separate, making ethnic churches "the fortress of their ethnic identity in the New World," where familiar language and customs kept one from feeling like a foreigner in their own interaction with their God. However, such ethnoreligious separateness remained only in the context of simultaneously synthesizing old ways into the new setting an individual occupied. Within this diverse and often new environment, a safe place for worship and musical expression unique to one's specific culture could flourish.[7]

Congregants worked to have both sermons and songs in their native language included in their religious experiences as a way to practice their identity in a new or changing environment. Some places of worship alternated their sermons in English, French, and German, as did the first Catholic Church in Carrollton, Louisiana, after protests by the minority non-German speakers. When Lafayette's new priest arrived in 1847, he was installed as "pastor of all nations in the City of Lafayette." An advertisement in one New Orleans newspaper printed in German announced a "German Protestant service" for Easter Sunday 1839, to "take place with the pleasure of singing accompanied by the organ." The German Orthodox Evangelical Congregation of New Orleans, established in 1840, had a German-language hymnal at least by 1849, and the city's German Catholic churches sung the "Te Deum" in German. The city's Jews met at a synagogue where their chanting reached the ears of passersby as well.[8]

In another case emphasizing the importance of native-language lyrics in religious music, missionaries took advantage of an already extant Native American religious music tradition to gain access, and potential converts, through hymn translations. Hymnals, which published Christian lyrics in Choctaw, had existed by the 1830s, and missionaries printed a collection of sacred songs specifically for the Baptist Native Christians of the Six Nations in an Indian language as well. These hymn books were almost completely in Choctaw, including a translation of the Ten Commandments, though some did include a few English titles. Although these translations were made by the missionaries to encourage conversion, Native singers utilized these new hymns within their already vibrant religious musical tradition, changing both the function and meaning of the hymns, as well as prior Choctaw religious music.[9] Singing praise in one's mother tongue allowed the region's diverse populace to assert its varied individualities when confronted with unfamiliarity.

Unlike the religious musical expressions of either the Native Americans or the immigrating Europeans, the enslaved's religious music often existed in a realm of only pseudo or hidden autonomy. Yet, they too expressed their own identity with religious music. Only in the sphere of the slave quarters, more than in mixed or even nominally supervised congregations, could slaves express their spirituality uncensored. Often, slaves who commented on singing at religious meetings on plantations placed songs in the context of something to be kept hidden from the master, done late at night under the cover of darkness. Elizabeth Hite, a slave on the plantation of a Louisiana Catholic, recalled how she and others "used to hide behind some bricks and hold church ourselves. You see, the Catholic preachers from France wouldn't let us shout." One Amite

County, Mississippi, slave remembered how after the whites went to sleep, slaves would "hide down under de hill and sing an pray fur de Lord tu cum an free 'em," and that slaves from other plantations would come to "sing an' pray" with them as well. Another slave who lived nearby recalled attending service with her mistress, but also singing religious songs when the "black African" came from a neighboring plantation to preach.[10]

Like the place of religion within the slave community, for some immigrants, churches also served as social and musical centers, where they solidified their group identity in a new setting through religious music. St. Patrick's Catholic Church of Cairo, Illinois, developed by the new Irish immigrants there, served as a center for the local Irish immigrant community. Parish-related associations in the Irish community often employed music, including the use of newly composed songs for the varied purposes of temperance leagues, repeal organizations, sodalities, and parochial and Sunday schools. In 1840, the German Glee club, a "sacred choir, . . . such as seldom [had] been heard in New Orleans before," participated in the dedication of a new "German Protestant Church," and two years later, twenty-five German musicians held a benefit concert for the church. The congregation of St. John the Baptist in New Orleans raised funds for a school by appealing to Irish ethnic identity in musical concerts. Songs, such as "The Harp That Once through Tara's Hall," performed to audiences of "many of the sons and daughters of Erin," resulted in a successful campaign. St. Patrick's Parish in New Orleans held concerts to raise money for various causes and invited traveling Irish musicians to perform, including "The Irish Skylark," Catherine Hayes, who gave a sacred concert there in 1852.[11]

St. Patrick's Day celebrations were of both national and religious importance to the Irish immigrants, and often revolved around the parish. These festivities simultaneously bolstered Irish identity in a new environment, while proving Irish culture's magnificence to the non-Irish. Irish music in this context was not performed "as in the homeland, but in ritualized concerts which recreated that home, if only for an evening, and displayed the 'glories of Irish culture' to America." For example, a song composed for St. Patrick's Day in 1836 hoped that:

Perhaps the day is drawing near,
When Erin's bitter tears will dry,
And in their stead a smile appear,
And from her lips be heard the cry,

'Come, pledge the free—we're freeman all—
Behold our country's peace an sheen'—
And e'er as freeman we'll recall
St. Patrick's mystic shamrock green.

New Orleans Irishmen met on St. Patrick's Day as early as 1811 for a dinner followed by toasts, "interspersed with appropriate and excellent songs." But as the celebration of St. Patrick's Day in New Orleans changed during this time, banquets became inadequate. With the new Irish came parades, singing in the streets, and dancing in the night, yet it remained the appropriate day to celebrate Irishness with music tied to religion.[12] In this way, the Irish immigrants to the lower Mississippi River Valley created and asserted an identity through their religious music culture within the context of an intensely changing diverse population that was attempting to do the same.

Despite the existence of uniquely ethnic religious music, newcomers did not transplant or retain in some pure form the music of their homeland past. Rather, they often created novel sounds to make sense of the new and diverse setting surrounding them. The regional population used this method, among many others, to navigate among the varied and unfamiliar people they encountered. Probably the most well known and well studied example is the creation of an entirely new genre of religious music by enslaved Christian worshipers known as slave spirituals. Although previously subject to much heated debate on their origins, Albert Raboteau describes them as "hybrids, born of mutual influence and reciprocal borrowing . . . from the Bible, Protestant hymns, sermons, and African styles of singing and dancing," that were, according to Lawrence Levine, "created or constantly recreated through a communal process." One ex-slave described her account of the creation of a spiritual, as recorded and published by Jeanette Robinson Murphy in the 1890s, in this way, "We'd all be at the 'prayer house' de Lord's day, and de white preacher he'd splain de word and read whar Esekial dome say—Dry Bones gwine ter lib ergin. And, honey, de Lord would come a-shinin' thoo dem paged and revive dis ole nigger's heart, and I'd jump up dar and den and holler and shout and sing and pat, and day would all cotch up he words and I'd sing it to some ole shout song I'd heard 'em sing from Africa, and dey'd all take it up and keep at it, and keep a-addin' to it, and den it wold be a spiritual." In this way, a new religious music emerged that was neither identical to nor completely divorced from the music of Africa, Europe, or America.[13]

Similarly, although working outside of the suppressive system of racial slavery, Irish immigrants transformed their own religious music in their new home. Although the Irish did not abandon the music of their homeland, even when entering Catholic communities with extant musical traditions, their religious music did change, reflecting both a tension and a coping mechanism of being simultaneously Irish and American. Because many Celtic rituals were linked to a particular site in Ireland, they lost their appeal in the new land, and the local parish cultures supplanted prior traditional ways. According to Robert Grimes in his study of the music of Irish Catholic immigrants, "In contrast to the silence of Irish worship services, the American church could call upon a variety of Catholic musical traditions," mostly unfamiliar to new immigrants. Although ecclesiastical authority mandated only canonical music, most of the music employed in the urban Catholic parishes reflected local popular taste. Even though this may have contradicted the spirit if not the letter of the canonical music law, either local ecclesiastical authority or popular approval sanctioned this musical choice. Irish immigrants sang the mass in Latin and Gregorian hymns, but also praised in English, to both Protestant tunes and familiar melodies of Ireland, although the latter were not without some controversy.[14] Through such techniques, a new music could be born, while retaining the solidarity of a particular group whose identity was being reshaped. Ethnic and racially specific religious music could reinforce the community although transformed to fit a specific need in its new diverse environment. Thus, the process of cultural production could continue to serve a group's needs although shaped by encounter with unfamiliarity in the region.

At other times, religious music directly responded to the stresses of uniquely American forces in the region. Lyrics that had originally mocked the French clergy, created in France at a time when the clergy exercised strict control, lost their humor in a frontier setting where settlers anxiously awaited their rare visits. St. Alphonsus, an Irish Catholic New Orleans church, organized an elaborate festival for the Fourth of July in 1855 to counter the Know-Nothing hysteria. Irish militia companies paraded, and the church held a high mass, as well as lectures and entertainment. Because the Irish were not encouraged to attend city-sponsored celebrations in Cairo, Illinois, the church held alternative celebrations for both American national and Irish holidays. In the midst of the Choctaw removal controversy of 1830, the "primordialist leaders," Mushulatubbee and Nittakaichee, forced Native American churchgoers to "dance away their religion." They reversed bans against ball games and dancing on the Sabbath, and passed decrees that encouraged these dances and games. Although some held dances and ballgames, the Choctaw Christians, "kept up their religious services of preaching, praying and singing every night to a late hour." Music and dancing both represented and reflected identity choices to the Choctaw during this critical moment of interaction with the American government, as these soon to be refugees dealt with their changing world.[15] The unique American environment prompted shifts in religious music culture from previous ways of expression.

In ways akin to religious groups, cultural organizations also made conscious efforts to allow for distinctive ethnic musical expression that served group needs in a new, changing, and diverse environment. A multitude of these ethnic organizations existed throughout the lower Mississippi River Valley, organized around a wide variety of functions including military, the arts (singing, literature, and theater), charitable, and political purposes. These cultural associations often used music as a way to express their group identity while familiarizing their fellow members with the ways of their new American home. In a private display of ethnic solidarity as early as 1812, the St. Andrew's Society of New Orleans, made up of those of Scottish heritage, gathered for a "meeting of brothers in a *chosen* and *adopted* country, whose hearts were warmed by the pleasing recognition of their native land. In the course of the evening, the following toasts, interspersed with national, patriotic and appropriate songs, were given." Such groups, organized around homeland, increasingly articulated a claim to public space and attention in the nineteenth century. Although some of the activities of these cultural associations were private, especially early in the century, gradually more and more occurred in very public settings.[16]

The public nature of music performances by ethnically labeled organizations reinforced the connection between music and ethnicity to the rest of the local population and heightened the sense of living in a place of great diversity. All the while, however, ethnically labeled public music performances allowed the foreign to seem more familiar, and potentially less divisive, through experiencing the music way of someone previously unknown. The success of cultural organizations in pursuing a public component is evidenced in the often-strong reactions to them. Some contemporaries condemned membership into these ethnic organizations, claiming they resulted only in "keeping up of national distinctions which should long ago have ceased." Another suspected that "the more an Irishman abstracts himself from these associations exclusively

Irish, the greater his chance of amalgamation," thought to be both positive and necessary. The formation of a Native American Society occurred as a reaction to the ethnic societies that already existed in New Orleans. "Are we not to enjoy the right of forming a Native American Association in an American city, where almost every foreigner nation is represented by a foreign society and some by *several*. We have a Hibernian and an Irish society. We have a German Union Society and a Scotch society, and French societies without number. . . . [W]e will assert our native rights and privileges in our own native land," declared their public organ the *True American*. Vicksburg residents who feared losing control of the city to outsiders and transients formed voluntary organizations to ease these people's transition into "legitimate" local society, including the creation of a singing club.[17] These tensions, hinted at here between American national and ethnic organizations in the region, highlight the instability diversity posed to those who assumed an American national culture should be fostered in the region as a way to solidify the diverse members' attachment to the nation. The public events held by these ethnically named groups contained the potential to alleviate their danger, as nonmembers could experience their ethnic cultural products, thus making both the product and the people more familiar.

Yet the lines between American and "other" identities were never as clear in this region as may have existed elsewhere. The *True American*, a nativist newspaper, carried advertisements for these ethnic clubs, such as for the annual meeting of the Swiss Society, where "all the Swiss citizens, and the friends of their nation, are invited to attend." In other instances, these ethnic organizations were publicly lauded for their patriotic activities, such as the *New Orleans Bee*'s commendation of the Spanish Club's "four hundreds and fifty sons of Castile, all good citizens and voters," who processed in "their picturesque and beautiful costume," in support of Zachary Taylor. Although like elsewhere in the nation, nativist cant found expression in sheet music, this, like so much else in the region, could have surprisingly heterogeneous connections. The "War Song of the Natives," dedicated to the American Party, written by Miss L. C., a "Creole of the city of New Orleans," and published by the German immigrant Philip Werlein in 1855, highlights the complex web of affiliations existing in the region's music culture at the time.[18]

Such ambivalent reaction to foreigners stemmed at least in part from well-organized associations of new immigrants in the region. Although such groups might initially appear divisive to national solidarity within the region, ethnic organizations could actually alleviate the risk diversity posed, since these groups laid the groundwork to expose a group's non-members to previously unfamiliar cultural ways. Throughout the early nineteenth century, but especially in the 1840s and 1850s, benevolent societies emerged within the lower Mississippi River Valley arranged along ethnic lines with the expressed purpose of assisting those of a shared homeland in America and as a way to create a group identity. As early as 1817, the New Orleans Hibernian Society organized for "charitable purposes" to relieve the "unfortunate Irishmen." An 1857 New Orleans city directory listed nine different benevolent societies, including those labeled Hebrew, German, Portuguese, Italian, Iberian, Jewish, Shamrock, Colored Female, and New England. Even the organization of New Englanders, although not specifically an ethnic organization, claimed as its purpose "to help the poor and destitute coming from New England," reinforcing the notion that a shared place of origin resulted in a bond of both affiliation and responsibility. New Orleans's free blacks strengthened their group identity through the over thirty social and benevolent societies they organized during the antebellum era, whose purposes included assisting the enslaved purchase their or their family's freedom. New Orleans Creoles of Color also organized two literary organizations in the early 1830s, the Société des Artisans and Société d'Economie. The Deutsche Gesellschaft, or German Society, organized in 1847, initially formed to help new German immigrants cope with acclimating themselves to their new home and later became a cultural organ for Germans in New Orleans. Other early New Orleans German benevolent societies included the Deutscher Verein, or German Club, as well as the Germania Lodge 46 of the Free Masons.[19] Hebrew, French, Swiss, German, and Irish benevolent societies all met in Memphis, and the Vicksburg Hibernian Benevolent Society met monthly in 1839. Even a town as small as Cairo, Illinois, boasted a Hibernian Fire Company, a Fenian Brotherhood and Sisterhood, and a St. Patrick's Benevolent Society. These organizations promoted ethnic mutuality as well as provided charitable services. But, the usefulness of any of these groups' activities was not the same for its members as to those who did not belong.[20] Exposure to the public activities of a group with an ethnic label that one did not identify with helped resituate what had been foreign into something more familiar.

These benevolent societies and other ethnic organizations frequently used musical activities to raise money for their causes, simultaneously celebrating and promoting their specific groups' music, and as a result, their group as a whole, within the larger community. Multiple societies employed the ever-popular ball to raise money for the support of their local ethnic community in need. In 1810, New Orleans's residents held a ball to raise money for the Committee of Benevolence to aid the Saint Domingue refugees. The city's Shamrock Benevolent Society held an annual ball for charity and the Hebrew Benevolent Association of New Orleans celebrated their anniversary in 1850 with a fundraising ball for their philanthropic work.[21] Artists from the Italian Opera Company volunteered at a concert hosted by the Italian Benevolent Society of New Orleans to raise money for their charitable activities, showing the association of specifically ethnic music with an ethnic organization. In 1820, a group of New Orleans free men of color organized a benefit concert to aid the free people of color victims of a recent fire in Savannah, Georgia. In 1850, the "Central Union for the Advancement of the Republic of Germany," gave a benefit concert for "Hungarian refugees," many of whom were German nationalist-liberals.[22] Helping one's own community through musical means, even if the exact sound is unknown, reveals group cohesiveness not only to the historian but also to the rest of the contemporary population, serving to reinforce the connection between music and race or ethnicity in the mind of the public.

Public parades celebrating ethnically specific anniversaries exposed a group's nonmembers to the sights and sounds of the group's expressions and identity, thus allowing the potential for a greater understanding of difference. St. Patrick's Day, as previously mentioned, was probably the most prominent of these and noted for its ability to express ethnic unity while demonstrating loyalty to the American nation. In 1850, the New Orleans Shamrock and St. Michael's Benevolent Associations paraded with "handsome banners and bands of music" through the city streets on St. Patrick's Day, and were lauded in the press for their charity to the suffering immigrants. New Orleans's annual Volks-und-Schuetzenfest, begun in 1854, featured a parade of German social and benevolent societies. The American, German, and Swiss flags, and several bands playing martial music, led the crowd to the Union Race Course for drinking, eating, dancing, games, and socializing.[23]

Despite the very public ethnic affiliation expressed by these organizations, they were prominent participants in celebrations of American national importance, especially with their musical contributions. It was not contradictory for members of ethnic societies in America to express affection for both one's original homeland and one's adopted homeland in song, especially during Independence Day celebrations or political events. This is similar to the way people in the early republic could express their dual identities of "both civic and craft pride," in parades that "asserted as much trade unionism as nationalism." Civic parades, formerly organized along occupational lines, began including groups structured around ethnic affiliation as well. For example, the Hibernian and German Union Societies both marched in the New Orleans Fourth of July Parade in 1836; and by 1849, a whole segment of the parade was composed of ethnic clubs.[24] Expressing group identity simultaneously with American national loyalty in such instances helped assure that even regions of great diversity such as the lower Mississippi cohered to the nation through a shared public music culture.

Yet to spectators, these public demonstrations seemed to promote ethnic identity as much as an American national identity, as their visual and aural expressions signified ethnic distinctiveness. It is important that an ethnic tag remain affixed in the minds of witnesses to these national events, if a public display was to succeed in familiarizing others to difference. On July 4, 1842, according to an observer at the New Orleans event, "the Shamrock Benevolent Society paraded about 20 persons, they looked very well in their uniform dress and green sashes, carrying banners and the 'Harp of Erin'—very Irish—but good music . . . altogether quite a pleasant spectacle." Other instances of public expressions of these dual loyalties emerged in the feasting accompanying such events. The local press noted how those at "the German Barbacue" held in Vicksburg for the Fourth of July toasted the United States, the flag, the memory of George Washington, and the President, each followed with the appropriate "American" song of "Hail, Columbia," "Star-Spangled Banner," "Washington's March," and the "President's March," while the toast to the memory of Baron Steuben, a Prussian military officer who assisted George Washington during the American Revolution, was followed with the appropriately "German" song "Dessassuer's March."[25] Such activities allowed participants to reconcile their past loyalties with those of their new home, all the while allowing observers to resolve what they perceived as ethnic with American ways.

The public funeral ceremony held in New Orleans for Henry Clay, Daniel Webster, and John Calhoun exemplifies the centrality such groups and their music played in events of national import. A pamphlet to commemorate the day remarked specifically how "the numerous Societies composed of natives of foreign countries, were by no means backward in the display of a spirit similar to that which animated our native and naturalized citizens." The "Fourth Grand Division" in the funerary procession included most ethnically arranged organizations. The French, Italian, Portuguese, German, and Italian Benevolent Societies headed this segment, including "a fine band of music." Later, the St. Andrew's Society, Hibernian, Shamrock, and St. Patrick Benevolent Societies, and the St. Michael Benevolent Burial Society followed with their own music.[26] Even without knowing what the music of these marching bands sounded like, the publicly performed sounds of these ethnically organized clubs at important national commemorations reinforced their ethnic distinctiveness while solidifying their national loyalty, not only to themselves, but within the community as a whole. Public performances by ethnically arranged musicians also solidified the connection between a soundway and a people in the minds of the listeners. In such instances, music performed for public consumption by people labeling themselves with a marker would be perceived as distinctively that of an ethnic "other," forcing a compartmentalization of music into ethnic genres by the audience.

Much of the preparation behind these public displays occurred within ethnically or racially defined gatherings, thus allowing the group's members to meet their own cultural needs and solidify their identity within a new and changing diverse environment. Immigrants, especially Germans, formed ethnically defined singing societies, often with the expressed purpose of promoting the music of the homeland. The German Casino Club of Memphis was one such group, "formed to cultivate German habits, customs and a taste for music and literature." New Orleans was the first American city with an all-German singing society when the Liederkranz formed in 1838. Another, the Turnverein Chorus, founded in New Orleans in 1851 was the first *männerchöre*, or amateur male choral society, in the city, with 140 members joining in only two months. A second *männerchöre* soon followed in the city's Second Municipality. These societies "brought together German-American men of all walks of life to sing, socialize, give concerts, participate in contests and otherwise enliven the activities of the community. . . . This mixture of social and musical elements gave the clubs a broad popular appeal and made them a significant force in the community." Because typically club events remained closed to nonmembers, German singing societies allowed these men an intimate safe space to experience their musical culture. Yet they also shared their sounds via public performances. The German Glee Club of New Orleans participated in the opening of the "new German church," while in 1857 a Turner Society formed in Cairo promoting music, sponsoring plays and speakers, and marching in parades. Seven known German music organizations had formed in the city of New Orleans before 1860, as had about ten different cultural and dramatic groups.[27]

Such ethno-specific music clubs were not limited to the Germans. Irish immigrants formed singing societies with varied repertoires of Catholic hymns, national airs, and the songs of Thomas Moore. The Société Philharmonique, also referred to as the Negro Philharmonic Society, formed in the late 1830s and consisted of over one hundred professional and amateur Creole of Color musicians. Making formal music accessible to free blacks who opposed the segregated seating of the theaters motivated these men, who gave concerts and arranged for the appearance of visiting performers. Some members of the Société Philharmonique played in the orchestra for the free black Theatre de la Renaissance that opened in 1840.[28]

The outsider status of free black musicians, like members of the Société Philharmonique, can be inferred not only from the legal and social limitations placed on their activities but also from the fact that many chose to move abroad either temporarily or permanently, an act usually attributed to their search for more equitable opportunities to express and promote their talents. One example of this is seen in the life of New Orleans free black musician Edmund Dédé, a child prodigy born of Saint Domingue refugee parents, who opted to spend much of his life in Paris with its more relaxed racial atmosphere. Dédé first left New Orleans for Mexico in 1848, possibly as a reaction to the changing racial climate in the city. He returned, however, due to an illness in 1851 and published "Mon Pauvre Coeur," the oldest known piece of sheet music by a New Orleans Creole of Color. Dédé worked a day job as a cigar maker, eventually saving up enough money (with the help of well-connected friends) to study at the Paris Conservatory in 1857. He spent the rest of his life, barring one visit to New Orleans in 1893, in France working as a composer and conductor. Other Louisiana free black musicians who struggled to make a career in music in antebellum New Orleans and then moved abroad include Victor-Eugène Macarty, Samuel Snaër, Thomas J. Martin, and Lucien and Sidney Lambert.[29] Although the place of free blacks in the region was different from that of new immigrants, both groups shared the experience of organizing themselves based on their own needs, and of being assigned into categories of affiliation by the rest of the population. Through the public cultural expressions of these ethnically and racially arranged groups, their distinctiveness was solidified in the minds of the rest of the region's population.

Other New Orleans free blacks gathered for more casual musical experiences than those offered by the Société Philharmonique, although it is difficult to assess to what degree their musical culture was because of self-identified group cohesiveness and how much was owing to both legal and social race segregation. Free blacks in the region were a diverse group, unified by their status as nonslave and at least one known ancestor of African birth. Their place of birth could be Saint Domingue, France, Africa, New York, or Louisiana, and their occupations, affluence, and educational levels varied. Although antebellum American legislation increasingly segregated them from the musical experiences of others with shared race or status, in the early part of the century it was not uncommon for free blacks to share musical experiences with both whites and slaves. Both slaves and free blacks attended the same theater and opera performances as whites, albeit in segregated seating. Venues for dancing, however, were increasingly chided for allowing mixture among the three groups. Despite the legally segregated dancing facilities for slaves, free blacks, and whites, in many instances these boundaries were not upheld, and encounters with socially defined "others" continued.[30]

As early as 1799, Bernard Coquet's dance hall on St. Philip Street catered to the city's free population, both black and white. Slaves, however, could also attend with a note from their master. After complaints from the Spanish Attorney General Pedro Barran that slaves too often attended without their master's permission and funded their lavish nights on the town by stealing in order to "impudently imitate" whites, the city council considered allowing black dances only in private homes with no whites whatsoever to be admitted. Coquet, however, negotiated a deal with the government, whereby the dances could continue for the free black population, although slaves could no longer attend. Such a law was still on the books in 1857, stating that any ball for free persons of color remained closed to slaves. This law clearly defined Creoles of Color as a distinct social group in the context of musical events, as racially segregated dance halls replaced the "tricolor" balls, open to the enslaved and free of any heritage, held during the Spanish period. Free blacks held dances at the St. Philip Street ballroom beginning during the Spanish period and continuing into the American one. The free black William Johnson of Vicksburg described a "Large Darkey Ball to Night at Parker's Ball Room," and another several years later when "Mr. Rose Gave a Ball Last Night at his residence, and it was a Darkey Ball So I am told." It is not clear if such events were reserved for the free or enslaved, although Johnson does not seem to have attended. The theater and concerts were more to his liking. His niece Emma Miller Hoggatt of New Orleans, however, wrote of being "all busy fixing to go to a ball tonight, Mardi gras as the French people call it and another one on Monday, all dress in costumes."

In Baton Rouge, the "Negro Temperance Society" held balls; however, some locals questioned their legitimacy, wondering whether "the whole negro population of Baton Rouge should be permitted to assemble at the garrison once or twice per week to pass the night in drinking and carousing."[31] Whether by choice or compulsion, free blacks in the region increasingly experienced a music culture defined to include only those of shared race and status. The awareness of this segregation by the rest of the region's population strengthened the assumed ties between a particular group and their music ways and heightened the awareness of diverse identities in the region via the music culture.

The most notable exception to an inclusive free black music culture would be the infamous quadroon balls of New Orleans, which were reserved for white men and free women of color. Various historians have likened these balls from settings for genteel mixed-race prostitution to coming-out parties where young free black ladies (and their mothers) could arrange marriage-like unions with white men, although formal marriages across the color line remained illegal. These balls captured the imaginations of many travelers to New Orleans who visited and then described them in multiple accounts.[32]

Such legalized segregation by both race and status struck visitors to the region as distinctive, and their comments reinforce and refine the connection of music with race and ethnicity, all the while describing such scenes as a way to emphasize regional diversity. As such, segregated dances held different meaning to the dancers than to the observing commentators. "The whites, the quarteroons or coloured people, and the blacks, have each their respective ballrooms," noticed Christian Schultz in 1808 New Orleans, basing the distinction purely on race. He continued, "That of the whites is sacred to themselves, nor can any white lady, who is known to be in the least degree tainted with the blood of Africa, ever gain admittance there. The coloured people have likewise their separate ballroom, from which all are excluded who have not some white blood in their veins. The white gentlemen of course are freely admitted, who generally prefer this assembly to their own." According to the visitor Amos Stoddard in 1812, the "dancing assemblies of the Quarterons, or free people of color," existed as distinct from both other blacks and whites.[33] Although the details of such accounts may seem questionable, commentators consistently recognized what they assumed to be a regionally distinctive dance culture. Through such labeling of public dances, the nature of music as rightfully attached to a particular people was reinforced in the minds of the public. Exposure to such carefully distinguished gatherings helped the regional population understand their diverse world.

Slaves, too, organized public dances, both in towns and on plantations. Beyond providing slaves with a way to express their shared identity, these dances also strengthened music's assumed ties to a particular group of people, in this instance those of shared race and status, and helped order the mixed population within regional residents' minds. Even before Congo Square became the designated area for expressions of various African musical traditions in New Orleans, slaves "assembled together on the levee, drumming, fifing, and dancing in large rings." In 1808, Christian Schultz described Africans in New Orleans who were organized into "twenty different dancing groups." Congo Square, variously used as a market, park, playing field, and circus, became the sanctioned public space where primarily African slaves, according to most commentary, gathered on Sunday afternoons to sing, dance, and socialize. This may have been the only place where African dance traditions were able to continue in the open on the mainland United States.[34] Descriptions of Congo Square were nearly as ubiquitous among commentators as the exotic quadroon balls, and historians have variously attributed the origins of jazz and modern dance to stemming from this ground. Although contemporary perceptions of the music and dance in the square will be dealt with in the following chapter, it is important to note here the existence of a specifically designated and officially sanctioned and regulated public space where the slaves of the city could express and experience the musical culture of their own choosing, and where nonslaves and nonblacks could witness clearly defined racial and ethnic expression. Although most descriptions are quick to note the Africanness of the dress, instruments, sounds, and dances of these participants, other commentators noted how the African and Afro-Caribbean music ways took on peculiarly American traits. Just as the European immigrants to the region built new music ways based on the remembered music culture of their homeland and informed by the reality of their new environment, so too did the African and Afro-Caribbean slaves. To take just one example, although these slaves might dance the Colinda, an Afro-Caribbean style repeatedly banned by white authorities as being too suggestive, lyrics to these songs responded to the local situation by satirizing the public figures in the city.[35]

Rural slaves living on plantations also organized musical activities, especially dances, often inviting those from neighboring plantations, which helped to solidify group cohesiveness.[36] The sugarhouse on one

Louisiana plantation in Ascension Parish became a dance hall for the slaves, as did the hospital on another in Jefferson County, Mississippi.[37] Extended musical activities within the slave community frequently occurred around Christmas, when a break in the seasonal labor cycle allowed for a general holiday. Solomon Northup described Christmas festivities on his Louisiana plantation as a "time of feasting, and frolicking, and fiddling," and his role "on these gala days always was to play on the violin." According to Ellen McCollam on her Terrebonne Parish plantation, at Christmas, "The Negroes have a holiday and a ball in the evening." In other instances, dances followed the "accomplishment of a particularly heavy task, such as the harvesting of a bumper crop, or the clearing of a large piece of land."[38] In fact, throughout the ex-slave narratives, "almost universally, instrumental music was discussed in the context of dancing." Although some plantation owners prohibited dancing, other slaves remembered dancing nearly every Saturday night with music from resident musicians purchased strictly for their skills.[39] Such dances not only allowed the slaves an outlet for expression but also reinforced the ability of a music way to signify race. By nonslaves' witnessing these slave dances, the possibility arose for difference to be perceived as more routine, if not necessarily better understood or respected, through exposure to an "other's" clearly identified cultural form.

Like the slave community, immigrant groups also held dances for themselves, again reinforcing this connection between musical genre and ethnicity among the general population, whose exposure to these dances helped them order and understand their varied world. Evidence that people made this connection can be seen in the ethnic language used to describe local dances. Some specific events for dancing were referred to solely by the name of the group in attendance. For example, William Johnson recorded in his diary of December 29, 1842, "Several Balls about town tonight. An Irish ball or two, then there were Darkey Balls." He noted a week later that "McDonald of the City hotel gives a small Dancing party to night, sort of French Doings." Two "German Balls" were held every Sunday in 1850, one at the Court Exchange and the other at Schrieber's Dance Hall. An ethnic or racial delineator was all that was needed in such cases to adequately describe the proceedings at each event. Although not originating out of any specific ethnic organization, the multitude of dances identified as "French," as has already been described in Chapter 3, emphasizes the connection between ethnic group and musical genre. The Germans too had particular places and times to dance as they saw fit. By 1836, a German Dance Hall existed in

New Orleans. Neighbors complained against the German Turner Society ballroom and theater, where "drinking and dancing and boisterous noise are carried on all night several times a week."[40] A wide variety of German organizations held balls as part of their activities. The German Society, the German Club, the Thalia Club, and the German Drayman's Club of Louisiana all held balls. The Festival of German Gymnasts culminated in an evening ball, and the Deutscher Verein of the First District had a Christmas ball in 1855.[41] Although these events helped create and solidify group identity, when seen within the context of a swiftly changing regional population, public awareness of such happenings assigned to them a different meaning. Cultural forms, such as a dance, became categorized as ethnic cultural forms, such as a German dance, as the regional population searched for meaningful ways to make sense of the diversity surrounding them. When one witnessed an ethnically organized music culture, the surrounding diversity seemed more benign.

Theaters, like dances, were also settings for ethnic expression and community. They too, however, could assume the additional meaning to witnesses as a site around which to arrange the varied populace through the music culture. Although theaters never catered to purely one ethnic group, the evidence does suggest that locals thought of theaters, at least partially, as promoting an ethnic taste. Likely, the main reason for this was the necessity of giving a performance in a specific language. Although flyers with translations might accompany certain performances, (French Opera Programs were printed with both French and English lyrics between 1843 and 1848), theaters usually stuck to a single tongue with their presentations.[42] This does not imply that an audience consisted purely of a single language group for any given performance; in fact the opposite seems more the case. The address given at the opening of the Camp Street Theater extended a "Welcome to All, American or Creole," and nearly all the theaters in the city at various times offered German-language productions. Vocal concerts with accompanying multilanguage texts became more prominent after 1850 when French-, German-, and English-language audiences more readily mixed company in the local venues. In 1845, the managers of the Orleans Theatre printed booklets of French librettos with their English translations from some of the most popular operas, and promised to do the same for each new opera for "those amateurs of good music, who do not understand French." A short-lived bilingual (English and French) arts publication in New Orleans, *The Opera Box, La Loge Opera: A Literary Journal*, was published to "treat of Theatres, Concerts, Balls, Exhibitions, Fashions,

Literature and the Fine Arts in a more special manner than such subjects are usually alluded to in our daily papers." The French and English
sections each had its own editor, who treated entirely different subjects,
and were not mere translations of each other. The St. Charles Theater ran
advertisements in both German and English in the New Orleans German-language newspaper *Tägliche Deutsche Zeitung.*[43] When the editor
of a New Orleans German-language newspaper proudly boasted that
"the Germans love the dramatic art, and when we attend the French or
English Theatre we find the house filled more with Germans than with
English or French, although there is a foreign language spoken," he revealed as much about local perceptions of the theater as an ethnic space
as he did about the German population. Whatever the makeup of any
given theater's audience, the local population identified each theater as
catering to a certain ethnic component of the population. The language
they used to describe the theaters is evidence of this. Theaters referred to
as the American Theater, the French Theater, and the German Theater
existed at various times in New Orleans.[44]

It is precisely because of the strong ethnic connection contemporaries
attached to cultural events and venues that the creation of a permanent
American Theater in New Orleans seemed especially important to some
local residents. The first French-language theater opened in New Orleans
in 1792, and at least one remained operational at all times throughout the
nineteenth century. In reaction, some Americans encouraged English-
language theater in the region. "The propriety of encouraging a national
theatre in this city," wrote one New Orleans editor just before Louisiana's
statehood, "is believed to be incontrovertible. . . . It is with regret every
friend to New Orleans will hear of the departure . . . of the American
players." For those who shared this editor's opinion, the theater was considered a possible integrating mechanism. They envisioned the English-
language theater as a way to "do something in forming the ear of foreigners who are learning to speak [English]. That part of our population
who speak the English language, increases fast—in a few years its wealth
and number will admit of as good support to an American Theatre, here
as New York or Philadelphia," forecast one writer in 1819. Following this
prediction, James H. Caldwell arrived in New Orleans with a troupe of
American players the next year. After renting space around town, he
eventually built his own theater on Camp Street in 1824, increasing the
competition of the French Theater in the city.[45]

Segregation of theater reviews and advertisements in the bilingual
New Orleans Bee implies that the two theaters must have appealed to

different audiences. Although both the French and English sections included an entertainment segment, they did not offer mere translations of each other, but included different information. The French *Feuilleton* most often announced and reviewed the French opera playing in the city, while the English section tended to discuss the happenings at James Caldwell's American Theater.[46] In 1838, a theater was built in New Orleans for the express purpose of performing German plays, and included "an orchestra of well known artists." This short-lived venture returned for seasons in 1842 and 1849 through 1855, when afterward only amateur German theater was available. Each German theatrical performance concluded with a dance, just as it did at the French Theater.[47]

Both free blacks and slaves could attend these theaters, although seating was segregated. In 1808, Christian Schultz reported that in the New Orleans theaters "the lower boxes are appropriated to the use of the whites, and the upper to the people of colour." According to one visitor's description of the French Theater, "Over the first row of boxes is a second, to which the free colored people resort, who are not admitted to any other part of the theatre, and above this row is the gallery, in which slaves may go, with the permission of their masters." The theaters of New Orleans, Natchez, Vicksburg, and Port Gibson consistently charged one dollar for whites and half price for free blacks, slaves, and children. The public took this segregation seriously. Caroline Church, whose racial identity remains unclear, was thrown out of a theater for attempting to sit in the white section. She took the theater to court and won a token one-dollar reward. Fueled by segregation, the Renaissance Theater, the first musical theater in New Orleans exclusively for Creoles of Color, opened in 1840 with an accompanying ballroom. The orchestra conductor, Jacques Constantin Debergue, came from a musically prominent Creole of Color family. In this way, as with the Société Philharmonique, the free black community could create performances to express their cultural needs.[48]

Like theaters, militia companies offered another opportunity for ethnic groups to both promote and express their identity through music, all the while, through public performances, exposing a group's nonmembers to previously unfamiliar ways. Because ethnic militia companies often appeared at public events of American national significance, their music culture served the multiple purposes of strengthening ethnic identity, reinforcing their cultural distinctiveness in the minds of outsiders, and demonstrating their American loyalty. Most towns in the region saw the formation of voluntary military units organized around ethnic lines.

New Orleans volunteer ethnic militia companies' decorative uniforms and social activities surely encouraged many to join, including the Spanish Cazadores, Volantes, and Catalanos; the German Jaegers, Rhinegold Rifles, and Fusileers; the Irish Emmet Guards, Montgomery Guards, and Emeralds; the Swiss Carbiners; and the French Chausseurs, Voltiguers, Mameluke de la Garde, Sapeurs de Genia, and Trailleurs d'Orléans. These men, with their accompanying bands, paraded on American national or ethnically significant holidays and sponsored balls, banquets, and excursions.[49] For example, the Spanish company of Cazadores used All Saints' Day to remember the departed brave with military honors, parading to the graves of their former members. The social season for both the Irish Montgomery Guards and Emmet Guards culminated with a grand military ball. Emile Johns, a New Orleans music dealer, even advertised a piece of sheet music, "'Jaeger Achtung! Pas redouple' for the German Jaeger Company." Memphis too had Irish and German militia companies. The Memphis Irish created three militia companies, including the Jackson Greens and the Jackson Guards, in honor of their hero who had defeated the British and was the son of immigrants. The St. Louis military band was better than any others, according to the Scottish tourist Charles Murray, because "it was composed, chiefly, if not altogether, of foreigners, Germans and others."[50] This public expression of music by military groups organized along ethnic lines reinforced the connection among witnesses between ethnicity and musical ways, while simultaneously proving their commitment to the nation and mitigating their potential to jeopardize, as a distinct cultural group, a nation attempting to unify culturally.

New Orleans free blacks continued the tradition begun under Spanish rule of forming their own militia units, though not without some resistance once the United States solidified their control over the region. These men also held social events, especially dances, as important components of their activities. Before American rule, members of a free black militia successfully petitioned the Cabildo in 1800 to hold weekly dances at the house of Don Bernard Coquet on Saturdays from November through the end of carnival season.[51] In 1812 Louisiana free blacks organized a militia, including by 1814 their own band of eleven men. In addition, each company had its own field musician, possibly a fifer or drummer. These musicians served the United States military for just over three months earning between thirty and thirty-six dollars for their services. Most of them had professions outside of music, and several had white fathers and mothers of mixed heritage. The composer Edmund

Dédé's father, a free black immigrant from Saint Domingue, was chef de musique of a local militia company.[52] In other instances, blacks served as musicians for white units, including the black drummers who worked for the Louisiana Legion. The most famous black drummer, Jordan Noble, who marched at the Battle of New Orleans, remained a favorite local celebrity throughout the era.[53]

Like the ethnic organizations that promoted distinctive musical cultures, the preponderance of foreign-born professionals in all aspects of the region's music industry reinforced the connection between music and ethnicity. Music sellers, teachers, and performers were the public face of the music culture among the regional population. Because the foreign-born, free black, and the enslaved dominated all parts of the region's music industry, people even more strongly associated a music way with a racial or ethnic group. Such a state contributed to the belief that a music way was distinctively ethnic or racial. The overabundance of those with ethnic or racial markers attached to them who worked in the music industry also reinforced the perception of intense regional diversity via the music culture. As such, according to some, their existence jeopardized the ability of an "American" music to develop that could bind this region closer to the nation. At the same time, however, these people working in the music industry helped facilitate the very American cultural experience of familiarizing oneself with a foreign "other" by consuming a musical product assumed to embody a particular ethnic meaning. In this way, the possibility of diverse cultural forms undermining national unity subsided.

Foreigners dominated the public face of music in the region, drawing even closer the connection between music and ethnicity through the diversity of people active within all components of the regional music industry. Those who made their living from music, whether performers, teachers, or businesspeople, lent a specifically ethnic air to the public experience of music and reinforced the perception of the ethno-specific nature of music in the region. This is not to imply that each foreign-born person played, promoted, or taught music of only one distinct ethnic tradition. However, the public face of music reflected a strong European visage. Those Americans with livelihoods connected to music were disproportionately enslaved or free blacks of mixed heritage. Their racial outsider status also reinforced the foreignness of music ways within the region, as racial blackness, unless it had been reimagined as blackface minstrelsy, remained outside the white definition of what was considered available to be American culture. Outsiders' sheer numerical presence in the professional music industry kept the population within the region from envisioning that native-born white Americans had something to contribute. Even those white American-born musicians who did gain musical popularity often sold their works with an ethnic component, as did Louis Moreau Gottschalk with his Caribbean and Creole titles and Stephen Foster's purposely racialized minstrel tunes. Although it may not have been a regionally specific characteristic that those considered outside the potential to create American music because of their heritage dominated the music industry (no comparison is made in this book with other regions), using the lower Mississippi River Valley as a case study reveals a dearth of white American-born people active in any part of the regional music industry.

Data expressing the percentages of these "outsider" musicians are impossible to provide with any degree of certainty for a variety of reasons. Complete information, including place of birth, style of performance, and precise musical contributions on most known musicians, is rare. Whenever possible, statistics have been included to buttress the argument that nonwhites and non-American-born predominated within the region's music industry. All other information is included to suggest the pervasiveness of "outsiders" in music selling, performing, and teaching. Census data, although revealing, present a very limited view of the region's music culture, since so many in the music industry may have participated temporarily, voluntarily, or under duress (like some slaves), were transitory to or within the region, or supplemented their primary livelihood with musical income. Despite this, by identifying those who advertised their musical skills or wares in the newspapers or city directories, or reported themselves to the census takers as working in music, the huge preponderance of foreign-born and free blacks in the region's music industry can be inferred.

The 1850 United States census, the first to include both place of birth and occupation, reveals a huge discrepancy between native and foreign-born musicians in the region. In the parishes of Ascension, Assumption, and East Baton Rouge, ten men listed themselves as musicians or music teachers. Only two of these were native born, both from Louisiana. The others listed as birthplaces Prussia, France, Italy, England, and Germany. In the city of New Orleans, of the 170 people who listed their occupation as being in the music industry 157, or 92 percent, were of foreign birth. Of these, seventy-eight were listed as German, thirty-eight French, nine Spanish, eight from Piedmont, eight Italians, and the remainder Irish, Neapolitan, English, Hungarian, or Danish. Of the fourteen

American-born, the census taker denoted five as "mulatto," all working as either musicians or music teachers. The music scholar Charles Kinzer has referred to one of those the census taker considered white, Adolphe Dantenet, as "mulatto," who lived in the home of the Italian orchestra conductor Ludovico Gabici. If he is correct, the entire 1850 federal census for the city of New Orleans lists only eight American-born whites in the music industry, five of whom were music teachers, one music dealer, one piano tuner, and the musician A. Muñoz, a "chanter" at the Roman Catholic Church.[54] Although such skewed ratios as presented in New Orleans may not hold true for the region as a whole, since it was the largest city with the most musical opportunities and the first stop for many immigrants, many of those listed as living in New Orleans in 1850 are known to have lived, taught, and performed in other parts of the region.

Data from the 1870 census again reveal the degree to which the foreign-born continued to dominate the music world of New Orleans. Of 222 people who listed themselves in the census as musicians, music teachers, or in the music business, 44 percent were German-, Austrian-, or Swiss-born, 15 percent French-born, and 10 percent Italian-born, out of a total of 80 percent of foreign birth. Of the 20 percent listed as American-born, 15 percent were white and 5 percent listed as black or "mulatto." Although in the census these men usually listed a career as musician, music teacher, or music seller, most fell into multiple categories.[55] The data suggest the degree of diversity within the music culture, reiterating the connection between music and ethnicity, and simultaneously reducing diversity's menace through facilitating exposure to what would appear to be the cultural product of an "other." The following delineation of individuals in the regional music industry organized by profession, as they appeared in the census, city directories, newspaper advertisements, sheet music, and a variety of secondary sources, highlights the centrality of the foreign-born and free blacks in the regional music industry.

European men opened and operated almost all of the major music stores in the region. Possibly the first was opened by Polish-born musician, teacher, printer, composer, and merchant Emile Johns in 1830, although he had been selling sheet music for several years prior. He sold his firm to the Massachusetts merchant William T. Mayo in 1846, who in 1853 sold it to the Bavarian immigrant Philip P. Werlein. Werlein had operated, for the previous decade, a music store out of Vicksburg, and his family would continue to run the New Orleans store until the twentieth century. Both Werlein and his fellow countryman Louis Grunewald, who also ran a New Orleans music store, began their careers in the

United States as music teachers, with the latter also playing the organ at Catholic churches.[56] Frederick Zambelli, another German, had opened a music store by 1840, which he continued to run for at least a decade. The Frenchman Eugene Chassaignac, who was a composer, teacher, and music critic in New Orleans, also ran a music store with his fellow countryman Adolphe Elie until a falling-out between the two men nearly ended in a duel. At least four other Frenchmen and two other Germans sold pianos and other musical instruments in New Orleans in 1850.[57]

Foreigners also dominated the musical instrument–making industry. As early as 1808, Thomas Hurdis, an English instrument maker, was working in Natchez. Between 1820 and 1852, six French immigrants listed their primary occupations as piano or musical instrument makers. Conrad Bregenzer, a German pianoforte maker, began working in New Orleans in the late 1840s, as did at least three other of his countrymen. Of all those who listed themselves in the 1850 census for the city of New Orleans as musical instrument makers, four were German, three French-born, two Italian, and one Spanish.[58] Music engraving began in New Orleans only in 1850 when the Parisian Charlotte Wehrmann came to the city and began working for Mayo. Her German husband, Henry, also an engraver and lithographer, opened his own sheet music business in 1852, where she continued her work at the family firm. Every music house in New Orleans, most of which were founded by German immigrants, commissioned their work.[59]

Gradually, during the first half of the nineteenth century, immigrant musicians, both as composers and as performers, began to dominate the musical activities of the country.[60] This same trend occurred in the region as well, reinforcing the non-American characteristics of music to the local population. Certainly, European performers dominated the touring groups who entered the region. Opera and theater companies as well as touring vocalists who appeared in increasing numbers were rarely Americans. But of equal importance were those performers who supplied the everyday music within the region. Local performers often filled the orchestras for these and other events, and the multitude of balls required a ready supply of bands prepared to accommodate the ever-changing dance fashions. Far more often than not, black musicians and those born overseas performed for these events. German immigrants especially seem to have filled the local demand for musicians. Of the 105 foreign-born residents of New Orleans who listed their career as musician in 1850, sixty-three were German-born. Germans, thus, dwarf the fifteen Italian musicians in the city, the second most numerous group.

Another thirteen of the city's musicians in 1850 had emigrated from France. At least eighteen French musicians had entered the port of New Orleans between 1820 and 1852. One especially visible French immigrant musician, the composer and conductor Eugene Prevost, born in France in 1809, lived in New Orleans from 1838 to 1858 conducting for the Theatre d'Orleans. Another, Jean-Baptiste Louis Guiraud, left France in 1832 for opportunities in the city after he had won the Prix de Rome in 1827. His son Ernest, born in New Orleans, made the return trip to Europe to study and later work in Paris. The Frenchman Monsieur Barbiere, a musician who also taught dancing, organized musical events, held balls and cotillion parties in Vicksburg, and played for dances with his band. He also performed in a "Grand Vocal and Instrumental Concert" in the city.[61] All these examples underscore the extensive role of foreign-born musicians in the region. Through their dominance, they lent an especially culturally specific nature to music in the region. Because people of all backgrounds witnessed their work in the especially diverse setting of the lower Mississippi River Valley, these musicians helped facilitate mediation between the varied populations who heard their musical ways.

As illustrated by Barbiere's diverse efforts, performance work could take a variety of forms. The German William Robyn organized and trained the St. Louis Brass Band, while a fellow countrymen played the steam organ on a boat out of Mobile, Alabama, for "a handsome salary." Several Piedmontese made their living in midcentury New Orleans as organ grinders. Bennett Barrow of the Florida Parishes hired an unnamed "Poleander . . . to repair his music boxes and perform for his family and guests." Barrow also noted hearing some *splendid* music" from "two Italians and one Swiss" who accompanied him on a serenade to a neighboring plantation. The German-born orchestra director for Noah Ludlow's touring theater, one Mr. Heidman, led a strike for increased wages just before a show opened in 1831 Natchez. His tactic failed, however, and Ludlow replaced the men within ten days with a new leader and group of musicians from New Orleans, very likely made up of fellow Germans. The English musician Thomas Cripps made his living in the late 1830s New Orleans as a church organist. The German organist Carl Weiss recalled some of the more interesting performances he felt forced to provide, shedding light on how some of these newcomers may have felt on their first arrival in a new home. On a visit to what he called an "English family" who discovered he was a pianist, Weiss was encouraged to enter their parlor, where he "had to drum out all sorts of nonsense for those present." He felt especially alienated from the social activities since he knew no English and they no German. He recalled having to make "quite a number of such visits, and at times I feel like a machine, that one transports from home and has to play everywhere. I am really glad, when we visit German families. . . . [W]e chatter German quite comfortably and old memories of home are freshened up." On his visits to the homes of other Germans, he made no mention of any forced exhibitions of his musical talents. Although the reputation for musical talent might benefit German immigrants looking for work, as a stereotype it could limit their sociability in a new home.[62]

Foreigners also dominated the music teaching business of the region, again emphasizing an especially ethnic nature to music. Many of the composers and performers mentioned above who worked as church organists, played in bands or orchestras, ran music stores, or made musical instruments supplemented their income with lessons, whereas others seemed to consider music instruction their primary career. In still other instances, immigrants arrived in the region with enough musical training to supply lessons, even if they had never done so in the past or had not intended to do so in their new home. In all cases, these teachers benefited from the vogue for music in the home of the growing American middle class. Although a national trend, this held true for the lower Mississippi as well. For example, Eliza Ripley, recalling her youth in 1840s New Orleans, noted, "Everybody was musical; every girl had music lessons and every mother superintended the study and practice of the one branch deemed absolutely indispensable to the education of a *demoiselle*. The city was dotted all over with music teachers, but Mme. Boyer was, par excellence, the most popular. She did not wander from house to house, but the *demoiselles*, music roll in hand, repaired to her domicile."[63] This phenomenon facilitated a growth of musical instructors in the region who were mainly foreign-born and reinforced music's nature as being particularly ethnic in the minds of the local population.

Other examples from outside of New Orleans also fit this trend. The 1850 Warren County, Mississippi, census, which included the city of Vicksburg, listed three "professors of music," F. W. Miller, born in Germany, and Francis Eberhardt Sr. and Jr., both born in France. The 1860 Mississippi state census listed forty foreign-born music teachers, whereas in 1850 New Orleans thirty-one music teachers instructed, all foreign-born except for five white American-born men and three Creoles of Color. P. Furvelle De Pontis, McDonald Reponey, and P. A. Rivarde, all Louisiana natives listed in the census as "mulattos," at least one of whom was a substantial property holder, listed "music teacher" as their occupation.

Of the 10,000 refugees who came to New Orleans from Saint Domingue via Cuba in 1809, at least four proposed giving music or dance lessons.[64] Between 1838 and 1852, at least three music teachers entered the port of New Orleans from France, including a Mrs. Huguet, Charles Meyer, and Jean Shneider, although it is likely this number is low since in 1850 fourteen music teachers lived in the city who had been born in France. One of these, Auguste Girault, kept in touch with friends back home who filled him in on all the theatrical and musical performances from Nantes. The remaining foreign-born music teachers in 1850 New Orleans included six Germans and two Spaniards. Although his birthplace is not known, one R. Santini listed his occupation in the 1846 New Orleans City Directory as "professor of the vocalist, Italian method," reinforcing the breadth of choice available for music pupils in the city at midcentury.[65] Assuming each instructor listed above did not cater only to those of his or her own heritage, one would learn the art of music from a professional somehow foreign to oneself, further reinforcing the ethnic nature of music to those in the region, while allowing the musical culture to be the site of encounter and exchange between previously unfamiliar people.

New Orleans was not the only place in the region where such a situation existed. The only music teacher listed in Assumption Parish in 1850 was the Frenchman Alexander Flandry, and for East Baton Rouge, the sole instructor was the German Theodore Bouran. In Adams County, Mississippi, home of Natchez, residents had a greater choice of music teachers: William Bayley, born in Ireland, or his sons, Thomas and Richard, ages twenty and nineteen, born in Virginia. The Bostonian William Nash taught music in the area as well, while Frederick Law Olmsted met two Italian musicians who were residents in Natchez, one of whom gave lessons on the violin.[66] Such teachers often traveled to the homes of their pupils, although in other cases, like Mme. Boyer, pupils might go to the teacher's home. It is not clear if students came to Mme. Boyer because she was a woman or because of her great popularity. Although much less visible in the antebellum records, some music teachers were women, including a "French widow lady" who desired employment giving lessons in her native language or on the piano. Still others found work in the local schools. Miss S. S. Hull's Young Ladies' Institute in New Orleans employed in the music department Monsieur and Madame Colignion from France and Monsieur Gabici from Italy, an orchestra conductor and musician in his own right.[67]

Similar to the role of music instructors in general, the dancing master occupied an important niche in the musical culture of the lower

Mississippi. Dance lessons had a long and vibrant history in a region where so much social interaction took place within the context of the ball. Many of these early dance masters were refugees of the Saint Domingue revolt who fled to the region directly or via a sojourn on the East Coast, whereas others arrived directly from France. In all cases, they were commonly referred to as "French dancing masters," reflecting both the style of dance and their place of origin or heritage. Just as some music teachers performed in orchestras and bands, so too did some of these dancing masters appear in the preponderance of stage productions, connecting the worlds of social and theatrical dance. Dancers, choreographers, and teachers of theatrical dance in New Orleans were usually French or were associated in some way with the Paris Opera, and they quickly became established as the tastemakers in America.[68] According to the dance historian Maureen Needham Costonis, "American theatrical dance was never the same after the French dancers' arrival. From 1791 on and for the next fifty years, French dancers, teachers and their students, choreographers and ballet masters" produced a French-derived ballet repertoire from New Orleans to Philadelphia.[69]

In one of the earliest examples, Jean Francisqui, a Parisian who had fled the Saint Domingue Revolution in 1793, performed and taught in Boston, New York, Richmond, Savannah, and Charleston before opening a dance school in New Orleans sometime before 1799. Throughout his time on the East Coast, Francisqui performed and worked with many other Parisian and Saint Domingue dancers. In New Orleans, he founded and directed an opera-ballet company, opened a dancing school, and sponsored subscription balls. In total, he produced 125 ballets and pantomimes in his fifteen years in America, a count no other ballet master in the country ever approached. A grand ball, "in order to commemorate the anniversary of taking possession of the Colony by the Americans," was given at his ballroom.[70] When he disappears from the historical record in 1811, Madame Placide, a former dancer from the Paris Opera, began training her own corps de ballet of local New Orleans dancers. Three years later, two new dancing masters from France, Edward Bertus, who taught for at least two decades, and one Chery, arrived in the city; in 1822, the French-born J. B. Forcade arrived in New Orleans from Havana to teach dancing as well.[71]

Although New Orleans's 1850 census listed only two dancing masters, both men had been born in France. However, based purely on newspaper advertisements and listings in the city directories, many more men and women found work as dance teachers. In the 1846 New Orleans

City Directory, four people listed themselves as "dancing masters" or as running a "dancing academy," including the Paris native G. Casimir. The others were Arraline Brooks, Dan Devoti, and A. Lavenant, whose origins are not known. In the same year, Mr. De Korponay, "the great teacher of the Polka dance," arrived in Natchez bearing the "highest testimonial as the satisfaction which he has given in other cities."[72] Both Jean Baptiste Badet and Antoine Cazebergue offered dancing lessons in early nineteenth-century New Orleans, and in the 1840s Mr. St. Maur Stuart's "Private Dancing and Waltzing Academy" gave locals a chance to improve their graceful maneuvers as well.[73] Previously, and as early as 1808, Natchez had welcomed Mr. Albert Lancelle's "French Dancing School" and the instruction of Henry Guibert, a "professor of dancing."[74] Eliza Ripley recalled "Mme. Angèlina, a new French importation whose specialty was the new dances that nobody else could teach." Ripley also attended J. Devotti's dancing academy, referred to by the Butler girls who received his instruction as "the distinguished Monsieur Devotee." He had previously taught in Baton Rouge.[75] "The Dancing Master" Mr. Gerardi taught at Bennet Barrow's plantation home, as well as two generations of the Butler family.[76] Because of the frequency with which dances or dancing instructors were labeled as "French" within regional commentary, a connection between ethnicity and music appears quite evident in these instances, as cultural forms became categorized as particularly ethnic cultural forms. Although such emphasis on the ethnic nature of music seemed to remove its availability to promote an American national culture in the region, encounters with ethnically labeled dance ways also helped facilitate the very American cultural experience of familiarizing oneself to a foreign "other" by consuming their cultural product.

Similarly, the frequency with which free black or enslaved musicians performed at all-white events in the region exposed people to difference through encounters with their musical ways. It is hard to know if these musicians were more often free blacks or enslaved because most who made written comments did so on their race rather than status. Henry Kmen suggests that in the first decades of American rule in the region, musicians ordinarily were black, even though the record is often silent on the racial composition of the performers (unless mentioned by a tourist), because black musicians were the status quo. One of the first written descriptions of an orchestra playing at a New Orleans ball mentioned that it consisted of "six Negroes, mainly fiddlers." Soon after American takeover, Benjamin Latrobe complained of a "tall, ill-dressed black in the music gallery, who played the tambourine standing up and in a forced and vile voice called the figures," at a French Creole ball in New Orleans. "The music was performed by negroes and coloured people, and was pretty good," noted the visiting duke of Saxe-Weimar-Eisenach of a subscription ball held at the French Theater in the mid-1820s. Gabe Emanuel of Claiborne County, Mississippi, recalled how some slaves on his plantation would make money singing at parties thrown by his master. Price Johnson remembered how "the same old fiddler played for us that played for the white folk." Because Solomon Northup "was considered the Ole Bull of Bayou Boeuf [m]y master often received letters, sometimes from a distance of ten miles, requesting him to send me to play at a ball or festival of the whites. He received his compensation, and usually I also returned with many picayunes jingling in my pockets."[77] Black musicians, such as Northup, performed for black, white, and mixed-race affairs in settings ranging from the slave quarters, plantation houses, urban dance halls, theaters, and ballrooms. Because of the centrality of dances within the slave community, black musicians enjoyed a special status, termed by one scholar a "folk elite," because of their important contribution to community life. Having musical talent ensured privileges to those enslaved in comparison with their nonmusical bondsmen, including increased freedom of movement, as well as a small personal income.[78]

The domination of all components of the region's music industry, either by the foreign-born or by those whose race reinforced their outsider status within American culture, resulted in a continued perception of white native American incapacity in the musical arts. A result of even greater significance, however, emerged from the sheer visible presence of these "outsiders" in the region's music culture. As foreign-born and blacks facilitated most daily musical experience, through either an individual professional or a group organization, they reemphasized the explicit connection between music and a particular cultural group, and made the regional population more apt to continue envisioning music ways as ethnically and racially distinct. The belief that music was uniquely attached to a distinctive group of people heightened the awareness of regional diversity every time music sounded and reminded locals of their tenuous cultural bond with the nation. This keen recognition of diversity led all people in the region to execute methods to help them chart a way through the varied populace surrounding them in order to familiarize themselves with whatever might seem foreign to them. One of the methods used to accomplish this goal was made available through the very music culture that continued to bring this diversity to their attention. By consuming the music culture of people outside one's realm of familiarity, their distinctiveness became less of a cause for concern, especially when the public celebrations of their identity coincided with American national events. By bringing ethnic expressions to nationally significant events, expectations and assumptions about what an American music culture could be began to change. As the particularly diverse regional population navigated among each other's musical ways in the lower Mississippi River Valley, they confronted the divisions among ethnic, racial, and national forms, and in doing so participated in a very American cultural experience.

5 /   Bounding Ethnicity: The Creation and Consumption of Ethnic Music Genres

On the Fourth of July, 1835, organizers of the day's events in New Orleans made a change to the parade route. In previous years, the festivities culminated with speeches and patriotic ceremonies outside the Catholic cathedral at the Place d'Armes. This year, the pomp would end outside the new Presbyterian church; it was less than a mile away, but a decision the Creole population interpreted as an attempt to limit their involvement at this national commemoration. The Louisiana Legion and Orleans Guards, militia companies composed of French-born and local French Creoles, protested and refused to continue processing across Canal Street, a symbolic boundary between the American and French districts of the city. This conflict, as expressed in the newspaper debates that followed, delineated not just the tensions between the American and French Creoles in the city, but even more tellingly, the Creole fear of being grouped with the "foreigners" in nativist discourse. This display, and many others like it in New Orleans and the rest of the region, illustrates the continued influence of ethnic differences, which reemerged during power struggles to exert or retain authority in a place of such fluid heterogeneity.[1] The dynamic population and the ethnic and racial diversity that made up the transforming demographics caused unease among much of the region's populace in the light of their own place within the region in relation to others, as well as this region's place within the nation.

The French Creoles and incoming Americans were not the only groups to feel the strain of cultural tensions. Between 1800 and 1860 the changing and diverse population of the lower Mississippi River Valley remained a cause of worry for all those living in the area. The swift influx of a population connected to the burgeoning cotton economy further dislocated the remaining Native American groups attempting to cope with their declining position within the frontier exchange economy. This caused tension not only among themselves, but also between them and the incoming settlers. In one 1802 instance, Governor James Claiborne reported to Secretary of State James Madison about the situation near Natchez as being "difficult to shield the Indians from much violence" perpetrated on them by the territorial colonists. These same inhabitants retained a "deep anxiety over black insurrection, Indian warfare, and even combined rebellion by the two groups." This stress resulted in increasingly racially defined laws limiting the rights of Native Americans and blacks, both free and enslaved. The colonists and then Americans organized better-armed militias in an overt attempt at "controlling subjugated ethnic groups."[2] Some of this fear stemmed from the incoming population, both black and white, that had fled the Saint Domingue slave revolt. Questions regarding the white refugees' loyalty to the United States and their extremist politics, as well as the fear that Saint Domingue blacks would foment race rebellion in the region, heightened suspicions toward this group on its arrival in the region. At times this concern was well founded. The Saint Domingue example did promote slave rebellions in the region, most notably the failed 1811 rebellion on the Louisiana German Coast, during which one hundred slaves were killed during and after their defeat by the local militia and federal troops. The Saint Domingan leaders of this rebellion fomented a catastrophic terror based on the Caribbean model, whose legacy haunted the region for decades.[3]

The experience of immigration within the region, especially during the decades after Louisiana's statehood, also caused stress not only to the new immigrants trying to find their footing in a new environment, but also between them, the local population, and the newly arriving native-born Americans coming from elsewhere in the nation. According to the historian Joseph Tregle, the "rich ethnic mixture" of New Orleans's population made it the "obvious battle ground in the strident conflict set off by the nativist crusade." The foreign-born worried the locals over competition for employment, supposed abolitionist leanings, political influence, and retention of their cultural heritage. In an 1836 address by the Louisiana Native American Association, nativists outlined the precise nature of the consternation these immigrants instigated: "When an Hibernian, or French, or German society, (*on the day of its foreign patron saint*) celebrates its annual fete, are the hallowed objects of American love and reverence the subject of their adoration? No! all their reminiscences emanate from 'the fader land.'" Although nativist methods for dealing with diverse foreigners were often little more than "simple primitive hostility to unfamiliar mores and lifestyles," at times they resorted to violence.[4] When two hundred Irish laborers arrived in Memphis in 1854 to begin work on a new railroad, and amid rumors of several hundred more to follow, Mayor A. B. Taylor ordered the militia to ready itself to preserve the "American way of life."[5]

The concern with diversity among the lower Mississippi River Valley's populace and vis-à-vis the region's attachment to the nation, the centrality of foreigners in the region's music culture, and the *belief* in authentically ethnic music, all remained intimately connected components of the regional music culture. The combination of these three facets resulted in the ability of local music ways to embody, express, and even alleviate the anxiety many felt while living among diversity. The population of the lower Mississippi River Valley recognized and signified the connection between a cultural group and a musical form by identifying each music way with a corresponding cultural label. Rarely, for example, was a ballad, quadrille, or jig written about that was not demarcated as Irish, French, or Ethiopian. Through such labeling techniques, people categorized and thus organized their diverse surroundings and created cultural forms that I have termed "ethnic music genres." These genres did not have to be, and in fact rarely were, accurate descriptors of a particular people's music, because as *genres* they were not created by or for any particular cultural group's members. Rather, they simply needed to be recognizable as culturally specific to the witnesses who would experience them. The public could then consume these ethnic music genres in a variety of ways, including purchasing a piece of sheet music, watching a parade, or attending an opera. Ethnically labeled musical forms appealed to those outside the particular cultural tradition represented, as ethnic music genres worked to assuage individual fears of difference, through exposure to what was considered an authentic cultural form. Experiencing an ethnic music genre resulted in a believable, if not actual, encounter with an "other." The concept of "the other" is not applied here in a hierarchical fashion, although most people saw certain cultures as inferior or superior during antebellum America. Rather, the term describes a way of defining a people perceived to be different from oneself, no matter who was doing the defining. Through contact with an ethnically labeled cultural form, the people its corresponding label signified became more familiar to the consumer.[6] This technique helped alleviate the uncertainty that diversity embodied by familiarizing difference. The creation and consumption of ethnic music genres also reveal an American music culture in flux, not as a deliberate response to cultural commentators, but much less self-consciously. Ethnic music genres helped the regional population navigate the realities of living in a particularly diverse region as it became increasingly attached to the American nation. The regional music culture developed through the shared experience of reconciling diversity within a nation attempting to unify.

The population of the lower Mississippi River Valley frequently categorized its music culture along ethnic lines, hinting at the anxiety many must have felt when surrounded by so many unfamiliar people and their strange ways. By organizing their diverse world into clear cultural categories, they were able to extend some order to their swiftly changing and, in many instances, entirely new surroundings. By defining the details of heterogeneity, it became more controllable and less threatening. The intention behind experiencing what was perceived to be an authentic ethnic music, then, was not so much to understand accurately unfamiliar people, but to find a way to deal with the difference, a difference that everyone encountered no matter what their race, status, ethnicity, nationality, or length of stay in the region. This concern with diversity resulted in bounding, or defining limits to ethnicity, through labeling and organizing into ethnic genres. A study of the language used within the music culture, including how performers were billed, sheet music sold, and teachers advertised, reveals the local population's concern with their diverse environment, and an attempt, even if a subconscious one, to make sense of the surrounding unfamiliar people and their accompanying sounds.[7]

This interpretation of the incessant labeling, appeal, and then consumption of ethnicity within the music culture relies on the assumption that music ways could be fashioned and bound into culturally specific commodities recognizable as such to the general population. Although an ethnic music genre might hold meaning to the in-group whose label was affixed, it did not have to do so. The usefulness of an ethnic genre came from its ability to signify this group to everyone else. Although the boundaries created by ethnic music genres appeared to separate people, they were in fact more like permeable membranes, which, although very real, allowed for enough movement between the groups to facilitate encounters. By temporarily crossing these boundaries through experiencing an ethnically labeled cultural form, the lines dividing each group from another were not removed. Rather, the transient experience provided a realistic way to cope with the potential confusion of unfamiliarity. The regional music culture bounded ethnicity and allowed people to temporarily cross these boundaries through the consumption of ethnic music genres.

Like the historian Eric Lott's suggestion that "the intercourse between racial cultures was at once so attractive and so threatening as to require a cultural marker," so too did ethnic labels, in addition to racial ones, signify a line of cultural demarcation between the varied groups in the region. In his study of blackface minstrelsy Lott refers to this as "love and theft," which "took the form of a simultaneous drawing up and crossing of racial boundaries." This is also similar to Samuel Kinser's interpretation of Mardi Gras as a way to deal with barriers "not by tearing them down . . . but by stepping over them and back again." Studying the boundaries of ethnicity owes much to the work of the anthropologist Fredrik Barth. According to Barth, "Boundaries persist despite a flow of personnel across them. . . . [E]thnic distinctions do not depend on an absence of social interaction and acceptance, but are quite to the contrary often the very foundations on which embracing social systems are built." With this in mind, then, to understand the social process of inclusion and exclusion, "the critical focus of investigation from this point of view becomes the ethnic *boundary* that defines the group, not the cultural stuff that it encloses."[8] The remainder of this study considers ethnic music genres as an example of one of these boundaries. In their attempts to define and stage ethnicity or "otherness" within the music culture of the lower Mississippi River Valley, all participants defined themselves as "not other." The appeal of ethnically labeled commodities in the regional music culture suggests that witnesses integrated "foreignness" into their own realm of understanding by consuming what they perceived to be unfamiliar authentic cultural ways that helped them better order and understand their multifarious world.[9]

People needed to have perceived a diverse music culture in the area in order for a reaction to this diversity to occur. In one example that highlights this, the editor of the New Orleans *Weekly Picayune* accentuated the region's particular diversity through a description of its music culture. He wrote, "Our city is the central point for all nations, and the proportion of those who come here, with a taste for sweet sounds, is to those who 'have no music in their soul,' as ten to three—*voila tout.*—The Frenchman, the German, the Neapolitan and the Spaniard, form two-thirds of our population, and the two last named nations, would, in the person of the lowest laborer, give their last dollar to the characters of their native airs."[10]

Travelers also made it a point to comment on regional music ways whose origins they explicitly, if romantically, connected to faraway places in times long past, in order to highlight the distinctively ethnic features of the diverse regional population. By doing this, they used music as a signifier of ethnicity, reinforcing the belief that music was inextricably tied to ethnicity, and the region was an especially diverse place. Although the amateur ethnological commentary of visitors may be fraught with problems for anyone studying the region's music, the usefulness of the comments in a cultural study such as this comes from the implicit assumptions the visitors' choice of language reveals about the ability of music to signify ethnicity to them. Travelers specifically wrote such descriptions to accentuate the diverse character they believed was unique to the region, in order to contrast it with more homogeneous and more "American" regions elsewhere. These descriptions of the *perceived* ethnic features of the music in the region and commentators' emphasis on the peculiar regional music culture resulting from this variety reveal a heightened recognition of diversity within the region, and thus a corresponding need to make sense of it.

In an early example of such categorization, during his 1806 visit, Thomas Ashe separated the New Orleans population along ethnic and national lines according to their taste in amusements. The Americans, for example, preferred "indulgence of the table, cards, and billiards"; the French filled their time with the "concert, dance, promenade, and *petit souper*"; and the Spanish strummed "the guitar under the window of a sleeping beauty, or the harp delicately touched under a corridore [*sic*] over which some charming girl attentively reclined."[11] His perceptions of the American lack of interest in things musical, the French love of social dances, and the Spanish lazy strumming exemplify how contemporaries connected a music way to the character of a people. These and other ethnomusical stereotypes and assumptions persisted throughout the era.

Instruments, especially the guitar, harp, and bagpipe, frequently signified ethnicity to commentators who consistently attached them to a particular cultural tradition. Although these instruments could hold a special place in a specific group's music culture, through ethnically labeled descriptions, instruments became ethnic signifiers to those outside the cultural tradition and were used as a way to emphasize and organize the region's particular diversity. In a New Orleans coffee house, "where the lower class amuse themselves," the visiting duke of

Saxe-Weimar-Eisenach reported hearing a workman singing in Spanish and accompanying himself with a guitar. Although the guitar was an important instrument in Spanish music, in this account and others like it, the guitar could simultaneously serve the purpose of a symbol of "Spanishness" to the reader, and as such provide a conduit of encounter between "Spanishness" and anyone who considered this way foreign to them. In another such account Bishop Whipple reported "listening to the sweet music discoursed to us by the Italian harpers who come here every evening to play for the crowd," again connecting through descriptive language an instrument to a particular people. The New Englander Henry Knight was surprised to meet on the New Orleans levee "a Highlander playing on his Scotch bagpipe." Bagpiping must have been foreign to his readers, since he felt the need to describe its music and performance as "something between a flute and violin with a humdrum drone to it." When Dan Rice led the "Ethiopian Serenaders" on the minstrel stage, he was advertised as performing with his "Congo Tambo," another instance of attaching an ethnic delineator to an instrument in order to signify ethnicity within the music culture.[12] By labeling musical instruments with an ethnic delineator as a way to symbolize the ethnicity itself, exposure to the instrument became an encounter with difference and a potentially familiarizing activity.

Many other instances exist where commentators recognized and signified a cultural group by identifying a music way with a corresponding cultural label. By explicitly connecting a sound with a place far away or a time long ago, they emphasized their perception of regional diversity and highlighted the potential of a music way to symbolize ethnicity. About fifty miles east of Natchez near the Pearl River, Joseph Holt Ingraham encountered a "Scotch community . . . most of whom or their fathers before them, emigrating from the land of primitive manners, still retain their national characteristics," where "the old popular Gaelic songs are sung, in their original purity and simplicity." At a funeral near Cape Girardeau, Missouri, Timothy Flint heard "a very ancient version of Luther's hymns, and they all began to sing in German, so loud that the woods echoed the strain; and yet there was something affecting in the singing of these ancient people, carrying one of their brethren to his long home. . . . It was a long, loud and mournful air, which they sung as they bore the body along." While visiting a plantation in the neighborhood of Natchez, the English traveler Adam Hodgson remarked, "While listening to some of our own favorite melodies on the harp and piano forte, I could have fancied myself on the banks of the Lune or Mercey, rather than on the Mississippi." One French traveler commented on a slave dance on the Washita River in Louisiana in the early 1830s; he described the "melancholy songs in which African slaves sigh of liberty . . . this sad and plaintive melody from another hemisphere."[13] In each of these instances, the authors used nostalgic descriptions of the diverse music ways connected to ancient homelands outside the United States to emphasize regional peculiarity. The use of language organizing the music culture along ethnic lines also meant that through exposure to one of these music ways with an ethnic label attached, the foreign had the potential to become more familiar to those who experienced it.

Commentators utilized dance, like song, for the same purpose of emphasizing that this region was considered a diverse sounding place by including ethnic labels within their musical descriptions. In these cases, the words African, Indian, Spanish, French, and American, clearly mark off aspects within the regional music culture noted for being culturally distinct. The tourist Arthur Singleton noted that "on Sabbath evening, the African slaves meet on the green, by the swamp, and rock the city with their Congo dances." Timothy Flint described the ethnic makeup of the city of Natchitoches through its dance ways. The city's "Indian *powwows*, its Spanish *fandangos*, its French balls, and its American frolics . . . and the character, costume, and deportment of the mottled damsels that attended them," clearly connected dance with characteristics of a people. According to Thomas Ashe, the residents of Ste. Genevieve, Missouri, in 1806 whom he called "French settlers," expressed "the vestige of Spanish customs" in the musical performances he witnessed, including groups of roving men singing and telling stories accompanied by the guitar and fiddle. Toward midnight, "the music of the village united" for a dance, which included the waltz, the pas de deux and the fandango, "the favorite of the few remaining Spaniards of the village." Evidently, Ashe considered the waltz as for the Americans and the pas de deux for the French of the village. The Polish travelers Francis and Theresa Pulsky observed a "squatter's ball," where "the unorthodox steps of the dances [had been] handed down from father to son, through so many generations that the original French and English measure is scarcely to be recognized."[14] Even in this later description of blending and dilution of culturally specific dance ways, the perception of ancient European origin remained clear enough for observers to attach a label. These descriptions of dance ways reveal a perception that the region was considered a diverse place that could be organized through embedding culturally specific markers within the language.

Native American dances and musical traditions seemed an especially useful way for writers to emphasize another distinctive feature of the mixed regional music culture. The sounds of the Native Americans, so peculiar to the ears of non-Native commentators, served as a way to call attention to their unique culture as well as the region's distance from the nation musically. According to the minister Timothy Flint, Native Americans "have various dances to which they are extravagantly attached; and which often have, as did the dances of the old time, a religious character. The aged council chiefs drum and the young warriors dance with great vehemence beating the ground with their feet. . . . The tunes are very monotonous, running only three or four notes, and constantly recurring to the same strain. In most of the tribes, the women take no part in the song or dance." Flint specifically described the Native Americans on the north shore of Lake Pontchartrain as singing a funeral song that "they are rather shy of exhibiting to strangers." He described this song as a "monotonous and most melancholy lament, in a kind of tone not unlike the howling of a dog. . . . One that appeared to lead in the business, would begin the dolorous note, which the rest immediately followed in a prolonged and dismal strain, for more than half a minute. It then sunk away. It was followed by a few convulsive sobs or snuffles, only giving way to the same dismal howl again."[15] The words Flint used to describe Native American music emphasize the unfamiliarity of this music to his ear, but they also show an attempt to make sense of it through describing it to others. Flint perceived ethnic features within the regional music culture and used descriptions of distinctiveness to contrast this region with what he considered more homogeneous and more American places elsewhere.

An examination of portrayals of the grassy public field on the edge of New Orleans, "where black New Orleanians gathered to dance, play and sing," also reveals how commentators used labeling of music to highlight regional distinctiveness, while familiarizing their readers with that which was foreign. The way writers spoke of this place in the nineteenth century, usually referred to as Congo Square, reveals how descriptions of the region's music culture could be used to show its distinctive diversity in comparison to other places as a way to emphasize the region's cultural distance from and hence precarious attachment to the nation.[16] The general assumptions by observers, both black and white, of the square's musical happenings included an emphasis of the participants' "Africanness." Choosing descriptive language such as "Congoese elite" to describe the dancers or "dulcet melody of a Congo banjo," to describe the music, shows conscious attempts to define these people by their ethnic heritage, rather than race or status alone.[17] By categorizing within the language in this way, commentators distanced the region's music culture from the rest of the nation, while using descriptors of ethnicity to help organize their world.

I am not emphasizing the touristic component of the square to imply that people participated in its music culture only to please the viewers; rather, during the early decades of the nineteenth century, Congo Square's activities simultaneously served a different function for the performing participant and the viewing participant, similar in this way to the potential multiple meanings of other ethnic music genres. Congo slaves made up the largest of the African ethnicities clustered in lower Louisiana in the nineteenth century. This is likely why some slave music and dance in Louisiana was described with the moniker; although it is also possible that the term Congo, or Kongo, was a European designation for diverse Central West Africans who arrived with even more precise identities of their own.[18] In either case, part of Congo Square's tourist appeal stemmed from its specific and generic "Africanness."[19] But what might be so appealing about this? Potentially, part of the appeal of witnessing the activities of Congo Square was similar to other encounters with difference described thus far—as a way to make the foreign more familiar. But in this instance, with the added context of racial slavery, white viewers might also interpret it as "proof" of the cultural inferiority of black Americans, via this reminder of their African roots, thus reassuring the need for the controlling mechanisms of slavery or racial hierarchy in America. Congo Square reiterated to white observers the distinctiveness of racial blackness from whiteness, while presenting the varied African ethnic groups who lived in the region. This combination safely distanced racial blackness even further from incorporation into American culture by connecting it not only to racial difference but also various versions of ethnic "Africanness." By witnessing the music at Congo Square, regional diversity, both racial and ethnic in this instance, was encountered, categorized, and defined, even if such acts of familiarization did not open avenues of acceptance.

One of the first extensive commentaries on Congo Square, made by Benjamin Henry Latrobe during an 1819 visit, is filled with his attempt to accentuate the "Africanness" of the proceedings he witnessed to show that this region was home to a particularly varied music culture that could be categorically arranged. He detailed the instruments he saw, including several drums and a stringed instrument with the body of a calabash that he believed "no doubt was imported from Africa." A man sang a song for the dancers that Latrobe "suppose[d] was in some African language, for it was not French." These "allowed amusements of Sunday," he believed, "perpetuated here those of Africa among its former inhabitants." Latrobe, in this two-page description, managed to connect the music culture he witnessed explicitly to Africa in three separate instances, and implied it in several others. He used skin color to imply a particularly close connection to the happenings he witnessed with "real" African culture, as he noted, "All those who were engaged in the business seemed to be blacks. I did not observe a dozen yellow faces."[20]

Other writers during the following decades frequently reemphasized Latrobe's commentary on the unique African music culture as expressed at Congo Square in New Orleans. John Paxton's 1822 New Orleans City Directory implied that the square's activities appealed at least to some viewers for its distinctively African nature, as these viewers attempted to familiarize difference. He preached, "On account of its being the place where the Congo and other Negroes dance," the "foolish custom" causes "great injury of the morals of the rising generation." However, "if it is not considered good policy to abolish the practice entirely, surely, they could be ordered to assemble at some place more distant from the houses, by which means the evil would be measurably remedied." In this condemnation, Paxton makes clear the voyeuristic appeal of what was believed to be Congo Square's distinctively African activities to some, while simultaneously revealing that whatever this music culture consisted of, "the most respectable persons who visit the city" found it distasteful.[21] In the mid-1840s Congo Square was spoken of, by this time somewhat nostalgically, as appealing to viewers for its distinctive ethnic component. *Norman's New Orleans and Its Environs* from 1845, which mentioned the "'unsophisticated' dances of the square's 'primitive days,'" attempted to distinguish the former African dances, which had by this time ceased, from the African-American dances, which continued in the same space. Norman recalled Congo Square as "the place where the negroes, in olden times, were accustomed to meet." However, the following year the *Daily Picayune* still recommended that "no stranger in this city of New Orleans . . . should fail to visit, of a Sunday afternoon, the square in Rampart Street, commonly called 'Congo Square.' The scene is novel, interesting, and highly amusing."[22] Such encouragement of cultural tourism reveals the appeal of Congo Square's perceived diversity within the regional music culture and the ability of seemingly authentically ethnic performance to act as an encounter with difference.

Tourist accounts of Congo Square reinforce the assumption that music ways could serve as ethnic markers during this era. It was in the Americas that various Africans made the transition from ethnicities to a race. Africans and their descendants in the United States did not simply forget their ethnic backgrounds, rather they "played a crucial role in determining the African American identity.... [E]thnicity had a direct impact on African Americans' self-perception," as well as the perceptions of non-Africans toward them.[23] In 1817, the German trader J. G. Flügel "witnessed a negro dance" at an unnamed location in New Orleans where he was informed that "three of the negroes in the group closest to us were formerly kings or chiefs in Congo," whose "more genteel address," was revealed in their ability to "dance extremely well." Arthur Singleton made the distinction in 1824 that it was the "African slaves" who met in the square to "rock the city with their Congo dances." "I judged it was African music," noted the free black witness James Thomas, "judging from the antics of those blacks on the congo green in New Orleans, I judge their dances, Juber and Partner, were imported from Africa, modified slightly," considering "the people looked as they, most of them, were the imported article." The local Henry Castellanos recalled Congo Square as the "favorite rendezvous of our African slaves on Sunday afternoons . . . where they would romp in African revelries . . . [with] . . . dances peculiar to their country." He made an additional distinction, but one nonetheless attempting to segregate participants by heritage when he wrote that the "*nègres 'Mericains* were not invited" to participate in the gathering.[24]

This "Africanness" inherent in Congo Square descriptions had remained so strong that even later in the century William Wells Brown recalled his own time spent in New Orleans by describing the various African groups who frequented Congo Square. His precise delineation of the varied African ethnic groups who used Congo Square for their leisure activities solidifies the perception that these slaves could not only be identified and categorized by their race but also by their ethnicity. This also emphasizes the distance Brown felt from the Congo Square performers. Brown recalled, "In Louisiana there were six different tribes of negroes, named after the section of the country from which they came, and their representatives could be seen on the square, their teeth filed, and their cheeks still bearing tattoo marks." According to Brown, these ethnic distinctions remained pertinent to the musical culture of these enslaved Africans in Congo Square. He described how at "about three o'clock the negroes began to gather, each nation taking their place at different parts of the square. The Minahs would not dance near the Congos, nor the Mandringas near the Gangas. . . . Each set had its own orchestra."[25] Using the word African, or any of the various ethnic groups, rather than black in the language describing Congo Square emphasizes that the codification by race alone was not how all contemporaries understood this diversity.

The activities of the square were appealing to locals and tourists alike for their ethnically defined musical uniqueness, and had become a commonly used symbol to represent the distinctiveness of the region. Such ethnic enclosures erected in language in order to mark off difference, as in this instance of Congo Square, should be read not only as delineating boundaries within the regional music culture but also as spaces where witness to difference could work as an ameliorating force, precisely because of the ethnic marker attached to a public cultural expression. Because Congo Square served both as a site for ethnic expression and as an attraction with ethnic appeal to nonperformers, the varied perceptions of this site reveal the intricate connection between the music culture and the categorizations of race and ethnicity in the region.

Such frequently made connections between the ethnic and musical components of this public culture reveal the implied belief in an ethnic nature of music, music's capacity to comment on cultural boundaries, and its ability to serve as a marker for regional distinctiveness in a place perceived to be peculiarly diverse. From such descriptions, a clear contemporary perception emerges that people who lived in the region belonged to specific ethnic groups with unique sounds. Instruments, dances, songs, and musical techniques and styles all served to signal that multiple ethnically distinctive music ways existed within the region. Although such categorization was meant to distinguish one group from another, these descriptions also aimed to differentiate the particular region of the lower Mississippi River Valley from other places in the nation with a more homogeneous and more "American" character. Although the connection these writers assigned to a specific music way and an ethnic group may lack accuracy from an anthropological perspective, such descriptions are more useful when viewed by the historian as contemporary organizational techniques, which illuminate the way they created boundaries around groups of people. Through such rhetoric, travelers into the region attempted to make sense of the varied sounds emanating from the diverse population they encountered. Outsiders, however, were not the only ones participating in such labeling. Those who lived in the region also considered it an especially diverse sounding place and found that it made sense to organize the world in which they lived into ethnic categories.

Although the appeal of music perceived as distinctively ethnic may be due purely to taste, other evidence suggests, as in the above case of Congo Square, that part of the appeal stemmed from the ability of ethnically labeled music to provide a seemingly authentic encounter with difference, and as such assuage the anxiety that diversity evoked. In just one example of this, the regional theater manager Sol Smith admitted to changing the name of the eight-year-old equestrian, singer, and actor Jimmy Robinson to Juan Hernandez in 1840 to sell more tickets. But what might be so appealing about experiencing a sound way previously unfamiliar or peculiarly "ethnic," that would make Smith's marketing technique effective? One possible explanation relates directly to the nationwide cultural phenomena whereby Americans denigrated their own cultural forms in favor of those of Europe. Instances of this did appear in the region as they had in other parts of the nation.[26] Although belittling American music culture certainly occurred, this explanation does not go far enough in explaining the deeper meaning embedded within the continued fascination with ethnically labeled cultural forms produced within the region.

A complementary and more plausible answer stems from the especially diverse and constantly shifting demographics of the lower Mississippi River Valley during the first half of the nineteenth century. Whether an African-born slave, a New York transplant, a fourth-generation French Creole, or a new European immigrant, a person's daily cultural encounters, both musical and otherwise, were filled with ways distinctively different from one's previously accustomed culture. Thus, experiencing a musical way outside one's comfort zone, served the purpose of familiarizing difference by making foreignness more manageable. This made difference less threatening and helped all people make sense of the diversity surrounding them. The appeal of music labeled as ethnic came from its ability to transform a stranger into someone familiar, even if done unconsciously and without breaking down all barriers of difference. This would have appealed to all the region's residents, making them feel more comfortable in their surroundings of shifting unfamiliarity.[27]

Because the regional population perceived their music culture as being organized within ethnically specific categories, they needed to be able to pass between these boundaries if they were to witness difference

and thus feel they understood it better. At times, this occurred by transforming music believed to be connected with one particular ethnic
group into ethnic musical genres. These ethnic music genres were accessible for experience by all, without shedding their implicit symbolic
meaning of being connected to a particular group of people. Ethnic
genre creation and consumption made safe the foreign; by consuming
the dissimilar, it became part of one's own repertoire of understanding.
Through this process of ethnic genre creation and then consumption,
music ways believed to be authentically ethnic were commodified.[28] The
consumption of ethnic genres could take place in a variety of ways, from
buying the sheet music of a "Spanish Dance" for the parlor piano, to
attending performances of an Italian opera, to watching the dancers at
Congo Square. This process of taking a music way, clearly identified by
an ethnic label, and choosing to perform, listen to, observe, or purchase
it for oneself, reveals that integration of the "other" occurred by familiarizing the foreign through consuming their perceived difference. The
frequency with which dances, performers, performances, sheet music,
and music instructors were advertised with an ethnic label implies that
the ethnic nature of their product particularly appealed to an audience,
who consumed each musical genre as a way to familiarize themselves
with the "others" in their midst.

The frequency with which dances were billed as ethnic suggests that
an ethnically defined dance way must have appealed to audiences. It also
implies that a particularly strong connection must have existed in the
minds of the consuming public between a dance style and a cultural
tradition for such an advertising technique to have worked. Describing
a dance as Spanish, for example, gave a particular meaning to the witnesses of this cultural form. This is not to imply that an advertisement
for a "Spanish Fandango" would necessarily be a dance created in Spain
performed by a Spaniard. By transforming a piece into an ethnic genre,
the mystique of ethnic authenticity could be retained, as ethnicity became performed and consumed. These ethnically labeled dances became
available to all when turned into genres, which could be safely consumed
by the general population and diminish the anxiety diversity generated.
In some instances, there was no illusion that an evening's ethnic dance
would be performed by one of the in-group, since multiple different ethnic dances were advertised on the same night to be performed by the
same person. During the course of one three-night stand in Natchez, the
"celebrated French dancers" performed eight different ethnically identified dances. In such instances the perception of authenticity, although

still important, could be staged through appropriate costuming or scenery, or "proven" by emphasizing performers' tutorial lineage. The preponderance of ethnically labeled dances billed in regional performances reveals an attempt to organize diversity through partaking of difference in the form of ethnic genres.

Madame Celeste, a frequent performer on the stages of the lower Mississippi River Valley, was particularly noted for her ability to perform ethnically labeled, or "characteristic," dances. Referring to ethnically labeled dances as "characteristic" may have stemmed from the belief that these dances revealed innate characteristics about the group of people who practiced a particular dance style. For example, a local newspaper described the polka, which took America by storm in the 1840s, as "equally popular in Bohemia, Hungary, Sweden, Norway," and "highly characteristic; it paints the northern inhabitant's highest joy in life." Like that of the "celebrated French dancers" (of whom she may have been a member), Celeste's ethnic repertoire was broad. During a single evening's performance in New Orleans in 1839, she danced a "Moorish Dance—The Alahambra," a "Spanish Dance—La Cachucha," and a "Greek Dance—The Romaika."[29] Celeste also appeared on the stage in dances labeled Chinese and Turkish; she could perform "the national Polish Dance of Liberty, called the Cracovienne," and a pas de deux in the Basque style, among others. An advertisement from her first American tour described these "National Dances" as imitating "the styles of various nations to a collection of popular airs." "The unrivalled Parisian Dancers, Mademoiselles Celeste and Constance" appeared at the American Theater in 1829 dancing "the Russian Mazurea Pas De Deux," and a "West Indian Dance."[30] Other dancers drew crowds with their ethnically labeled performances as well. In 1828 Mr. Nicolas Barabino, whose newspaper advertisement appeared in both English and French, performed a "Spanish Dance called the Cachucha . . . with the accompaniment of *castanetos*," while in 1845 Mr. Bonnie and Miss Oceana danced "the Spanish Bolero," between two plays at the American Theater. Lola Montez advertised her intent to dance the "Spanish Tarantella for the first time in St. Louis" in 1853, while later that year Senorita Soto and Mr. G. W. Smith performed a "Grand Bolero Espagnol" for the city's Varieties Theater.[31]

The theater manager Sol Smith advertised a particularly diverse repertoire for the dancers associated with his 1829–1830 tour in the region. On March 23, the "first night of the French Dancers," the program ended with "a Spanish Dance," and the March 26, 1830, program included an

"English national dance, a national Scottish dance, the comic Scotch song of Little Wot Ye Wa's Commin and a Grand Italian Dance." The following night, the "third night of the celebrated French dancers," included "a grand Turkish dance," "a Chinese dance," and an "Allemande Dance." The "last night of the celebrated French dancers" added a "Grand Swiss dance" and a "Brazilian Dance" to the ethnic movements of the following weeks.[32]

Other references to "Indian Dance," "Various Negro Dances," an "English Dance," and "A Grand National Scotch Dance" appeared in advertisements within the region. Interestingly, when Mr. Vilallave promoted his upcoming fandango performance the *New Orleans Bee* printed advertisements in English, French, and Spanish; however, only the English-language advertisement used the descriptor of "Spanish" before fandango. After the "characteristic dance" by the ballet corps at the American Theater, one Mr. Wells danced a "Scotch Strathspey." On a Scottish-themed night at the St. Charles Theatre in 1845, "the true Highland Fling will be danced to the stirring strains of the Scotch Bagpipes, by the Child Eliza, only six years old." By utilizing these now familiar representations of ethnic others, such performances played on audience expectations of experiencing the unfamiliar through these ethnic genres. In this way, what had been foreign became less so. Surrounded by diversity, the appeal of dances labeled as ethnic grew from a shared desire to understand the unfamiliar, resulting in the creation of ethnic genres as a surrogate for authenticity.[33]

Dancing masters also promoted their ability to teach "characteristic dances" and usually listed their ethnic specialties within their advertisements.[34] For example, an instructor in Vicksburg let his clients know that he could teach both the French and German Quadrille, whereas one New Orleans dancing master advertised his knowledge of German, Cossack, and Russian waltzes, among others.[35] "French dancing masters," as they frequently called themselves, made sure to advertise their success or training in Paris to legitimize their authenticity. Mr. Lavenant, "*Elere* of the Royal Academy at Paris," taught dancing in Baton Rouge and New Orleans and proclaimed his competency by marketing his "correspondence with the principal professors of Paris, . . . [from whom] . . . he receives all the new music of every dance and the engravings, introduced in the most fashionable society." Lavenant worked to reach a larger audience by advertising in both English and French. Professor St. Maur Stuart proposed "in accordance with the custom of Mobile and New Orleans," giving semimonthly soirées and Tuesday night Quadrille Parties.

To do so, he advertised a "long experience in his profession, acquired in the principal cities of Europe."[36]

Other musical instructors found ways to emphasize their own legitimacy to teach "characteristic" music either by emphasizing the place of their training or experience as a teacher. This technique continued the illusion of authenticity through ethnic genre creation and an ability to encounter difference on one's own terms. Many dance teachers advertised themselves as "French dancing masters" and traveled the river towns looking for new pupils. Although it is not clear if these instructors were French or Saint Domingue immigrants, local French Creoles, or others teaching a certain dance style commonly known as "French," the frequency with which this label appeared shows that it had a certain meaning to the regional population and that their product must have appealed to at least some people.[37] New Orleans French dancing master Professor J. Vegas advertised his dancing academy on the back of an 1853 French opera program, noting the "new dances for this season, [the] Varsovia and Hungarian." Later, the local music house of Blackmar published a piano solo with the inscription on the title page, a "*Nouveau Quadrille des Professeur de Danse de Paris*, as taught by Prof. J. Vegas," and a description, printed in English and French, of the dance steps meant to accompany this quadrille. Eliza Ripley recalled her youth in New Orleans when Mme. Angelina, a "new French importation, whose specialty was the new dances that nobody else could teach," ran a dancing academy.[38]

Some instructors advertised their former success in different European places in order to emphasize the ethnic authenticity of their offerings. Through these advertisements, music teachers in the region helped create ethnic music genres available for consumption; disseminating these forms labeled with ethnicity held the potential to familiarize their students with perceived difference. "A Young Lady, recently arrived from London," included singing and piano lessons as her areas of expertise in a New Orleans advertisement from 1837, while in 1818, A. C. van Hirum, sold his skills in St. Louis as a professor of music "late from Amsterdam."[39] The Natchez music teacher Mrs. Armstrong advertised how after "having resided some time with the Spaniards, [she] has acquired their method of performing on the Guitar, and will teach pupils to perform in the Spanish style." "Professor A. F. Cykoski and Lady" advertised in the 1860 Vicksburg City Directory as being "from Paris." She "teaches music on the Piano and Singing and French in its Purity," while he "teaches Music on the Piano, Guitar and all wind instruments."[40] These music teachers believed the ethnic appeal of their training was strong enough among their audience to include mention of it in their advertisements. In doing so, they facilitated the promotion of ethnic music genres in the region.

The appeal of an ethnically perceived music culture can also be seen in the multitude of performers who were billed as ethnic. The monikers given to these touring performers consistently connected the musical product they were selling with a distinctive cultural tradition, so much so, that whole new genres labeled by ethnicity emerged, in some instances, based on the performance of one particular artist. Although most of these traveling performers originated from the places they were sold as representing, the consistency with which the ethnic component of their performance trumped so many other potential categorizations implies an appeal of the ethnic to the local audiences being courted to attend. Although advertisements often revealed distinctions in age, gender, and even race to make a performer uniquely appealing, ethnicity remained a central element in how acts were sold. Jenny Lind became the "Swedish Nightingale" thanks to the marketing techniques of P. T. Barnum, and Catherine Hayes, by Barnum imitators, the "Swan of Erin" or the "Irish Skylark." According to the performance scholar Joseph Roach, "the two divas—'The Swedish Nightingale,' and the 'Irish Skylark'—staged a drama of ethnic assimilation. . . . Race-conscious New Orleans provided a particularly promising setting for this drama of social mobility and inclusion versus social death."[41] Within this context, the African American singer Elizabeth Taylor Greenfield became the "Black Swan" in her billings, and although she never performed in the region, her birthplace of Natchez expressed a continued interest in her career. One Buffalo, New York, announcement read, "There is no doubt that the novelty of hearing a colored woman perform the most difficult music with extraordinary ability will give *éclat* to the concert," and another from Columbia, Ohio, believed, "She is indeed a remarkable swan. Although colored as dark as Ethiopia she utters notes as pure as if uttered in the words of the Adriatic." Even Ole Bull was almost always labeled as a "Norwegian violinist" in his advertisements. After hearing Lind's performance in New Orleans, young Lizzie Randall wrote, "I was delighted, entranced and felt as if I were transported to 'music land' of German tradition."[42] Barring time spent in Germany, Randall's exposure to the ethnic music genres that formed a foundational part of her cultural world very likely sold the girl on this conclusion. Through advertising themselves as ethnic, touring performers reveal their ethnic appeal, all the while creating ethnic genres, easily consumable and helpful at familiarizing the region with diversity.

The Swiss Rainer Family, who toured the United States in 1839 in their "national costume," provides another excellent example of touring performers who marketed themselves as distinctively ethnic, thus creating ethnic genres available for consumption by the regional population. The Rainers' advertisements consistently connected their performances to the peculiarity of their homeland sound. According to the historian Scott Gac, "The Rainers understood the power and value to their music of nationalism and posed as organic entertainers whose music and talents sprang forth from their native land." Editors throughout the country commented on their performances and consistently tied their sound to their peculiar Swiss or Tyrolean nature. The Rainer style appealed so strongly that others mimicked it, including, ironically, the Hutchinson Family Singers from New Hampshire. Despite the Hutchinsons' prior tours emphasizing themselves as particularly American, even going so far on their playbills as to encourage audiences to support native American talent, after hearing the Rainers in concert, the older boys dressed up their eleven-year-old sister in a "Swiss costume" and boasted of their "Tyrolean style of singing." From then on, the Hutchinson Family appeared on stage dressed in Alpine folk costume and added Aeolian-style yodeling à la Rainer to their repertoire. The Hutchinsons' mimicry shows how strongly these ethnic genres must have appealed to audiences, if these American performers so carefully attempted to tap into this ethnic appeal. Although the Rainer family toured the South, no specific details of their route have been uncovered. Other of these performers who did tour the region riding the wave of the Rainers' ethnic appeal include "The Campanologian Band of Swiss Bell Ringers," the Peak Family, billed as "Germanian bell ringers," and the "French Mountaineer Singers."[43]

Other lesser-known ethnically labeled performers were part of this same trend. Although some mimicked the success of more prominent entertainers, others found their own ethnically appealing niche. The *New Orleans Bee* lauded Madame Hammerskoldn for the "Swedish airs" she sang. After the Austrian ballerina Fanny Elssler's tour in 1841, other nationalities tried their luck tapping into this ethnic market, including a "Swiss Fanny" named Gabrielde Korpomay, "a Hungarian polka specialist," "Viennese children," and a "Spanish Troupe," who all toured the region in the 1840s.[44] A Vicksburg report that "the Hungarians will appear in their NATIONAL COSTUME," left little room to debate this band's perceived authenticity and its appeal to the audience. Mr. Templeton

performed in Natchez as "the first of English tenors," while Mr. Slo-
man sang in New Orleans as "the celebrated English buffo singer."[45] Mr.
Gustave Krollmann, "the celebrated German violinist," graced the stage
of Baton Rouge's Market Hall, and Mr. Grossman, a "pianist from Germany" did the same in Vicksburg. Even Master Diamond, "this young
prodigy in the African line," a young blackface performer managed by
Barnum, performed in New Orleans and Vicksburg in 1841 in the context of representing an ethnic genre via his performance.[46] The frequent
use of ethnic labels in musical advertisements shows how authenticity
could be signaled with cues in the written language. The ethnic music
genres created as a result needed not so much to present actual as believable expressions of ethnicity in order for consuming difference and
familiarization to occur.

The frequent use of ethnic labels in the titles of performance pieces
helped accomplish this same goal. The consistent choice of performing
ethnically identified pieces reveals their appeal to the regional population and the potential to make the foreign more familiar through such
perceived encounters with difference. Professional stage productions,
like individual performers, advertised ethnically labeled performances,
and in doing so created ethnic genres. An 1830 program for the Scottish
"romantic operatic play" *Rob Roy* included several Scottish songs not part
of the original score but introduced in New Orleans by Mrs. Knight, including "Draw the Sword, Scotland," and "All the Blue Bonnets Are Over
the Border," among others. "An Italian cavatine," an "English Dance, and
A Grand National Scotch Dance" followed this stage performance. Such
genre pieces played on their ethnic appeal in the advertisements for their
performances. Following a play at the New Orleans American Theater
in 1827, one "Mr. Crampton, who has been eminently successful in singing Scotch and Irish Songs," advertised his intent to "sing the admired
Scotch Ballad of Little Wot Ye Wha' Comin, and the popular Irish Song
of Larry O'Gaff." The existing theater programs from Sol Smith's Company for the 1829–1830 season, consistently advertised song selections
as being "Scotch." At least twenty of the performances listed in the programs included phrases such as "introducing the popular Scotch Song"
and "will sing for the first time a new Scotch Song." Also included in
Smith's advertised performances was "The Irish National Song of the
'Exile of Ireland.'" A "New National Dance" was performed between
School for Scandal and *The Irish Tutor* in New Orleans, likely referring to
an Irish dance in this case, while the *Englishman in India* was followed
by "national airs," most likely representing England or India in song.[47]

Newspaper announcements for local amateur performances reveal the ability of ethnic music genres to embody a potent cultural meaning among the region's population, as musicians frequently chose to perform songs with ethnically labeled titles. Potentially, by performing a song identified with a particular cultural group, its prior novelty became customary once part of one's familiar repertoire. The "Amateur Concert" given for the benefit of the Vicksburg Catholic Church in 1845 included a variety of "ethnic" songs, including the "Canadian Song," "Erin in My Home," "To Greece We Give Our Shining Blades," "Tyrolese War Song," among other Scotch, Irish, French, and Italian pieces. A "Soirée Musicalle," given by Madame Caradori Allan in New Orleans, included several Italian opera pieces but also a "Bolero Français" and a "Scottish Ballad." Her third night included an Italian opera piece, a "Scottish Air," a "German Air," and an "Air Français." As early as 1813, the Natchez amateur theater group advertised a performance of "the celebrated comic opera called the Highland Reel, With the original Overture, [and] appropriate Highland Dresses."[48] When the students at the Elizabeth Female Academy in Washington, Mississippi, near Natchez gave their "Musical soiree," the performance included the songs "Blue Bells of Scotland," "Egyptian Rondo," "Air Russo," and "Swiss Boy."[49]

That such represented ethnicity remained linked in the minds of locals with a population in their midst shows how ethnic music genres existed not only in the abstract but remained powerfully real symbols of an "other" with whom they were striving to come to terms. Tyrone Power, an Irish character actor, frequently appeared on the local stage in any number of his Irish characters replete with "brogue, blarney and botheration," in "his exquisitely faithful delineation of the Irish character." Power's staged Irishman became a point of reference for actual "Irishness" among the non-Irish population, who were searching for ways to understand this strange new people surrounding them, and found at least some answers through the ethnic genres of the stage. In 1839, a New Orleans *Picayune* police report mockingly described how "Mr. Philip Power and Mrs. Philip Power were arrested for going through an amateur performance of the farce of 'Family of Jars,' or as the watchman vulgarly expressed it for fighting and disturbing the peace." A few years later, an Irishman arrested on the levee was reported as smiling "in a most bewitching manner, *a la Power.*" There was also some reaction against this sort of stereotyping. The *Daily Delta* of New Orleans regretted that too often audiences went home believing that negative stage caricatures were authentic portrayals of "Irishness."[50] Ethnic music

genres entrenched by staged ethnic characters like those Power performed, helped the regional population organize their diverse surroundings, even though the ensconcement of negative stereotypes may have
limited the acceptance of the group being portrayed.

The choice of sheet music titles reveals another instance of music's
ability to signify ethnicity to the regional population. The sheet music
industry used ethnic labels to create genres defined by perceived ethnic
boundaries and produced cultural consumers based on a heightened
awareness of ethnicity. Whole volumes of sheet music were devoted to
Irish melodies or Spanish airs, reinforcing in the minds of witnesses the
ethnic nature of music, the diverse nature of their world, as well as their
ability to define and control it through choosing exposure to such forms.
Sixteen of the Rainers' songs were published as sheet music in the United
States, including "The Alpine Horn," "The Alpine Hunters," "The Mountain Maid's Invitation," "The Tyrolese in America," and "The Tyrolese
War Song."[51] Local music sellers carried an especially varied collection
of music with ethnic titles. The New Orleans music seller T. E. Benoit advertised a selection of "French Songs for the Piano"; John Klemm, a "Bohemian Melody"; and Benjamin Casey sold sheet music with the words
Tyrolese, English, Switzer, Spanish, and Italian in the titles.[52] The young
Ste. Genevieve, Missouri, native Zoé Vallé enjoyed "The Celebrated Ty-
rolian Waltz" enough to transcribe it in a book among several Parisian
scores and pieces of American popular sheet music. "The Chinese Bell
Quadrilles" must have signaled ethnicity with the sound of the piece,
for it contained no lyrics to explain its "Chinese-ness" to the consumer.[53]

The familiarity of these pieces to the local audience is clear from the
frequency newspapers published new lyrics to some of these works.
For the readership to have enjoyed these new works, the original songs
would have to have been quite familiar. Newspapers printed new lyrics
to "Gaelic Song," "Scotch Song," "Song of the Ancient Choctaws," "Cossack Song of 1814–'15," and "The Irish War Song."[54] The "Spanish Air"
must have been familiar enough to the Vicksburg newspaper audience
for the "Hymn to the Mississippi" to be set to its tune.[55] The preponderance of sheet music sold with ethnic labels in their titles suggests the
appeal of these ethnic music genres within the American sheet music
market. Songs titled "Spanish," "French," "Scotch," or "Irish" were most
common; however, many other ethnicities could be purchased as well.
Published songs represented nearly every potential categorization of humanity to the regional population, making presumed knowledge about
people they represented available as well.

The prevalence of ethnically titled sheet music found in bound collections suggests that ethnicity appealed not only to the producer of the genre but also to the purchaser, who could then familiarize himself or herself with strangers by performing the musical genres thought to express their distinctive ways. The sheet music collection of the free black Natchez family of William Johnson included "Erin Is My Home," "The Irish Milkmaid's Song," "Dance Espagnole," "Le Tyrol Variations Elégantes," and a book of "Favorite Scotch Melodies."[56] Matilda Kinney, wife of a Mississippi River steamboat captain, received a copy of "The Lament of the Irish Immigrant" after her husband returned from a trip to St. Louis. This piece of sheet music describes exactly how the performing consumer of this work should understand the Irish in their midst. The cover notes this piece as "portraying the feeling of an Irish peasant previous to his leaving home, calling up the scenes of his youth under the painful reflection of having buried his wife and child and what his feelings will be in America." Such an addendum made the Irish experience more accessible to anyone else performing the work. Enna Massey Walker's teacher instructed her by teaching a sampling of songs from a variety of ethnic genres. Her piano lesson book included "Air Savoyard," "The Guaracha, a Spanish Dance," "Russian Air," "Hungarian Air," "Polacca, a Polish Movement on Three Crotchets," "A Favorite Italian Air," "Foliad Espagna," and "A Fine Specimen of the Welsh National Music."[57]

In order for a personal experience with difference through consuming an ethnic music genre to be an effective technique to alleviate some of the anxiety associated with living in a place full of unfamiliar ways, a music way believably, if not accurately, had to express ethnic distinctiveness. The ability of a musical way to be transformed into an ethnic music genre was predicated on the belief in authentically ethnic music. Otherwise, experiencing a musical form could not have helped anyone familiarize themselves with difference. Many prior examples have alluded to this issue; however, what follows is a more detailed description of instances whereby the perceived belief in various authentically ethnic sounds occurred within the region. Although scholars today consider the concept of authenticity a historical construct, it appears that at this time and place, ethnic authenticity was an assumed reality. By "misremembering" the past in order to reorganize a group's relationship to nongroup members and the nation, the regional population participated in a collective process the sociologist Richard Peterson has called "fabricating authenticity." As the following examples show, musical expression seemed at the time to be necessarily, not incidentally, a result of one's ethnicity.[58]

Because there was no consistent term used in the early nineteenth century to describe the concept we today would call ethnicity, I have settled on using the word "ethnicity" despite its not being used at the time. People variously referred to this idea with terms such as nationality, characteristic, or race. However, these words now have changed meaning in the modern context, and the closest vocabulary in current usage to convey what I believe nineteenth-century Americans meant and understood about difference is "ethnicity." The language commentators used to categorize the regional music culture reveals the assumed link between an authentic and discrete cultural heritage and a person's music. This link had to remain strong enough for an encounter with musical difference to serve the purpose of assuaging diversity's danger.

Writers often used descriptive words such as "national" and "real," to signify authenticity. For example, an 1827 American Theater performance advertised that "a gentleman, a native of Scotland, who has kindly volunteered his services, will play several Scotch airs on a real Scotch harp," while the Camp Street Theater in New Orleans advertised for "the Real Bedouin Arabs." When describing the "twenty different dancing groups of wretched Africans, collected together to perform their *worship* after the manner of their country," Christian Schultz made sure to note how "they have their own national music," to imply the authenticity of such an expression.[59] The New Orleans *Daily Picayune* noted that the actor Barney Williams performed "the genuine Paddy, the true Irish peasant," while "performances on the Scotch and Irish Bagpipes by Mr. Ferguson" were given an air of legitimacy as audiences were assured he would "appear clad in true Highland Costume."[60] When the French danseuse Madame Celeste performed for the "first time in New Orleans, The national Polish Dance of Liberty, called the Cracovienne," its ethnic authenticity was validated by noting that "this beautiful dance was presented to Celeste by Col. Bertrand, a distinguished Polish officer, and performed by her in London on the Polish Anniversary, before the Committee, and 100 of the brave exiles."[61] Slaves in the region also recognized the potential for authenticity in music and dance. Isaac Stier of Lauderdale County Mississippi, remembered that although some of the men clogged and pidgeoned, when he attended a dance they were "real cotillions, lak de [sic] white folks had." In other instances, emphasizing ancient heritage signified authenticity as did a copy of "Foliad Espagna" described as a "Spanish Air of Great Antiquity." The "ancient Irish Airs," one 1809 Natchez newspaper described in an article on Irish music, commends Thomas Moore's ability to convey "the ancient freedom and valor of the sons of Erin."[62] Such choice of language reveals inherent assumptions about the belief in ethnic authenticity in the regional music culture and, as such, the ability of music to be transformed into ethnic music genres.

To audiences, a fine line existed between the actual and the contrived. In a review of Felippe Cioffi's benefit concert, the reviewer criticized a piece for being "too English in manner to make an impression, especially when the concert as a whole consisted of Italian music." The concert program for the touring Irish musician P. F. White, billed as a friend of Thomas Moore, the Irish poet popular with both the Irish and non-Irish population in America, announced, "Mr. White will sing as Mr. Moore himself sings his melodies." A quote from Thomas Moore in the next column of the newspaper lent more authenticity to the event for anyone hoping to experience "Irishness" at the performance. Moore noted, "It has always been a subject of some mortification to me, that my songs, as they are set, give such an imperfect notion of the manner in which I wish them to be performed, and that most of the peculiarity of character, which I believe they possess as I sing them myself, is lost in the process they must undergo for publication. . . . [T]he hand that corrects their errors is almost sure to destroy their character, and the few little flowers they may boast of are generally pulled away with the weeds." This "character" he spoke of was the "Irishness" believed inherent in each performance.[63]

White locals recognized the ability of slaves to perform authentically, through their condemnation of "inauthentic" expression. On a plantation outside of Natchez, Henry Miller commented on the slave balls of Christmas week when the slave "apes his betters." Miller interpreted certain aspects of music and dance as mimicry and as such a false cultural expression that necessarily led to a decline in "original" slave culture. "Such occasions," he noted, "often times destroy their rural festive pastimes; instead of giving us the niggah in his originality, they give us the White man niggahfied; . . . When the Negro leaves his hoedown and goes to dancing Cotillions, there is something truly ludicrous in the figure he cuts. When the dignified air and importance in every jesture [sic] as he swells around the circle or moves through the figure of the dance, what stiffness, what pomposity."[64] As implied in these examples of performances in the region, music could be performed in ways that were considered more or less authentic. When a performance strayed too far from its creator's presumed ancient heritage, it was believed to have lost some of its validity, making the performance either tame or a joke. In either case, the once "true" expression had moved into the realm of mere imitation. Only when the perception of authenticity remained could experiencing a music way work toward familiarizing oneself with difference and making diversity less frightening.

Another instance revealing the local belief in authentically ethnic musical forms is seen in the parodies of legitimate musical concerts, which carried assumptions of being attached to either German or Italian traditions. A clear link between a music way and the corresponding ethnicity had to remain fixed in the public's mind for the humor to work. An 1843 *Daily Picayune* announcement for the next "sheet iron band" performance of a local *charivari* troupe, parodied both the look and sound of common concert programs at the time. Not only does this caricature imply a familiarity with the visual layout of concert programs, but also an awareness of the likelihood that performers in a legitimate local concert bill would be Italian or German. This burlesqued advertisement played up the "Italianness" and "Germanness" common in many local concerts, similar to the way minstrel shows mimicked Italian opera, by using fake Italian and German names and titles. For example, in this sheet iron band exhibition "Von Blast," performed "Fantasia on a Valve Stove Pipe," while "Screameroari," played "obligato on the Railroad Alarm Whistle." For the humor to work in this parody, the connection between the regional concert music culture to "Germanness" and "Italianness" had to be secure in the minds of the audience. The fact that the sheet iron band performed noise rather than music during their *charivari* deepens the humor of the spoof. In a similar instance, the New Orleans press referred to the popular local black street vendor Old Corn Meal, who appeared in a few stage performances, as "Signor Cornmeali."[65] In order for the humor of these parodies to make sense, locals must have assumed that authentically ethnic musical expression, in these instances of Germans and Italians, existed in the region. Through exposure to their strange ways, even through a spoof, the ethnic "other" might become tamed.

One of the best examples showing the *belief* that a music way could be authentically ethnic, and as such turned into an ethnic music genre available for consumption, is seen in the language used to discuss blackface minstrelsy. When white minstrel performers first appeared on the American stage, "they thought they were imitating African or Ethiopian behavior, at least this is what their playbills announced." In fact, according to the minstrel scholar Eric Lott, "Early audiences so often suspected that they were being entertained by actual Negroes that minstrel sheet music began the proto-Brechtian practice of picturing blackface performers out of costume as well as in."[66] An article on minstrelsy in *Putnam's Monthly Magazine* showing the belief in minstrelsy's authenticity, speculated on the "origins of this ancient and peculiar melody" as either from the banks of the Mississippi or "a relic of heathen rites in the Congo." However, they were sure that "the true secret of their favor with the world is to be found in the fact that they are genuine and real." "Why may not the banjoism of a Congo, an Ethiopian or a George Christy aspire to an equality with the musical and poetical delineators of all nationalities," wondered a writer to the *New York Tribune*; "it expresses the peculiar characteristics of the negro as truly as the great masters of Italy represent their more spiritual and profound nationality." In fact, the use of the term "Ethiopian" was not limited to discussions of minstrelsy. Writers also employed it to describe generic "Africanness" within black American culture or a particular African ethnicity within "scientific" discussions of race during the mid-nineteenth century. Use of the word "Ethiopian" within minstrelsy and the insistence of blackface performers that their acts were "genuine" further buttressed the perception of ethnic authenticity inherent in minstrelsy and bolstered its ability to make the unfamiliar known.[67]

Much of minstrelsy's appeal stemmed from the fact that the audience assumed the forms expressed on the stage were based on actual black culture, likely because the minstrels themselves, who "claimed to be authentic delineators of black life," sold it as such. This is why the use of the term "Ethiopian" within the music culture, although not accurate, can be read as another example of genre creation. The minstrel scholar Robert Toll writes that much of blackface minstrelsy's appeal stemmed from the perception of its racial and ethnic authenticity. He writes of "the promise of satisfying white Northerners' growing curiosity about blacks and especially slaves at a time when slavery was becoming a major national controversy. . . . Although most northerners did not know what slaves were like, they believed or wanted to believe that black slaves differed greatly from free white Americans. Thus, minstrels emphasized Negro 'peculiarities,' described themselves exotically as 'Ethiopian Delineators,' and/or 'Congo Melodists,' and called some of their acts 'Virginia Jungle Dance,' 'Nubian Jungle Dance,' 'African Fling,' and 'African Sailor's Hornpipe.'" There was also a strand in American culture, which, in opposition to emphasizing the exoticness of blacks through minstrelsy, emphasized the minstrel performance, and hence black culture, as particularly American. According to Eric Lott, "The motivating idea here is a Herderian notion of the folk, articulated in the year of *Leaves of Grass* for much the same reason: to celebrate the popular sources of national culture." In either case, "Ethiopian" music could serve as an ethnic music genre, as did music with the labels Irish, French, or Spanish, and hence serve the purpose of familiarizing difference.[68]

Without this perception of authenticity, blackface minstrelsy lost much of its humor and symbolic usefulness. This is most clearly evidenced in the effort put forth by blackface minstrels to connect their performance style with an actual song or dance they had seen or heard by an "authentic" black slave. A body of literature resulted detailing the origins of blackface performance techniques, which always began with the minstrel watching a black man's performance. E. P. Christy, leader of Christy's Minstrels, claimed to have studied black speech and song at Congo Square. Ben Cotton, recollecting his days as a minstrel, described taking a job on the Mississippi steamer *Banjo* to study "the darky type more closely and carefully." Dan Rice allegedly learned the dance he mimicked for his "Jim Crow" performance from a black stable hand whose clothes he bought for a more authentic portrayal. Even the English actor Charles Matthews, who did not appear in blackface, emphasized the authenticity of his stage impersonations of black Americans by noting how he had carefully studied their dialect and songs, including a performance of the African Theater Company in New York.[69]

Off the stage, other methods were employed to signify this same difference considered on the minstrel stage. The frequent use of dialect in printed sheet music lyrics served, like the burnt cork and spoken dialect on the stage, as signifiers of boundaries between people, which could also be sold as ethnic music genres to consumers hoping to order their varied world. The common use of black dialect in song lyrics, or "literary blackface," according to the historian David Waldstreicher, served as a way to keep the black race culturally marginalized by ridiculing "black pretensions to speak (and write) as whites did." Although sheet music titles and lyrics mimicking black dialect were most common, other "ethnics" could be represented by dialect in the printed word as well, most commonly Scots, Irish, German, and Chinese. Such technique signaled an ethnically bounded musical form to the consumer of sheet music, even if none of these dialect pieces in reality were part of a particular group's heritage. To the historian, this reveals another version of staged authenticity and the existence of ethnic genres. The press, like music publishers, solidified ethnic boundaries through dialect as well.

The *Memphis Enquirer* printed lyrics to an unnamed comedic song in a German dialect, in the form of a letter to the editor by the German immigrant "Schake." After a New Orleans performance, the *True American* critiqued Mr. Brown, who "could have dispensed with a little of the cockney, for the simple reason we thought it out of character."[70] Through such public commentary, music could be "proven" as authentic through the use of dialect lyrics. Through exposure to these ethnic music genres, diversity's menace seemed more benign, as witnesses believed themselves to be experiencing an ethnic music way.

The appeal of music, labeled and sold as ethnic, no matter if it was actually affiliated with the particular cultural traditions whose name remained affixed or not, arose from its ability to assist a nation searching for its identity, while helping individuals make sense of the diversity surrounding them. Creating consumable ethnic musical genres was just one more coping mechanism for dealing with the potential danger of diversity to a national culture in formation. As the presence of "others" seemed to undermine the unity assumed needed to create a secure nation culturally, at least according to East Coast Anglo-Americans, these "others" were made safe, their existence defused, by placing them into clearly definable, understandable, and acceptable cultural units. In this way, the "other" was marked, marketed, and consumed throughout the regional music culture.[71] For those individuals living in regions of particular diversity, the same technique could serve a more practical purpose, that of making sense of the unfamiliar in their midst. The reason for the appeal of staged ethnicity or consumable ethnic music genres was not to understand any particular group's cultural traditions so much as it was to deal with their difference. How any group might then be dealt with would depend on a variety of already formed and still forming assumptions as understood within the racial and cultural hierarchy of the time.

By singing the "Lament of the Irish Immigrant," attending a minstrel show, hiring a German music instructor, or watching a "Spanish dancer," the Irish, African American, German, or Spaniard was made more familiar and hence less menacing to anyone not identifying themselves with that particular group. Differentness did matter during the early republic and antebellum eras, and as a result, codification of groups became helpful ways to make sense of the continually shifting diverse surroundings within the lower Mississippi River Valley. By studying the way contemporary language demarcated the "other" from the "self," perceptions of ethnicity are revealed. Only by considering the process of and motivation for bounding cultural entities will what has historically been labeled cultural conflicts, mixings, and retentions be more clearly understood.

According to Berndt Ostendorf, "Minstrelsy anticipated on stage what many Americans deeply feared: the blackening of America." Because of "the threat of intermixture and acculturation," white American culture created coping mechanisms to deal with this perceived threat. Minstrelsy used the technique of creating a "symbolic language," which allowed for a safe cultural intermingling yet retained social isolation. The bounding of ethnicities in general, including separating African Americans into and considering them as an ethnic group, performed much the same function. This "symbolic language" within the regional music culture, which connected a music way to a people, allowed for a safe cultural encounter and a useful structural framework for a person to use to organize their diverse world. Although the way each person utilized this framework might differ, it was an available cultural structure for all in the region. This ethnic order could then serve as a portal into acceptance within the larger American national culture or a continuation or even entrenchment of outsider status. "By intermingling with a self-created symbolic Ethiopian he meant to forestall actual assimilation"; however, by intermingling with a self-created Spaniard, German, or Choctaw, the choice for inclusion could be reconsidered in each case by the individual.[72]

The creation and consumption of ethnic music genres within the regional music culture provided a cultural mechanism through which safe encounters could be facilitated between previously unfamiliar people. These interactions had the potential to diminish the regional population's feelings of anxiety brought about by living in a quickly changing diverse world precariously attached to the rest of the nation. Although the music culture created in this way differed strikingly from the aspirations of cultural commentators, desirous of fashioning a unified and homogenous American culture to counter the threat of diversity, it nonetheless built a music culture reacting to diversity, albeit through individual encounters with difference. This regional music culture grew organically from the specific needs and the individual choices of the local population. Yet, this regional culture nonetheless managed to accomplish the same objectives of the commentators: alleviate the danger ethnic and racial variety posed to the youthful nation with only tentative unity between its varied peoples and regions.

Conclusion

The political and cultural founders of the new American nation were never able to solidify a unifying national culture that extended beyond a shared revolutionary heritage. As a result of this failure, the memory of the Revolution remained the strongest cultural tie that bound the diverse people of this vast land together, both ideologically and through commemorative acts. Because localism and regionalism had been embedded within American culture since before the Revolution, a unity based solely on this shared creation story never completely erased other loyalties. A shared national culture founded on memory meant that certain segments of the nation might remember differently. Although public celebrations of the Revolution "continued to enhance Americans' sense of national identity," according to the historian Sarah Purcell, it was increasingly an "identity without the power to cover over real divisions in American society." Seen in the context of already extant regionalisms, distinctively northern and southern sectional identities could more easily solidify in opposition to each other because of the failure of a unifying national culture beyond amorphous memories of a singular shared revolutionary experience.[1]

As sectional issues became more pronounced throughout the 1850s, concerns of national unity took on new and different meanings. The ethnic and racial variety that had seemed to undermine national unity no longer appeared to pose the same danger as it had during the first half of the nineteenth century. Rather, the threat a heterogeneous population posed to the nation was subsumed by more pressing concerns over the solidification of two clearly divisive regional interests, one North and one South. Despite this new urgency, ethnic and racial diversity remained an underlying, if supplemental, concern embedded in regional interests. With both northern and southern politicians making claims as sections to the heritage of the founders' vision, the creation and recognition of cultural products designed to bolster each section's claims as the legitimate inheritors of the national culture became increasingly significant.[2]

During the early republic and antebellum eras, Americans from all regions engaged in efforts to define the nation's culture. Some people made very conscious attempts to do so, as in the case of the cultural commentators and artists striving to recognize and promote forms expressive of the national experience, as they understood it. In other instances, people responded to cultural difference much less self-consciously, as in the creation and consumption of ethnic music genres, through which the nation's inhabitants altered cultural products in response to their experience with the nation as a dynamic and tessellated place. The latter informal experiences exemplify the United States's functioning as what Gordon Wood describes as "a very democratic and egalitarian society, dominated as it was by common, ordinary people," who "in their separate and strenuous pursuits of happiness dictated and shaped values and contours of life to an extent never before or since seen."[3]

Gradually, however, a new understanding entered the nation's cultural rhetoric—one that increasingly used "northern" and "southern" to define cultural authority within America. Neither of these two sections, though, recognized their perceived cultural distinctiveness as stemming from divergent memories of the same events; rather they both considered their cultural memory to be the founders' true vision. As earlier Americans previously had done with Europe, northerners increasingly defined northern American identity as national by using the South as a negative reference point. In contrast, Southerners, who believed their declining power in the national government would undermine the slave labor system on which their society was grounded, increasingly defined themselves as an American culture under siege. By 1860, these two oppositional views had solidified to the point that they "believed the United States to be composed of two incompatible civilizations."[4] Just as oppositional identities erupted in violence during the transfer of Louisiana to the United States, a time of particularly fluctuating identities within the region, so too did the sectional conflict ignite during national redefinition of the 1850s.

The lower Mississippi River Valley's strategic importance to both southern identity and lifestyle and the North's efforts to undermine southern unity once the war began heightens the significance of this region in the context of sectionalism. Throughout the 1850s, voices within the lower Mississippi River Valley gradually began to make more explicit comparisons between tastes within the nation they defined as "southern" and "northern." This definitional process was not unlike the care given to label all things uniquely American against those clearly not American, or "ethnic," during earlier years. These writers expressed their claims of northern and southern distinctiveness with rhetoric similar to that employed by early American nationalist writers attempting to distinguish the character of the United States from other places. For example, a review of the *Southern Ladies Book* appearing in the *Mississippi Free Trader* encouraged the region's inhabitants to "build up a Southern literature that we may no longer fear literary comparison with our northern countrymen." The author of this 1853 review emphasized not only its literary merit as deserving patronage but also its "peculiar claims on Southern support." Three years later, the *Opera Box,* a New Orleans literary journal, complained that the northern and southern book publishers would have nothing to do with the books of the other section. Once the war began, southerners emphatically derided their dependency on northern books and periodicals and proclaimed that their new nation should foster its own national literature.[5] Such statements strongly echo those of American cultural nationalists from the early republic, and suggest that their audience was in the process of realigning and redefining its identity.

Gradually, even the music culture began to reflect this realignment of identities and loyalties. Although all parts of the nation shared some aspects of a national music culture, thanks in large part to a fruitful print culture, patriotic commemorations, and touring performers, during the 1840s and 1850s instances of the *belief* in a distinctive northern and southern music culture, which included the lower Mississippi River Valley in the latter, began to appear. In 1856, the *Opera Box* complained that northern music publishers hardly supported southern compositions. While southern merchants "buy thousands of dollars worth of music published in the North ... it is rather mortifying to the pride and legitimate ambition of composers and publishers that their productions ... should be so feebly received beyond Mason and Dixon's line." A claim by the *Daily Picayune* in 1856 again emphasized the increasing solidification of the perception of a distinct northern music culture. The "musical periodicals of the North . . . ignore the very existence of such an establishment here," bitterly complained one writer in reference to the exclusion of New Orleans from discussions of the nation's music culture. This occurred to such an extent, he claimed, that operas, which had been performed as "a stock piece at the Theatre d'Orleans for two seasons," might still be advertised in New York as "the first production of the opera in America."[6] To these commentators at least, the lower Mississippi River Valley was being redefined as part of a regional southern culture and rejected from a northern definition of the nation. Many regional commentators found this recategorization distasteful, as they envisioned themselves and their cultural activities as no less American than the balls of Philadelphia, the operas of New York, or the symphonies of Boston. The region's distinctiveness, which had previously and consistently been emphasized by commentators, was now subsumed to its shared connection with the particular "southern" space being increasingly defined in opposition to the nation by northerners.

Although this book ends with the coming of the Civil War and does not deal with the realignment of national and regional identities that occurred as a result, the cursory examples described above suggest that an extension of this study chronologically would continue to illuminate the threat diversity, in this instance sectional more so than ethnic or racial, posed to the United States. At least to some degree, some shared aesthetics existed throughout the nation by 1860, yet claims of regional loyalty if not peculiarity remained divisive within the music culture. The *Magnolia Weekly* in 1863, for example, was especially dismayed that songs written by "Yankees," had been "palmed off upon the people as Southern productions." Even during increasing sectionalism and eventual disunion, the music culture remained an available channel through which to codify and express difference within an era of redefining identities.[7]

The founders' fears that diverse interests throughout the nation might threaten their republican experiment seemed to be coming true as states began to withdraw from the union in 1860. Was this a result of the failure to create an American national culture strong enough to bind together the multiple diverse interests throughout the country? Could a more useful and all-encompassing national culture have been able to prevent the divisions threatening the United States in 1860? Would a more forceful national culture have had greater success in dealing with the threat diversity of all sorts posed to national unity? Although such speculative questions can never be adequately answered, it is likely that these differences could never have been completely erased no matter how explicit and successful the organized and concerted efforts were in dealing with the various diversities the new nation encountered. The technique of creating and consuming ethnic genres within the regional music culture succeeded in alleviating some of the stress caused by encountering diversity. By 1860, however, other overwhelming factors submerged though never erased the anxiety many felt while navigating within the ethnic and racial mixture surrounding them. At least temporarily, the emphasis on oppositional sectional societies during the Civil War consumed the national consciousness. Apprehension surrounding ethnic and racial diversity's opposition to national cultural unity did not disappear with the war, however, and it resurfaced as problematic in the postbellum years. Because the founders had created an especially flexible and vague document to guide the nation's development, they left room for multiple political visions within the framework. Because of this, cultural commentators of every era saw their work of creating a unified national culture as all the more necessary.

Notes

Introduction

1. Hoffman, Sobel, and Teute, *Through a Glass Darkly* 2–3; Kerber, "Revolutionary Generation," 53; Kersh, *Dreams of a More Perfect Union*; Eastman, *Nation of Speechifiers*, 1–3.

2. Kornfeld, *Creating an American Culture*, vii; Watts, *American Colony*, 39; Anderson, *Imagined Communities*; Hobsbawm and Ranger, *Invention of Tradition*, 279–80; Cox, *Traveling South*, 9.

3. Tamarkin, *Anglophilia*, xxvi.

4. Kermes, *Creating an American Identity*, 1.

5. Barth, *Ethnic Groups and Boundaries*; Dain, *Hideous Monster*, viii.

6. Dain, *Hideous Monster*, vii–viii; Painter, "Was Marie White," 3–30; Thompson, *Theories of Ethnicity*; Smedley, *Race in North America*, xi, 30–32, 37–41.

7. Knobel, *Paddy and the Republic*, xi–xii, 4; Nagel, "Constructing Ethnicity," 152–53.

8. Gjerde, "Here in America," in *Race and the Early Republic*, ed. Morrison, 96, 103–4; Roediger, *Wages of Whiteness*, 144; Jacobson, *Whiteness of a Different Color*, 42–48; Ignatiev, *How the Irish Became White*.

9. Hall, *Slavery and African Ethnicities*; Hall, *Africans in Colonial Louisiana*.

10. Baer, *Trial of Frederick Eberle*, 15, 21; Nolt, *Foreigners in their Own Land*, 1–4; Gjerde, "Here in America," in *Race and the Early Republic*, ed. Morrison, 103–4; Sarna, "New Theory of 'Ethnicization,'" 372.

11. For a good historiography of this see Smedley, *Race in North America*, 114–18, 131–40.

12. Hobsbawm and Ranger, *Invention of Tradition*, 279–80; Bercovitch, *Rites of Assent*, 14.

13. Tamarkin, *Anglophilia*, 1–3.

14. Levine, *Highbrow/Lowbrow*, 33.

15. Knobel, *Paddy and the Republic*, 10–11.

16. Tamarkin, *Anglophilia*, xxvi; Bercovitch, *Rites of Assent*, 14.

17. Tamarkin, *Anglophilia*, xxvi.

18. Tawa, *High-Minded and Low-Down*, ix–xii.

19. Richards, *Drama, Theatre, and Identity*, 8–10, 22.

20. Some historians who emphasize this changing diversity include Tregle, *Louisiana in the Age of Jackson*; Usner, *American Indians in the Lower Mississippi Valley*; Brasseaux, *French, Cajun, Creole, Houma*; Kastor, *Nation's Crucible*. For this contemporary example see "Description of New Orleans," 39–42.

21. Usner, "Between Creoles and Yankees," 2.

22. Knight, "Cart War," 319–22.

23. Rath quote found in Buisseret and Reinhardt, eds., *Creolization in the Americas*, ix–x, 3, 99–100; Dawdy, *Building the Devil's Empire*, 5–7.

24. Bauer and Mazzotti, *Creole Subjects in the Colonial Americas*, 3–7, 52–53; Tregle, *Louisiana in the Age of Jackson*, 25–26, 337–44.

25. Dominguez, *White by Definition*, 9–10.

26. Kornfeld, *Creating an American Culture*, 67; Shaffer, *Public Culture*, x.

1 / Insecurity and Nationalism: The Call to Create a Unified American Music Culture

1. Tamarkin, *Anglophilia*, xxvi.

2. Knobel, *Paddy and the Republic*, 8–9; Waldstreicher, *In the Midst of Perpetual Fetes*, 2.

3. Kornfeld, *Creating an American Culture*, 66–68; Said, *Orientalism*; Pearce, *Savagism and Civilization*, v; Cobb, *Away Down South*, 3; Knobel, *Paddy and the Republic*, 3–4.

4. Frost, *Never One Nation*, xiii–xv; Tellefsen, "Case with My Dear Native Land," 459.

5. Richards, *Drama, Theatre, and Identity*, 9–10, 14, 22.

6. Morrison, *Playing in the Dark*, 52; Frost, *Never One Nation*, x–xi.

7. Thomas Jefferson to unknown, in *The Life and Selected Writings of Thomas Jefferson*, ed. Koch and Peden, 363–64.

8. Wood, *Rising Glory of America*, 1–2, 8, 20–21.

9. Chmaj, "Fry versus Dwight," 63–64; Richards, *Drama, Theatre, and Identity*, 14; Webster, "On the Education of Youth," 77; Wood, *Rising Glory of America*, 21; Simpson, *Politics of American English*, 3–4.

10. Travers, "Paradox of 'Nationalist' Festivals," 275.

11. Kornfeld, *Creating an American Culture*, vii; Kammen, *Mystic Chords of Memory*, 50; Simpson, *Politics of American English*; Cremin, *American Education*; Cohen, *Revolutionary Histories*; Shaffer, *To Be an American*.

12. Somkin, *Unquiet Eagle*, 4; Nagel, *This Sacred Trust*, xii; for first and third quote, Appleby, *Inheriting the Revolution*, 5, 25, 239–40; for second quote, Power, "Crusade to Extend Yankee Culture," 638.

13. Ingersoll, *Inchiquin*, 113, 136.

14. Mathews, *Memoirs of Charles Mathews*, 382–83.

15. White, ed., "Notes and Documents," 319.

16. "Review of Adam Seybert's *Statistical Annals of the United States of America*," *Edinburgh Review* (January 1820): 78–80, quoted in Gruver, *American Nationalism*, 274–76; Tocqueville, *Democracy in America*, 544; Fearon, *Sketches of America*, 368; Buckingham, *America*, 373.

17. "Present and Future of American Art," 85; *Vicksburg Daily Sentinel*, July 9, 1838.

18. Reprinted in *Baton Rouge Gazette*, March 13, 1841.

19. Fuller, "American Facts," 126–27; Fuller, "Dispatch 18," 441–42; Watts, *Writing and Postcolonialism*, 5.

20. Emerson, "American Scholar" and "Nature," 23–24, 58, 70–71, 73; Rohler, *Ralph Waldo Emerson*, 46–47.

21. Ingersoll, *Inchiquin*, 134; Gannett and Willis quotes found in Lowens, *Music and Musicians*, 213.

22. Ziff, *Literary Democracy*, xiii; Watts, *Writing and Postcolonialism*, 5; Simpson, *Politics of American English*, 33; Hawthorne, *Marble Faun*, vii; *Vicksburg Daily Sentinel*, November 21, 1838; for "fabricating authenticity" see Peterson, *Creating Country Music*.

23. Neil, *Toward a National Taste*, x, 49; quote found in Ingersoll, *Inchiquin*, 143; Levine, *Highbrow/Lowbrow*, 85–168.

24. Merchant, *American Environmental History*, 77; Reynolds, *Walt Whitman's America*, 5.

25. Dougherty, review of *Literary Democracy*, 472–75; *Mississippi Free Trader*, September 7, 1847; Levine, *Highbrow/Lowbrow*, 4.

26. Whitman, "Music That IS Music," 138; Knobel, *Paddy and the Republic*, xi.

27. Knobel, *Paddy and the Republic*, xi.

28. *Louisiana Gazette* (New Orleans), January 28, 1806; Von Glahn, *Sounds of Place*, 5; "Music in Boston"; "Present and Future of American Art," 94;

29. Whitman, "Art-Singing and Heart-Singing," 202; "National Music," *American Quarterly Review*, 276–77.

30. "Musical Authors and Publications," 86; Hastings, *Dissertation on Musical Taste*, xiv, 148; "National Music," *American Quarterly Review*, 277.

31. "National Music," *American Quarterly Review*, 277–78.

32. "Present and Future of American Art," 94.

33. "National Music," *North American Review*, 5.

34. For quotes see "National Music," *American Quarterly Review*, 277–79; Finson, "Romantic Savage," 203–32; Levine, "American Indian Musics," 28.

35. *Southern Quarterly Review* (July 1842).

36. Upton, *William Henry Fry*, 141; Hatch, "Music for America," 583; quote from "Complaint on Behalf of Native Composers," 94.

37. Ingersoll, *Discourse*, quoted in Gruver, *American Nationalism*, 278; *Southern Quarterly Review* (July 1842); "Prospects for a National Music in America"; for acquisitiveness quote see "Music in Boston"; for Dwight quotes see "Popular Amusements," 117.

38. Williams, *National Music*, 4–5; Macartney, *Embassy to China*, 21–22, 364.

39. First quote from "Prospects for a National Music in America"; following quotes from "National Music," *North American Review*, 3, 9–13.

40. "Art in America," *North American Review*, printed in *Baton Rouge Gazette*, May 5, 1841.

41. "On Singing in Sabbath Schools."

42. First quote from Upton, *William Henry Fry*, 38; second quote from "Musical Talent of the Americans," 82.

43. "Letter from A.W.T. on Oratorio Practice," 170; "National Music," *North American Review*, 2.

44. Hastings, *Dissertation on Musical Taste*, xiv, 109; Whitman, "Templeton the Singer," 29 and "Music That IS Music," 137.

45. *Musical Magazine* (July 1835): 78; "On Singing in Sabbath Schools."

46. "Musical Talent of the Americans," 83; "Music in America," 327; "Present and Future of American Art," 94.

47. *Virginia Warbler* quoted in Stuyvesant, *Early Songs of Uncle Sam*, 17–18; "Editor's Address."

48. For first quote see "Musical Talent of the Americans," 82; Tischler, *American Music*, 5–6, 20; for second quote see Hastings, *Dissertation on Musical Taste*, 109.

49. Heinrich, *Dawning of Music in Kentucky*, 122; Woodward, *Old World's New World*, xvii–xxi.

50. Heinrich, *Dawning of Music in Kentucky*, 71–76, 252–69; Fuller, "Ole Bull," 244.

51. *Dwight's Journal of Music* 1 (June 12, 1852); "National Music," *Dwight's Journal of Music*; Nicholls, *Cambridge History of American Music*, 250; *Mississippi Free Trader*, April 28, 1847; for Bull's announcement see Howard, *Our American Music*, 200–201; for *Port Folio* quote see Neil, *Toward a National Taste*, 197.

52. "Prospects for a National Music in America"; Whitman, "Art-Singing and Heart-Singing," 202; "Thought of Ours about Music," 322; "American Music, New and True," 233; and "Hutchinson Family," 176.

53. Hatch, "Music for America," 579, 581; Upton, *William Henry Fry*; Chmaj, "Fry versus Dwight," 64, 68–70.

54. Hatch, "Music for America," 580; *Dwight's Journal of Music* 3 (August 27, 1853): 167; "National Music," *Dwight's Journal of Music*, 140; Chmaj, "Fry versus Dwight," 66, 69.

55. Adorno quoted in Gilroy, "Sounds Authentic," 111–36; Honestus quote found in Upton, *William Henry Fry*, 38; Richards, *Drama, Theatre, and Identity*, 33.

56. "On Singing in Sabbath Schools"; *Vicksburg Daily Sentinel*, March 7, 10, 1845, and June 17, 1844; "Hungarian Orchestra," 19.

57. "National Music," *American Quarterly Review*, 273; Schultz, *Travels on an Inland Voyage*, 198; "Chinese and Scotch Music"; "Art in China," 116.

58. "Original Communication"; Fuller, "Celestial Empire," 259–61; *Louisiana Courier* (New Orleans), June 16, 1829.

59. *Mississippi Free Trader* (Natchez), April 28, 1847; "Original Communication."

60. "Letter from A.W.T. on Oratorio Practice," 170; "Prospects for a National Music in America."

61. "National Music," *North American Review*, 3.

62. For first quote see "National Music," *North American Review*, 3–4; for second quote see "National Music," *American Quarterly Review*, 27; for another example see "Prospects for a National Music in America."

2 / The Threat of Diversity: The Lower Mississippi River Valley as a Case Study

1. Kastor, *Nation's Crucible*, 4–5; Morris, *Becoming Southern*, xiv–xv, xviii–xix.

2. Clifford, *Predicament of Culture*, 344; White, *Middle Ground*, ix.

3. Ayers et al., *All Over the Map*, 4.

4. Gayarré, *History of Louisiana*, 1, 276; McMichael, *Atlantic Loyalties*, 169–75;

James, *Antebellum Natchez*, 75, 109; Polk, *Natchez before 1830*, 5–6; Carter, *Lower Mississippi*, 155–56; Rodriguez, *Louisiana Purchase*, 267; Reps, "Great Expectations and Hard Times," 14–21; Biles, *Illinois*, 47; Arnold, *Colonial Arkansas*, 179; Harrison, *Kentucky's Road to Statehood*, 131; Bergeron, Ash, and Keith, *Tennesseans and Their History*, 77; Kleber, *Kentucky Encyclopedia*, 460–61; Monette, *History of the Discovery and Settlement*, 339–518, 542–60; Kastor, *Nation's Crucible*, 3.

5. First quote from Joseph Patrick Key and second quote from Walter Nugent, both found in Williams, Bolton, and Whayne, *Whole Country in Commotion*, xv–xvi, 91.

6. Usner, "Between Creoles and Yankees," 2–4.

7. Baird, *View of the Valley of the Mississippi*, 87; Monette, *Discovery and Settlement*, 21, which paraphrases Flint, *History and Geography*, 135–37; "Historie de la Louisiane par Charles Gayarré," 362–63.

8. Usner, *American Indians*, 82–83; Cuming, *Sketches of a Tour*, found in Thwaites, *Early Western Travels*, 339; Schultz, *Travels on an Inland Voyage*, 217; Flint, *Recollections of the Last Ten Years*, 366.

9. Ashe, *Travels in America*, 3:115–16; Cuming, *Sketches*, in Thwaites, *Early Western Travels*, 339.

10. Martin, "People of New Orleans," 361–75; Mitchell, *All on a Mardi Gras Day*, 8; Berquin-Duvallon, *Travels in Louisiana*, 78.

11. Fontenay, *L'Autre Monde* quoted in Reinders, *End of an Era*, 33; Wilhelm, *Travels in North America*, 32–33; Usner, *American Indians*, 112.

12. Hodgson, *Remarks during a Journey*, 161; Ingraham, *South-West*, 99.

13. Ingraham, *South-West*, 99; Berquin-Duvallon, *Travels in Louisiana*, 48; Grimes, *How Shall We Sing?* 24; Tregle, *Louisiana in the Age of Jackson*, 12–16; Tregle, "Creoles and Americans," 153–57; Olmsted, *Journey in the Seaboard Slave States*, 593.

14. Creecy, *Scenes in the South*, 18; Hodgson, *Remarks during a Journey*, 161; Paxton, *New Orleans Directory*, 45; Norman, *Norman's New Orleans*, 73–76.

15. Kelman, "Boundary Issues," 695–703.

16. Ingraham, *South-West*, 90; Vandenhoff, *Leaves from an Actor's Note-book*, 206; Latrobe, *Journal of Latrobe*, 161; Murray, *Travels in North America*, 189; Whipple, *Bishop Whipple's Southern Diary*, 95–96, 119; Samuel Clemens to Ann E. Taylor, June 1, 1857, from New Orleans, Louisiana, in Branch, *Mark Twain's Letters*, 72.

17. Latrobe, *Journal of Latrobe*, 161; Berquin-Duvallon, *Travels in Louisiana*, 48; Flint, *History and Geography*, 138–45; Olmsted, *Seaboard Slave States*, 593–97.

18. Lachance, "Growth of Free and Slave Populations," 204–43; Martin, *History of Louisiana*, 205–6.

19. Usner, *American Indians*, 14, 33–34, 55; Usner, "Frontier Exchange Economy," 173–74.

20. Brasseaux, *French, Cajun, Creole, Houma*, 10, 11, 15, 17–23; Holmes, *Gayoso, 1789–1799*, 23–24; Johnson, "Colonial New Orleans," 46–49; Ancelet, *Cajun Music*, 16; McMichael, *Atlantic Loyalties*; Kinnaird, "American Penetration into Spanish Louisiana," 214–16.

21. Hall, *Africans in Colonial Louisiana*, 10, 277, 278, 281, 286, 288; Brasseaux, *French, Cajun, Creole, Houma*, 12.

22. Blume, *German Coast*, 130–34, 143; Deiler, *Settlement of the German Coast*, 16–17; Kondert, *Germans of Colonial Louisiana*; Arnold, *Rumble of a Distant Drum*,

143; Arnold, *Colonial Arkansas*, 68, 70; Dormon, *Creoles of Color*, ix; Blassingame, *Black New Orleans*, 21.

23. Usner, *American Indians*, 112–16; Martin, *History of Louisiana*, 206–7; Guice, "Face to Face in Mississippi Territory," 157.

24. Brasseaux, *French, Cajun, Creole, Houma*, 22–24; Dessens, *From Saint-Domingue to New Orleans*, 1; Dormon, *Creoles of Color*, 6; Blassingame, *Black New Orleans*, 9–10, 221; quote from Lachance, "1809 Immigration," 109–33.

25. Dessens, *From Saint-Domingue to New Orleans*, xi–xii, 34, 46, 54, 62; Brasseaux and Conrad, *Road to Louisiana*, 7.

26. Brasseaux, *"Foreign-French,"* vol. 1, xii–xiii, xxv; vol. 2, ix, xvii; vol. 3, xvi.

27. Bromwell, *History of Immigration*, 145–65; quote from Berlin and Gutman, "Natives and Immigrants," 1176–77; Curry, "Urbanization and Urbanism," 43–60; Goldfield, "Urban South," 1015.

28. Spletstoser, "Back Door to the Land of Plenty," 45; quote from Tregle, "Creoles and Americans," 166.

29. Niehaus, *Irish in New Orleans*, 25.

30. Weaver, "Foreigners in Ante-Bellum Towns," 63–67.

31. Morris, *Becoming Southern*, 115.

32. Weaver, "Foreigners in Ante-Bellum Towns," 63–67.

33. Tregle, "Creoles and Americans," 164; Weaver, "Foreigners in Ante-Bellum Towns," 151; James, *Antebellum Natchez*, 164–65; Morris, *Becoming Southern*, 115.

34. James, *Antebellum Natchez*, 164–65; Niehaus, *Irish in New Orleans*, v, 11.

35. Nau, *German People of New Orleans*, 4, 7, 14; Eskew, "German Contributions," 25; Clark, "German Liberals in New Orleans," 137–38, 141; Kamphoefner, *Westfalians*, 94.

36. Niehaus, *Irish in New Orleans*, v, 11; James, *Antebellum Natchez*, 164–65; Berkeley, *"Like a Plague of Locusts,"* 16; Capers, *Biography of a River Town*, 44, 108.

37. Gleeson, *Irish in the South*, 23–25.

38. Nau, *German People of New Orleans*, 4, 7, 14.

39. *Report of the Superintendent*, 18; Merrill, *Germans of Louisiana*, 11.

40. De Bow, *Statistical View of the United States*, 249.

41. *Report of the Superintendent*, 18–19.

42. Ibid., 16–19, 160; Treat, "Migration into Louisiana."

43. Tadman, *Speculators and Slaves*, 2, 5, 31, 44; Deyle, *Carry Me Back*, 283–89; Libby, *Slavery and Frontier Mississippi*, 61, 68.

44. Lachance, "1809 Immigration," 114–15, 119.

45. Tadman, *Speculators and Slaves*, 226; Kulikoff, "Uprooted Peoples," 152; Libby, *Slavery and Frontier Mississippi*, 23, 52; Robinson, "Louisiana Purchase," 112–13; Schafer, *Slavery, the Civil Law*, 149–79; quote from Taylor, "Foreign Slave Trade," 36–43.

46. Obadele-Starks, *Freebooters and Smugglers*, 31, 60–61.

47. Kulikoff, "Uprooted Peoples," 149–52.

48. Tadman, *Speculators and Slaves*, 12.

49. Logsdon and Bell, "Americanization of Black New Orleans," 211.

50. Hall, *Africans in Colonial Louisiana*, 278; Bolton, *Arkansas*, 11; Carter, *Territorial Papers*, 9:702.

51. *Aggregate Amount*, 1.

52. The 1830 river counties include, for Missouri, Ste. Genevieve, Perry, Cape

Girardeau, Scott, and New Madrid; for Tennessee, Dyer, Tipton, and Shelby; and for Kentucky, Hickman. *Abstract of Returns*, 25, 28–29, 32–33, 36, 41, 43 50, 51.

53. All statistics compiled from *Abstract of the Returns*, 25, 28–29, 32–33, 36, 41, 43, 50–51, and De Bow, *Statistical View*, 193–95, 200–201, 236–37, 242–43, 260–61, 266–69, 272–73, 302–3, 308–9; Bolton, *Arkansas*, 127.

54. *Report of the Superintendent*, 160; Treat, "Migration into Louisiana."

55. The 1850 river counties for Missouri, Kentucky and Tennessee are the same as above with the additions of Mississippi County in Missouri, Lauderdale and Obion in Tennessee, and Ballard and Fulton in Kentucky. All statistics compiled from De Bow, *Statistical View*, 193–95, 200–201, 236–37, 242–43, 260–61, 266–69, 272–73, 302–3, 308–9.

56. *Report of the Superintendent*, 160.

57. Logsdon and Bell, "Americanization of Black New Orleans," 206; Hanger, *Bounded Lives*, 18.

58. Logsdon and Bell, "Americanization of Black New Orleans," 206; Dominguez, *White by Definition*, 116–17.

59. Hanger, *Bounded Lives*, 6; quote from Logsdon and Bell, "Americanization of Black New Orleans," 207.

60. Curry, *Free Black in Urban American*, 250; Reinders, "Decline of the Free Negro," 89–90. Reinders's numbers for the city's free black population are slightly higher than those of Curry's that are cited in the text. Logsdon and Bell, "Americanization of Black New Orleans," 192, 207–8.

61. Logsdon and Bell, "Americanization of Black New Orleans," 209; *Report of the Superintendent*, 160.

62. Whayne, "Shifting Middle Ground," 60–61; McNeilly, *Old South Frontier*, 6; Libby, *Slavery and Frontier Mississippi*, 60.

63. Morrison, *Slavery and the American West*.

64. Dormon, *Creoles of Color in the Gulf South*, 29; quote found in Williams, Bolton, and Whayne, *Whole Country in Commotion*, xiii–xiv.

65. Spitzer, "Monde Créole," 57–72.

3 / The War of the Quadrilles: Ethnic Loyalty and American Patriotism

1. Kastor, *Nation's Crucible*, 15.

2. LeMenager, "Floating Capital," 407–8.

3. For references describing New Orleans as "Babel" see Berquin-Duvallon, *Travels in Louisiana*, 48; Ingraham, *South-West*, 90; Murray, *Travels in North America*, 189; Latrobe, *Journal of Latrobe*, 161; Flint, *History and Geography*, 264; Whipple, *Bishop Whipple's Southern Diary*, 95–96, 119; Walter Foster Diary, January 2, 1842; Vandenhoff, *Leaves from an Actor's Note-book*, 207.

4. Quotes from Mitchell, *All on a Mardi Gras Day*, 27 and Schroeder, *Opening the Ozarks*, 18–19; Kastor, *Nation's Crucible*, 4; Aron, *American Confluence*, xv; Hatfield, *William Claiborne*, 124; Usner, "Between Creoles and Yankees," 1–2.

5. Kmen, *Music in New Orleans*, viii.

6. Ibid., 30; Mitchell, *All on a Mardi Gras Day*, 11–12.

7. Waldstreicher, *In the Midst of Perpetual Fetes*, 6.

8. Tregle, *Louisiana in the Age of Jackson*, 25–26, 337–44; Watts, *In This Remote Country*, 2–4.

9. Quote from Watts, *In This Remote Country*, 2–4; Bernhard, *Travels through*

North America, 72; Gilpin, Letter from New Barracks, New Orleans, February 18, 1837, in "Dragoon Letters from the Western Frontier," bound volume, 1835–1838; Tregle, *Louisiana in the Age of Jackson*, 23–32.

10. Needham, "War of the Quadrilles," 66–72; Costonis, "War of the Quadrilles," 63–81; Kmen, *Music in New Orleans*, 3, 27–29.

11. Tregle, *Louisiana in the Age of Jackson*, 23–32.

12. Laussat, *Memoirs of My Life*, 85–86.

13. Claiborne, *Official Letter Books*, 331.

14. Ibid., 351–52.

15. Costonis, "War of the Quadrilles," 71–72.

16. Quotes from Laussat, *Memoirs of My Life*, 94–95. These songs sung by the Americans were highly nationalistic for the era. The word "Columbia" was used at this time to mean "America" (the nation was almost named Columbia), while "God Save the King" (or Queen) continued as a popular air in the United States even after the Revolution. Sonneck, "Critical Notes on the Origin," 139–66; Schlereth, "Columbia, Columbus, Columbianism," 939; Larner, "North American Hero?" 50; Rosenberg, *Jenny Lind in America*, 12.

17. Laussat, *Memoirs of My Life*, 96; Claiborne, *Official Letter Books*, 354–55.

18. Quotes from *New York Herald*, March 10, 1804; *Washington Federalist*, March 16, 1804; *Democrat* (Boston), March 24, 1804; Wilkinson, *Memoirs of My Own Times*, 2:264–65.

19. Carter, *Territorial Papers*, 178–79, 185.

20. Quotes from ibid., 178, 181; Lachance, "Foreign French," 101–30; Brasseaux, *French, Cajun, Creole, Houma*, 2.

21. Kastor, *Nation's Crucible*, 10; Quotes from *Louisiana Gazette* (New Orleans), January 11, 1805. Another article referred to Claiborne as a "certain American Governor, who could not dance French Country Dances!" *Louisiana Gazette* (New Orleans), January 22, 1805.

22. *Louisiana Gazette* (New Orleans), January 25, 1805.

23. Mitchell, *All on a Mardi Gras Day*, 11; Kastor, *Nation's Crucible*, 12; Carter, *Territorial Papers*, 185; Tregle, *Louisiana in the Age of Jackson*, 80–81; Waldstreicher, *In the Midst of Perpetual Fetes*, 3, 279–80.

24. Carter, *Territorial Papers*, 185, 191.

25. First quote from "Copy of the Telegraphe," 299–302; second quote from *Louisiana Gazette* (New Orleans), March 15, 1805.

26. Carter, *Territorial Papers*, 185.

27. Kmen, *Music in New Orleans*, 3, 5–7, 10; Nicholls, *Cambridge History of American Music*, 192.

28. Stoddard, *Sketches, Historical and Descriptive*, 321, 325.

29. McNeilly, *Old South Frontier*, 13; Perin du Lac, *Travels through the Two Louisianas*, 44, 83; unknown observer quoted in Arnold, *Colonial Arkansas*, 70–71; Worley, "Letter of Governor Miller," 389–90; Flint, *Recollections of the Last Ten Years*, 263–64; Nuttall, *Journal of Travels*, 88, 262; Schultz, *Travels on an Inland Voyage*, 60.

30. First quote from Berquin-Duvallon, *Travels in Louisiana*, 42; Wood, "Life in New Orleans," 688–89; Ashe, *Travels in America*, 267; Murray, *Travels in North America*, 163, 188; Latrobe, *Journal of Latrobe*, 172; Paxton, *New Orleans Directory*, 40; "Letters of Nathaniel Cox to Gabriel Lewis," 187; Spence, *Settler's Guide*, 330.

31. Marigny, "Reflections on the Campaign," 77–79.
32. Berquin-Duvallon, *Travels in Louisiana,* 28–30.
33. Price, "Le Spectacle de la Rue St. Pierre," 219; Gayarrè, *History of Louisiana,* 3:327; Le Gardeur, *First New Orleans Theatre,* 4.
34. Allain and St. Martin, "French Theatre in Louisiana," 140.
35. Claiborne, *Official Letter Books,* 369; Claiborne to Madison, October 20, 1804, in Hackett, *Papers of James Madison,* 8:191.
36. Claiborne, *Official Letter Books,* 35; *Louisiana Gazette* (New Orleans), December 21, 1804.
37. *New Orleans Bee,* January 26, 1828; *New Orleans Bee,* February 22, 1828; quote about the theater from Price, "Le Spectacle de la Rue St. Pierre," 219; Kmen, *Music in New Orleans,* 60–61.
38. Grimsted, *Melodrama Unveiled,* 67n103; Levine, *Highbrow/Lowbrow,* 26; Trollope, *Domestic Manners,* 134; Kmen, *Music in New Orleans,* 60–61; for the Astor Place Riot see Berthold, "Class Act," 430, and Cliff, *Shakespeare Riots,* xxi.
39. Castellanos, *New Orleans as It Was,* 224–26.
40. Claiborne, *Official Letter Books,* 249–50, 368–69; *Louisiana Advertiser* (New Orleans), July 7, 1823.
41. Latrobe, *Journal of Latrobe,* 174; Whipple, *Bishop Whipple's Southern Diary,* 99–101, 119; Flint, *Recollections of the Last Ten Years,* 307; Reiff Journal, January 23, 1856; Bernhard, *Travels through North America,* 57.
42. Quotes from Ingraham, *South-West,* 121–22; Kmen, *Music in New Orleans,* 25–26. For a few selected advertisements for children's balls see *New Orleans Bee,* December 27, 1827, April 21, 1845; *Louisiana Gazette* (New Orleans), January 16, 1811; *Mississippi Free Trader* (Natchez), January 1, 1851.
43. For Morgan see Mitchell, *All on a Mardi Gras Day,* 14; for Orleans Theater see Paxton, *New Orleans Directory,* 17; for mixed languages see Jones, *America and French Culture,* 348–49; "Letters of Nathaniel Cox," 187.
44. Letter from Anna B. Cox (New Orleans) to Louisa Cox (St. Louis), May 1, 1819; second quote from Wilhelm, *Travels in North America,* 33, 35; final quote from Kmen, *Music in New Orleans,* 138, 175.
45. For the opera competition see Dizikes, *Opera in America,* 30–31; quotes found in Kmen, *Music in New Orleans,* 102; Lavasseur, *Lafayette in America,* 92.
46. Hatfield, *William Claiborne,* 119; Tregle, *Louisiana in the Age of Jackson,* 82; Kastor, *Nation's Crucible,* 2, 55–75.
47. Hobsbawm and Ranger, *Invention of Tradition,* 279–80.
48. Claiborne, *Official Letter Books,* 2, 236.
49. Quotes from *Louisiana Gazette* (New Orleans), February 25, 1806; Waldstreicher, *In the Midst of Perpetual Fetes,* 2; for leading citizens see one example from *Vicksburg Register,* February 25, 1836.
50. Gerstäcker, *Wild Sports in the Far West,* 220–23.
51. Miller, "Journal of Henry Miller," 213–86; Nuebling Letterbook, 1825; Williams, *Old Times in West Tennessee,* 171.
52. Advertisements for some celebrations of Washington can be found in *Louisiana Gazette* (New Orleans), February 12, 1805; *Vicksburg Register,* February 25, 1836; *New Orleans Bee,* February 20, 1828; *Mississippi Free Trader* (Natchez), March 1, 1848; *Baton Rouge Gazette,* February 27, 1847.

53. Flugel, "Pages from a Journal," 427; *New Orleans Bee,* February 20, 21, 1828, and January 28, 29, 1829; Kmen, *Music in New Orleans,* 8; *Weekly Chronicle* (Natchez), July 13, 1808; for Henry Clay see *Baton Rouge Gazette,* February 18, 1843; for Andrew Jackson see *Louisiana Gazette* (New Orleans), February 21, 1815, and *New Orleans Bee,* January 7, 10, 22, 1828.

54. Kmen, *Music in New Orleans,* 6; Nolan, *Lafayette in America,* 282; Bank, *Theatre Culture in America,* 9–23; Lavasseur, *Lafayette in America,* 89–144.

55. For a few general examples see *Louisiana Gazette* (New Orleans), December 17, 20, 1805, December 23, 1806, March 8, April 26, 1805; for Baton Rouge quote see *Baton Rouge Gazette,* January 11, 1845, January 10, 1846; for Rapides quote see *Louisiana Gazette* (New Orleans), April 23, 1805.

56. Waldstreicher, *In the Midst of Perpetual Fetes,* 3; *Louisiana Advertiser* (New Orleans), July 7, 24, 1823.

57. *Weekly Chronicle* (Natchez), July 6, 1808. Other descriptions can be found in *Baton Rouge Gazette,* July 11, 1840, June 29, 1844, June 14, 1845; *Memphis Enquirer,* June 22, 1836; *Vicksburg Daily Sentinel,* July 10, 1840, July 6, 1841; *Louisiana Advertiser* (New Orleans), July 24, 1823 (describing ones in the Parrish of Terrebonne); Invitations Collection, "Fourth of July ball and barbeque at Bonhomme Settlement," 1836.

58. First quote from *Louisiana Advertiser* (New Orleans), July 7, 1823; for just one example of such song titles see *Vicksburg Register,* July 14, 1836; Los Angeles example from Bell, *Reminiscences of a Ranger,* 132–33.

59. Waldstreicher, *In the Midst of Perpetual Fetes,* 11–14; Tower Diary, entry for November 7, 1845; *New Orleans Bee,* September 20, 1848; quote from *Vicksburg Daily Sentinel,* July 9, 1838.

60. Kmen, *Music in New Orleans,* 203–5; for quote see Kinzer, "Band of Music," 348–69.

61. *Vicksburg Daily Sentinel,* July 6, 1841; *New Orleans Bee,* January 28, 29, February 18, 20, 1829; Bernhard, *Travels through North America,* 72.

62. *Baton Rouge Gazette,* February 27, 1841.

63. *Baton Rouge Gazette,* May 25, 1844, May 29, 1841, June 14, 1845, February 16, 1850.

64. *Louisiana Gazette* (New Orleans), December 21, 1810, December 21, February 23, 1811.

65. Tregle, *Louisiana in the Age of Jackson,* 132–33.

66. *New Orleans Bee,* January 22, 1828.

67. *New Orleans Bee,* January 7, 10, 11, 22, 1828; Bank, *Theatre Culture in America,* 9–23.

68. Davis, "Printing and the People," 65–66; Newman, *Parades and the Politics of the Street,* 3, 93, 187–88; Waldstreicher, *In the Midst of Perpetual Fetes,* 10–11, 109–12.

69. *Louisiana Advertiser* (New Orleans), August 1, 7, 1823; *Vicksburg Daily Sentinel,* March 5, 1839, June 5, 1841, August 6, 1845; *Mississippi Free Trader* (Natchez), September 8, 1852.

70. For quote see Waldstreicher, *In the Midst of Perpetual Fetes,* 2; for an example see *Vicksburg Daily Sentinel,* July 6, 1841.

71. *Baton Rouge Gazette,* June 20, 1840; Guion, "Felippe Cioffi," 24–25; Tawa, *High-Minded and Low-Down,* 200–203; Waldstreicher, *In the Midst of Perpetual Fetes,* 8–9.

72. Waldstreicher, *In the Midst of Perpetual Fetes*, 11–14; Tregle, *Louisiana in the Age of Jackson*, 80; Anderson, *Imagined Communities*, 44–45.

73. These songs were at times played in the homes of local residents, as was "Tip and Ty a New Comic Whig Glee," among others. See Conner Family Papers for this example. *Baton Rouge Gazette*, July 6, August 10, September 28, October 19, December 7, 21, 1844; *Mississippi Free Trader* (Natchez), August 16, September 20, 1848, August 27, September 15, 1852; *Vicksburg Daily Sentinel*, October 21, 1839, November 26, 1841, April 5, 8, 1844, July 1, 1844.

74. *Baton Rouge Gazette*, May 18, 1844, June 8, 1844, reprinted from the *New York Journal of Commerce*.

75. For the Natchez examples see *Vicksburg Daily Sentinel*, December 7, 1840; for the parrot example see Tawa, *High-Minded and Low-Down*, 202; for the newspaper accounts see *New Orleans Bee*, September 19, 1848; for more on the 1840 election music see Davis, *Recollections of Mississippi*, 110.

76. *Louisiana Advertiser* (New Orleans), August 6, 1823; *Mississippi Free Trader* (Natchez), September 20, 1848; *Baton Rouge Gazette*, July 6, 1844; "Fillmore and Donaldson: Songs for the Campaign," 1856; *Songs for the Campaign*.

77. *Baton Rouge Gazette*, September 28, 1844; *Mississippi Free Trader* (Natchez), May 16, 1849; *New Orleans Bee*, December 28, 1830; Mason, *Singing the French Revolution*, 93–103; Waldstreicher, *In the Midst of Perpetual Fetes*, 12; Newman, *Parades and Politics*, 120, 152, 177–83; Leary-Warsaw, "Nineteenth-Century French Art Song," 48–49.

78. Smither, "History of the English Theatre," 29; for French Opera Company quote see Allain and St. Martin, "French Theatre in Louisiana," 147; for Louisiana assembly quote see *Mississippi Free Trader* (Natchez), April 26, 1848; *New Orleans Bee*, December 24, 1830; for "Southern Marseilles" see Leary-Warsaw, "French Art Song," 49–50.

79. *Baton Rouge Gazette*, June 8, 1844.

80. *Vicksburg Daily Sentinel*, January 30, 19, 1844, reprinted from the *New Orleans Picayune*; *Baton Rouge Gazette*, April 24, 1827.

81. Quotes from Kmen, *Music in New Orleans*, 195, 195n83, 224; for Cioffi's ancestry see Guion, "Felippe Cioffi," 1–2; for Guiraud's ancestry see "Review of Piccolino," *Musical Times* (February 1, 1879): 84.

82. Guion, "Felippe Cioffi," 23–25.

83. Conner Family Papers; Boudreaux, "Music Publishing in New Orleans," 1.

84. La Hache, "Musical Album for 1855"; Bremer, *Homes of the New World*, 223; *Daily Delta* (New Orleans), May 31, 1850; Guion, "Felippe Cioffi," 24–25.

85. Kmen, *Music in New Orleans*, 223–24; Leary-Warsaw, "French Art Song," 57.

86. For Francisqui see Costonis, "American Career," 430–42; for Desforges see Kmen, *Music in New Orleans*, 224–25.

87. Kastor, *Nation's Crucible*, 15; Waldstreicher, *In the Midst of Perpetual Fetes*, 259.

4 / "Other" Musicians: Ethnic Expression, Public Music, and Familiarizing the Foreign

1. Dickey, "Music of a Louisiana Plantation Family."

2. Ibid., 28, 33, 34, 36, 37, 41, 65, 66, 103. Dickey describes Gaertner as German. For Elie and Vegas see Bureau of the Census, *Population Schedule of the Seventh Census of the United States*, Louisiana, 1850. For Madame Angelina see Ripley, *Social Life*,

5, http://docsouth.unc.edu/fpn/ripley/ripley.html (accessed January 27, 2009). For Benoit see Brasseaux, *Foreign French*, vol. 2. For Werlein see Conrad, *Dictionary of Louisiana Biography*, 2:835.

3. Dickey, "Music of a Louisiana Plantation Family," 39, 59, 73, 76–77.

4. Ownby and Joyner, *Black and White Cultural Interaction*, x–xviii.

5. Fiehrer, "From Quadrille to Stomp," 25.

6. Ryan, *Civic Wars*, 78; *Cohen's New Orleans*; *Letters of Fredrika Bremer*, 274–81.

7. Dvorak, *African-American Exodus*, 1; James, "Biracial Fellowship," 37–57; Raboteau, *Slave Religion*, 205; Niehaus, *Irish in New Orleans*, 15–17; quote from Miller, "Church in Cultural Captivity," 12, 30–37; Gleeson, *Irish in the South*, 87; Doorley, "Irish Catholics and French Creoles," 34–54; Konrad, "Diminishing Influences of German Culture," 130, 137, 148; Deiler, *History of the German Churches*, 8; Capers, *Biography of a River Town*, 109.

8. Deiler, *History of the German Churches*, 13–14, 31, 59; for Lafayette see Niehaus, *Irish in New Orleans*, 15–17; Eskew, "German Contributions," 33–34; for synagogue see Reiff Journal, February 15, 1856.

9. *Chahta, uba*, 2nd ed. and *Chahta, uba*, 3rd ed; *Collection of Sacred Songs*; McNally, "Practice of Native American Christianity," 840; McNally, *Ojibwe Singers*, 43–80; O'Grady, "Singing Societies of Oneida," 67–91; Draper, "Abba isht tuluwa," 43–61.

10. For Hite quote see Saxon, Dreyer, and Tallant, *Gumbo Ya-Ya*, 242, quoted in Levine, *Black Culture and Black Consciousness*, 41–42; Epstein, *Sinful Tunes and Spirituals*, 191–237; for Amite County quote see Sparks, "Religion in Amite County, Mississippi," 37–57.

11. For Cairo see Hays, "Way Down in Egypt Land," 69–70; Grimes, *How Shall We Sing?* 9, 112–18; Free, "Theatre of Southwestern Mississippi," 1:146, 204; for the German glee club quote see Deiler, *History of the German Churches*, 13–14; for St. John the Baptist quote see Kelley, "Erin's Enterprise," 234; for "The Irish Skylark" see Niehaus, *Irish in New Orleans*, 104.

12. Grimes, *How Shall We Sing?* 171; *Memphis Enquirer*, April 20, 1836; *Louisiana Gazette* (New Orleans), March 18, 1811.

13. Raboteau, *Slave Religion*, 243; Levine, *Black Culture and Black Consciousness*, 18–24; ex-slave account from Levine, "Slave Songs and Slave Consciousness," 64; Murphy, "Survival of African Music," 60–72.

14. Grimes, *How Shall We Sing?* 3, 10–11, 53, 57, 112–14, 183; Gleeson, *Irish in the South*, 6–8, 55.

15. For French example see Brandon, "Socio-Cultural Traits," 30–31; for Know-Nothing example see Niehaus, *Irish in New Orleans*, 105; for Cairo example see Hays, "Way Down in Egypt Land," 69–70; for Choctaw quote see Carson, *Searching for the Bright Path*, 120–21.

16. *Louisiana Gazette* (New Orleans), January 16, 1812; Ryan, *Civic Wars*, 78.

17. Ethnic organization quotes from Niehaus, *Irish in New Orleans*, 113; *True American* (New Orleans), August 3, 1835; Vicksburg quote from Morris, *Becoming Southern*, 123, 125.

18. *True American* (New Orleans), April 5, 1839; *New Orleans Bee*, October 25, 1848; "War Song of the Natives," http://www.louisianadigitallibrary.org/cdm4/item_viewer.php?CISOROOT=/APC&CISOPTR=75&CISOBOX=1&REC=2 (accessed January 30, 2009).

19. Free, "Theatre of Southwestern Mississippi," 5; Niehaus, *Irish in New Orleans,* 13; *Mygatt's New Orleans*; Blassingame, *Black New Orleans,* 13; Kinzer, "Band of Music," 361; Miller, "Slaves and Southern Catholicism," 147; Clark, "German Liberals in New Orleans," 141–42; "Nineteenth Century Immigration," http://www.hnoc.org/collections/gerpath/gersect2.htm (accessed January 30, 2009).

20. Capers, *Biography of a River Town,* 109–10; Tracy, "Immigrant Population of Memphis," 74; Chapman, "Literature and the Drama in Memphis," 9; *Vicksburg Daily Sentinel,* November 16, 1839; Hays, "Way Down in Egypt Land," 206.

21. *Louisiana Gazette* (New Orleans), April 21, 1810; Dessens, *From Saint-Domingue to New Orleans,* 47; Office of the Mayor Complaint Book, July 12, 1856; *New Orleans Bee,* February 26, 1850.

22. *New Orleans Bee,* May 6, 1845; Tower Diary, March 17, May 7, 1845; Kinzer, "Tio Family," 77; Clark, "German Liberals in New Orleans," 142, 145.

23. *Baton Rouge Gazette,* March 23, 1850; Moss, "St. Patrick's Day Celebrations," 137; Gleeson, *Irish in the South,* 60–61; Davis, *Parades and Power,* 47; Nau, *German People of New Orleans,* 121.

24. Ryan, *Civic Wars,* 70–72, 80–81; for quote see Foster, *Moral Visions,* 43–44; *True American* (New Orleans), July 4, 1836.

25. Dennis, *Red, White, and Blue,* 39; for Irish parade example see Thomas F. Jenkins to James Emile Armor, July 11, 1842; for German barbecue example see *Vicksburg Daily Sentinel,* July 16, 1845.

26. "History of the Proceedings," 21, 26–27, 37, http://nutrias.org/~nopl/spec/pamphlets/clay/clay1.htm (accessed January 30, 2009).

27. Chapman, "Literature and the Drama in Memphis," 9; for German American society quote see Morrow, "Singing and Drinking in New Orleans," 5, 11, 23n2; Nau, *German People of New Orleans,* 104; Merrill, *Germans of Louisiana,* 272; Morrow, "Somewhere between Beer and Wagner," 100n6; Hays, "Way Down in Egypt Land," 68–69.

28. Grimes, *How Shall We Sing?* 57; Kinzer, "Band of Music," 361; Kmen, *Music in New Orleans,* 234; Trotter, *Music and Some Highly Musical People,* 351–52; Fiehrer, "From Quadrille to Stomp," 29.

29. Sullivan, "Composers of Color," 54–71; Wyatt, "Six Composers," 125–40; Desdunes, *Our People and Our History,* 82–89; Trotter, *Music and Some Highly Musical People,* 333–52.

30. Reinders, "Decline of the New Orleans Free Negro," 88–98; Kmen, *Music in New Orleans,* 232–33; Kmen, "Singing and Dancing," 90; Hanger, *Bounded Lives, Bounded Places,* 143, 145.

31. Jerde, "Black Music in New Orleans," 19; Leovy, *Laws and General Ordinances,* 259; Hanger, *Bounded Lives, Bounded Places,* 143, 145; Kmen, *Music in New Orleans,* 42–48; Johnson, *William Johnson's Natchez,* 253, 557; for Hoggatt quote see Gould, *Chained to the Rock of Adversity,* 30; *Baton Rouge Gazette,* September 24, 1842.

32. Kmen, *Music in New Orleans,* 42–55; Martin, "Plaçage," 57–70; Gould, "In Full Enjoyment," 224–30; Vandenhoff, *Leaves from an Actor's Note-book,* 208–9; Bernard, *Travels through North America,* 61–62; Holmes, *Account of the United States,* 333; Sullivan, *Rambles and Scrambles,* 223; Olmsted, *Seaboard Slave States,* 245.

33. Schultz, *Travels on an Inland Voyage,* 195; Stoddard, *Sketches, Historical and Descriptive,* 321.

34. Cuming, *Sketches of a Tour*, 363; Schultz, *Travels on an Inland Voyage*, 197; Johnson, "New Orleans's Congo Square," 117–57; Epstein, *Sinful Tunes and Spirituals*, 85–98, 133–35.

35. Johnson, "New Orleans's Congo Square," 117–57. For some specific descriptions of Congo Square see Ingraham, *South-West*, 162; Creecy, *Scenes in the South*, 20–23; Latrobe, *Journal of Latrobe*, 180–81; Thomas, *From Tennessee Slave*, 109; Brown, *My Southern Home*, 121–24. For Colinda see Bernard and Girouard, "Colinda," 42–43; Epstein, *Sinful Tunes and Spirituals*, 30–33; Cable, "Dance in Place Congo," 527–28.

36. Abrahams, *Singing the Master*, xviii, 45–46; Epstein, *Sinful Tunes and Spirituals*, 32, 52, 100, 104–5, 136; Holmes, *Account of the United States*, 332; Emery, *Black Dance*, 103–8.

37. Russell, *My Diary North and South*, 175; Rawick, *American Slave*, Mary Jane Hones, supplement series 1 (Mississippi), vol. 8, part 3, 1245.

38. Northup, *Twelve Years a Slave*, 163–65; McCollam Diary, June 21, 1845, August 3, 4, December 25, 1847; bumper crop quote from Cade, "Out of the Mouths of Ex-Slaves," 333; Nissenbaum, *Battle for Christmas*, 264–85; Abrahams, *Singing the Master*, 32, 56–60, 88, 203–328; Emery, *Black Dance*, 103, 108–16.

39. Winans, "Black Instrumental Music," 51; Rawick, *American Slave*, Sally Dixon and Virginia Harris, supplement series 1 (Mississippi), vol. 7 and vol. 8, part 3, 627, 942.

40. Johnson, *William Johnson's Natchez*, 469, 473; *Tägliche Deutsche Zeitung* (New Orleans), April 27, 1850; "Typed Autobiography," 26; *Daily Picayune* (New Orleans), December 15, 1839, quoted in Nau, *German People of New Orleans*, 72; Office of the Mayor Complaint Book, July 25, 30, 1856.

41. *Tägliche Deutsche Zeitung* (New Orleans), September 26, 1850, January 17, 1854, April 28, 1855, January 12, 1856, February 12, 1856, May 2, 4, 6, 1856, April 28, 1858, May 4, 1858. For Christmas balls see *Tägliche Deutsche Zeitung* (New Orleans), December 11, 23, 25, 27, 1855.

42. French Opera Programs; Collection of Miscellaneous Librettos.

43. For Camp Street Theater quote see *True American* (New Orleans), October 24, 1838; Konrad, "Diminishing Influences," 156; Leary-Warsaw, "French Art Song," 103; *New Orleans Bee*, November 19, 1845; *Opera Box*, November 15, 1856. See multiple advertisements throughout the 1850s in the months of December, January, and February in *Tägliche Deutsche Zeitung*.

44. *Tägliche Deutsche Zeitung* (New Orleans), October 28, 1853, quoted in Nau, *German People of New Orleans*, 101; *Cohen's New Orleans*.

45. Allain and St. Martin, "French Theatre in Louisiana," 139–51; *Louisiana Gazette* (New Orleans), April 25, 1818, March 19, 1819, quoted in Bogner, "Sir Walter Scott," 429, 432, 434; Kmen, *Music in New Orleans*, 93–103.

46. *New Orleans Bee*, December 18, 1827; *Baton Rouge Gazette*, March 13, 1841.

47. Nau, *German People of New Orleans*, 96; Clark, "German Liberals in New Orleans," 147–50.

48. Schultz, *Travels on an Inland Voyage*, 196; Holmes, *Account of the United States*, 333; for second visitor quote see Bernard, *Travels though North America*, 8; Free, "Theatre of Southwestern Mississippi," 450; *Louisiana Gazette* (New Orleans), February 8, 11, 1811; for Church case see Gould, "In Full Enjoyment of Their Liberty," 143–44, 263; for Renaissance Theater see Jerde, "Black Music in

New Orleans," 20, Kmen, *Music in New Orleans*, 235, and Kinzer, "Band of Music," 358.

49. Lavar, "Rethinking the Social Role," 780; Reinders, *End of an Era*, 81–84; Kohn Letterbook, April 23, 1832.

50. *True American* (New Orleans), November 1, 1838; *Actas de la Compania de Casadores de Orleans*; Niehaus, *Irish in New Orleans*, 115–16; for Emile Johns see *True American* (New Orleans), November 27, 1838; Tracy, "Immigrant Population of Memphis," 74; Brady, "Irish Community," 37–38; Murray, *Travels in North America*, 91.

51. Hanger, *Bounded Lives, Bounded Places*, 132–33. For an edited and translated copy of this petition see Morazan, "'Quadroon' Balls," 311–15.

52. Kinzer, "Band of Music," 348–49, 351, 357; Kinzer, "Tio Family"; Sullivan, "Composers of Color," 54.

53. *Mississippi Free Trader* (Natchez), June 27, 1846; Dunbar-Nelson, "People of Color in Louisiana," 25n62; Southern, *Music of Black Americans*, 133; Noble Manuscript.

54. These statistics include those listed as a musician (either in general or of a specific instrument), music instructors (including dance), music sellers, and manufacturers of instruments. It excludes those proprietors of places where music was performed, such as theaters, ballrooms, and dance halls. Statistics compiled from Bureau of the Census, *Population Schedule*, Louisiana, 1850. This takes into consideration wards one through three, including the Third Representative District, for the city of New Orleans. To put this in some perspective, according to William Bromwell, between 1820 and 1829, 137 immigrants to all U.S. ports listed themselves as musicians. In the 1830s, 164 musicians arrived, in the 1840s, 189, and between 1850 and 1853, when he stopped compiling, 140 immigrants reported themselves as musicians. Compiled from statistics in Bromwell, *History of Immigration*. Between 1820 and 1839, at least eighteen musicians, four instrument makers, and one dancing master immigrated into Louisiana from France. During the following thirteen years at least twenty-two more French-born music teachers, instrument makers, and musicians arrived. The statistics on the French entering at Louisiana are compiled from passenger manifests in Brasseaux, *Foreign French*; Kinzer, "Tio Family," 92–93. Of those musicians listed as "mulattos," all were born in Louisiana except for Charles Lambert, of New York, and Charles Paisson of France. Gushee, "Black Professional Musicians," 61.

55. Gushee, "Nineteenth-Century Origins," 6; Nicholls, *Cambridge History of American Music*, 187.

56. Conrad, *Dictionary of Louisiana Biography*, 1:436, 835; Baron, "Paul Emile Johns," 246–50; Boudreaux, "Music Publishing in New Orleans," 42, 72; Eskew, "German Contributions," 26–27.

57. *New Orleans Directory*; *Cohen's New Orleans*; Conrad, *Dictionary of Louisiana Biography*, 1:170; Bureau of the Census, *Population Schedule*, Louisiana, 1850.

58. Free, "Theatre of Southwestern Mississippi," 34; Cuming, *Sketches of a Tour*, 348; Brasseaux, *Foreign French*; *Cohen's New Orleans*; Bureau of the Census, *Population Schedule*, Louisiana, 1850.

59. Leary-Warsaw, "French Art Song," 106–8.

60. Arrington, "Nationalism and American Music," 4; Howard, *Our American Music*, 211–25; Nicholls, *Cambridge History of American Music*, 136–37, 146, 193–207.

61. Bureau of the Census, *Population Schedule*, Louisiana, 1850. Other musicians

were from Spain, Hungary, Denmark, Ireland, and England; Brasseaux, *Foreign French*; Conrad, *Dictionary of Louisiana Biography*, 1:367 (Prevost), and 2:664 (Guiraud); *Vicksburg Daily Sentinel*, May 5, 6, 11, 1841; Free, "Theatre of Southwestern Mississippi," 408. Barbiere rented William Johnson's State Street store to hold dance classes in 1841. Johnson, *William Johnson's Natchez*, 355–56.

62. "Typed Autobiography," 33; Nichols, *Forty Years of American Life*, 229; Bureau of the Census, *Population Schedule*, Louisiana, 1850; Barrow, *Plantation Life*, 54, 226, 258, 259; Free, "Theatre of Southwestern Mississippi," 231; Ludlow, *Dramatic Life*, 373–75; Cripps Papers; Clark, "Bavarian Organist," 36.

63. Nicholls, *Cambridge History of American Music*, 178–81, 192–93; Tawa, *High-Minded and Low-Down*, 68–77, 93–105; Ripley, *Social Life*, 10–11, http://docsouth.unc.edu/fpn/ripley/ripley.html (accessed January 30, 2009).

64. Weaver, "Foreigners in Ante-Bellum Mississippi," 159; Bureau of the Census, *Population Schedule*, Louisiana, 1850; Lachance, "1809 Immigration," 132.

65. Girault Papers; Bureau of the Census, *Population Schedule*, Louisiana, 1850; Brasseaux, *Foreign French*; quote from *New Orleans Annual*.

66. Bureau of the Census, *Population Schedule*, Louisiana, 1850; Olmsted, *Journey in the Back Country*, 40.

67. For French widow see *Baton Rouge Gazette*, September 11, 1841; for Hull's Institute see *Mississippi Free Trader* (Natchez), August 8, 1852; Bureau of the Census, *Population Schedule*, Louisiana, 1850.

68. Costonis, "Ballet Comes to America," 20, 112, 149–58.

69. Needham, *I See America Dancing*, 134–35.

70. Costonis, "American Career of Jean Baptiste Francisqui," 435–41; *Louisiana Gazette* (New Orleans), December 26, 1806; Sanjek, *American Popular Music*, 2:92–93. For Francisqui's advertisements see *Louisiana Gazette* (New Orleans), November 30, 1804, January 18, 1805, October 2, November 17, December 22, 1807, January 15, 1808.

71. Costonis, "Ballet Comes to America," 4, 170, 174; Needham, *I See America Dancing*, 146–47; Brasseaux, *Foreign French*, 1:212; Paxton, *New Orleans Directory*.

72. *New Orleans Annual*; *Baton Rouge Gazette*, June 14, 1845; *Mississippi Free Trader* (Natchez), March 18, 1846; *New Orleans Bee*, December 9, 1845.

73. *Moniteur de la Louisiane* (New Orleans), October 21, 1807, January 23, 1808; *New Orleans Miscellany*, December, 1847; *Mississippi Free Trader* (Natchez), January 1, 1851.

74. *Weekly Chronicle* (Natchez), September 28, 1808, September 30, 1809; *Southern Galaxy* (Natchez), January 7, 1830.

75. *New Orleans Bee*, November 6, 1845; Ripley, *Social Life*, 5, http://docsouth.unc.edu/fpn/ripley/ripley.html (accessed January 30, 2009); *Baton Rouge Gazette*, September 26, 1840, September 4, 1841; Dickey, "Music of a Louisiana Plantation Family," 35.

76. Barrow, *Plantation Life*, 259; Dickey, "Music of a Louisiana Plantation Family," 27, 42.

77. Epstein, *Sinful Tunes and Spirituals*, 112; quote from Kmen, *Music in New Orleans*, 231; Latrobe, *Journal of Latrobe*, 172; Bernhard, *Travels through North America*, 58; Rawick, *American Slave*, Gabe Emanuel and Price Johnson, supplement series 1 (Mississippi), vol. 7 and vol. 8, part 3, 46, 1172; Northup, *Twelve Years a Slave*, 165.

78. Winans, "Black Instrumental Music," 46; Butler, "Music in Slave Era Mississippi,"

46; Ownby and Joyner, *Black and White Cultural Interaction*, 160; Kmen, *Music in New Orleans*, 231–36; quote from Cimbala, "Black Musicians," 15–16.

5 / Bounding Ethnicity: The Creation and Consumption of Ethnic Music Genres

1. Tregle, *Louisiana in the Age of Jackson*, 304–5.

2. Usner, *American Indians*, 81, 88.

3. Dessens, *From Saint-Domingue to New Orleans*, 110–17; Dormon, "Persistent Specter," 389–404.

4. Tregle, *Louisiana in the Age of Jackson*, 302–3, 310; Niehaus, *Irish in New Orleans*, 77–78.

5. Berkeley, *"Like a Plague of Locusts,"* 15.

6. Richards, *Drama, Theatre, and Identity*, 8–10, 22.

7. Ostendorf, "Minstrelsy and Early Jazz," 583; Knobel, *Paddy and the Republic*, xi–xii.

8. Lott, *Love and Theft*, 6; Kinser, *Carnival American Style*, xvii; Barth, *Ethnic Groups and Boundaries*, 9–10, 15–16; Frith, *Sound Effects*, 57.

9. Levine, *Highbrow/Lowbrow*, 23; Tamarkin, *Anglophilia*, xxvi.

10. *Weekly Picayune* (New Orleans), December 17, 1838.

11. Ashe, *Travels in America*, 263–65.

12. Bernhard, *Travels through North America*, 55; Whipple, *Bishop Whipple's Southern Diary*, 121; Singleton, *Letters from the South and West*, 125; Carlyon, *Dan Rice*, 51.

13. Ostendorf, "Literary Acculturation," 577–586; Ingraham, *South-West*, 66; Flint, *Recollections of the Last Ten Years*, 234; Hodgson, *Remarks during a Journey*, 170; Théodore Pavie, *Souvenirs Atlantiques: Voyages aux États-Unis et au Canada*, vol. 2 (Paris: Roret, 1833), 319–20, in Epstein, "Folk Banjo," 336.

14. Singleton, *Letters from the South and West*, 127; Flint, *Recollections of the Last Ten Years*, 366; Ashe, *Travels in America*, 117–18; Pulszky, *White, Red, Black*, 2:238.

15. Flint, *History and Geography*, 123; Flint, *Recollections of the Last Ten Years*, 141.

16. Johnson, "New Orleans's Congo Square," 117–57. For works by historians emphasizing the African dimension of the music culture at Congo Square see Kmen, *Music in New Orleans*, 61–91; Epstein, *Sinful Tunes and Spirituals*, 84–85.

17. Castellanos, *New Orleans as It Was*, 157–58; Creecy, *Scenes in the South*, 20–23; Ingraham, *South-West*, 162.

18. Hall, *Slavery and African Ethnicities*, 44, 57, 74–79.

19. Roach, "Deep Skin," 107.

20. Latrobe, *Journal of Latrobe*, 180–81.

21. Paxton, *New Orleans Directory*, 40.

22. *Daily Picayune* (New Orleans), 1846, quoted in Shenkel, *Archaeology of the Jazz Complex*, 25; Norman, *Norman's New Orleans*, 182, quoted in Donaldson, "Window on Slave Culture," 67; Johnson, "New Orleans's Congo Square," 148, 149n47.

23. Quote from Gomez, *Exchanging Our Country Marks*, 13; Hall, *Africans in Colonial Louisiana*, xiv, 29–30, 403–4.

24. Flugel, "Pages from a Journal," 432; Singleton, *Letters from the South and West*, 127; Thomas, *From Tennessee Slave*, 49, 109; Castellanos, *New Orleans as It Was*, 157–59.

25. It is unclear if this description was original to Brown or if he took it from another source. These exact words had appeared in the *Daily Picayune* (New Orleans), October 12, 1879, with no author named, while Brown's work was published in 1880. Brown, *My Southern Home*, 121–24.

26. Hamm, *Yesterdays*, 99; Jones, *America and French Culture*, 336; Smith, *Theatrical Management*, 155; *Mississippi Free Trader* (Natchez), January 13, 1847.

27. Ostendorf, "Minstrelsy and Early Jazz," 575; Reiss, *Showman and the Slave*, 149.

28. Peterson, *Creating Country Music*, 4–5.

29. "Polka of the Bohemian Girl to Her Lover: A National Ballad," *Vicksburg Daily Sentinel*, June 24, 1844; *True American* (New Orleans), March 23, 1839.

30. Costonis, "Ballet Comes to America," 202; *True American* (New Orleans), April 24, 1839; *Louisiana Courier* (New Orleans), April 21, 23, May 13, 1829.

31. *New Orleans Bee*, February 12, 13, 1828, January 1, 1845; Varieties Theater Programs, October 6, March 25, 1853.

32. Smith, Theatre Collection, Bound Theatrical Programs from 1829 to 1830, Sol Smith Company from Huntsville, Tuscaloosa and Natchez; Free, "Theatre of Southwestern Mississippi," 212; Smith, *Theatrical Management*, 63.

33. *New Orleans Bee*, January 19, 1830, January 6, 1845, April 17, 1845. For more examples see Smither, "History of the English Theatre," *Vicksburg Daily Sentinel*, January 23, 27, 1841, and Bogner, "Sir Walter Scott in New Orleans," 476–77.

34. *Mississippi Free Trader* (Natchez), November 1, 1848; *New Orleans Bee*, January 6, 1845; *Baton Rouge Gazette*, January 27, 1844.

35. *Vicksburg Daily Sentinel*, December 15, 1843; Kmen, "Singing and Dancing in New Orleans," 34.

36. *Baton Rouge Gazette*, April 24, May 8, June 5, 12, 1847; for Stuart see Invitations Collection.

37. Neil, *Toward a National Taste*, 30; *Weekly Chronicle* (Natchez), September 30, 1809; *Baton Rouge Gazette*, April 24, 1847, June 12, 1847.

38. French Opera Programs, Don Juan Opera, 1853; Leary-Warsaw, "French Art Song," 21.

39. *True American* (New Orleans), April 12, 1837; Writer's Program, *Missouri*, 160.

40. *Mississippi Free Trader* (Natchez), February 7, 1849; Clard, *City Directory*.

41. Roach, "Barnumizing the Diaspora," 39.

42. *Mississippi Free Trader* (Natchez), February 18, 1852; Trotter, *Music and Some Highly Musical People*, 66–87. For Bull see *Vicksburg Daily Sentinel*, March 27, 31, 1845; *Mississippi Free Trader* (Natchez), March 23, 1853; Lizzie Randall Letter.

43. Gac, *Singing for Freedom*, 136–37, 161; Nathan, "Tyrolese Family Rainer," 63–79; *Vicksburg Daily Sentinel*, March 7, 1845; *New Orleans Bee*, February 20, 1845; Olshausen, *Forty Years Ago*; Opera Box, La Loge Opera, November 15, 1856.

44. *New Orleans Bee*, January 29, 1845; Costonis, "Ballet Comes to America," 322; Kmen, *Music in New Orleans*, 163.

45. *Vicksburg Daily Sentinel*, May 20, 21, 1840; *Baton Rouge Gazette*, May 9, 1840; *Mississippi Free Trader* (Natchez), March 18, 1846; *New Orleans Bee*, March 4, 1829.

46. *Baton Rouge Gazette*, May 8, 1847; *Vicksburg Daily Sentinel*, December 20, January 15, 1841; Lott, *Love and Theft*, 112–15.

47. Bogner, "Sir Walter Scott in New Orleans," 476–77; *New Orleans Bee*, December

19, 1827; Smith, Theatre Collection, Bound Theatrical Programs from 1829 to 1830, Sol Smith Company from Huntsville, Tuscaloosa and Natchez; *True American* (New Orleans), April 27, 1839, October 9, 1838.

48. *Vicksburg Daily Sentinel,* March 7, 10, 1845; *True American* (New Orleans), February 25, March 13, 1839; Free, "Theatre of Southwestern Mississippi," 38.

49. *Mississippi Free Trader* (Natchez), April 26, 1848.

50. Niehaus, *Irish in New Orleans,* 124–26; *New Orleans Bee,* January 21, 1850.

51. Nathan, "Tyrolese Family Rainer," 70, 78–79 Leary-Warsaw, "French Art Song," 32, 45–46.

52. *New Orleans Bee,* February 3, 1845, November 8, 1830; *True American* (New Orleans), September 6, 1838.

53. Sheet Music, Ste. Genevieve Collection; Bound Collection of Steph F. Bonbright, vol. 1, St. Louis Mercantile Library.

54. *Louisiana Courier* (New Orleans), April 24, 1829; *Vicksburg Register,* January 21, 1836; *Vicksburg Daily Sentinel,* November 14, 1838; *Mississippi Free Trader* (Natchez), July 4, 1849; *Baton Rouge Gazette,* July 8, 1843.

55. *Vicksburg Daily Sentinel,* June 17, 1844.

56. Bailey, "Music in the Life of a Free Black"; William T. Johnson Memorial Collection.

57. Sheet Music Collection, Missouri History Museum; Walker, Piano Lesson Book.

58. Vianna, *Mystery of Samba,* xiii, 14–16, 113–14; Bendix, *In Search of Authenticity,* 17; Peterson, *Creating Country Music,* 5, 6n5; Hobsbawn and Ranger, *Invention of Tradition.*

59. For Scottish example see Bogner, "Sir Walter Scott in New Orleans," 442; for Arabs see *True American* (New Orleans), March 8, 1839; Schultz, *Travels on an Inland Voyage,* 197.

60. *Daily Picayune* (New Orleans), December 28, 1855, quoted in Niehaus, *Irish in New Orleans,* 126; *New Orleans Bee,* April 17, 1845.

61. *True American* (New Orleans), April 24, 1839.

62. Rawick, *American Slave,* Isaac Stier (Mississippi), 7:145–46; Walker, Piano Lesson Book; *Weekly Chronicle* (Natchez), December 9, 1809.

63. Guion, "Felippe Cioffi," 14; Grimes, *How Shall We Sing?* 55–56.

64. Miller Journal.

65. McKnight, "Charivaris, Cowbellions," 412–13; Levine, *Highbrow/Lowbrow,* 13; Kmen, "Old Corn Meal," 29–34.

66. Ostendorf, *Black Literature in White America,* 71; Lott, *Love and Theft,* 6, 20.

67. "Negro Minstrelsy," 72–73; *New York Tribune,* quoted in Lott, *Love and Theft,* 15–16. For examples of the term "Ethiopian" being employed as an ethnic delineator outside of music culture see *Southern Quarterly Review* (October 1842): 321–22, (October 1851): 459, (January 1852): 159, (November 1856): 164; *De Bow's Review* (July 1851): 66–68.

68. For more on the necessity of a perception of authenticity in minstrelsy see Ostendorf, "Minstrelsy and Early Jazz," 580; Holmberg and Schneider, "Daniel Decatur Emmett's Stump Sermons," 27–38; Toll, *Blacking Up,* 26–27, 34, 40; Lott, *Love and Theft,* 16. For some contemporary examples of Lott's suggestion see "Who Are Our National Poets," 31–41; Nichols, *Forty Years of American Life,* 396–97.

69. "Authentic Memoir of E. P. Christy," *New York Age*, 1848, found in Toll, *Blacking Up*, 46; "Interview with Ben Cotton"; Lott, *Love and Theft*, 51–52; Mathews, *Memoirs of Charles Mathews*, 382–83; Sanjek, *American Popular Music*, 158–59; Toll, *Blacking Up*, 26–27; Hodge, *Yankee Theatre*, 3, 65, 70.

70. Bean, Hatch, and McNamara, *Inside the Minstrel Mask*, 38; Waldstreicher, *In the Midst of Perpetual Fetes*, 337; *Memphis Enquirer*, September 16, 1836; *True American* (New Orleans), January 30, 1830.

71. Richards, *Drama, Theatre, and Identity*, 214–26.

72. Ostendorf, *Black Literature in White America*, 67–69.

Conclusion

1. Kammen, *Season of Youth*, 15; Kammen, *Mystic Chords of Memory*, 41; Waldstreicher, *In the Midst of Perpetual Fetes*, 246–48; Purcell, *Sealed with Blood*, 210; Grob and Billias, *Interpretations of American History*, 414.

2. Kammen, *Season of Youth*, 56–57.

3. Wood, "Significance of the Early Republic," 20.

4. Grant, *North Over South*, 1–6; Potter, *Impending Crisis*; McPherson, "Antebellum Southern Exceptionalism," 422.

5. *Mississippi Free Trader* (Natchez), February 16, 1853; *Opera Box, La Loge Opera* (New Orleans), December 20, 1856; Fahs, *Imagined Civil War*, 5; Watson, *From Nationalism to Secessionism*.

6. *Opera Box, La Loge Opera* (New Orleans), December 20, 1856; *Daily Picayune* (New Orleans), 1856, reprinted in *Dwight's Journal of Music* (Boston), December 13, 1856.

7. Fahs, *Imagined Civil War*, 6; Mullenix, "Yankee Doodle Dixie," 34.

Bibliography

Newspapers and Periodicals

Baton Rouge Gazette, 1840, 1845–1850.
The Cairo Daily Democrat, 1865–1866.
The Cairo Delta, 1848–1849.
Cairo Weekly Times and Delta, 1855.
De Bow's Review (New Orleans), 1851.
Dwight's Journal of Music (Boston), 1852–1860.
Louisiana Advertiser (New Orleans), 1823.
Louisiana Courier (New Orleans), 1829–1830.
Louisiana Gazette (New Orleans), 1804–1807.
Memphis Enquirer, 1836–1837.
Mississippi Free Trader (Natchez), 1845–1853.
Moniteur de la Louisiane (New Orleans), 1807–1808.
The Natchez Weekly Courier and Journal, 1837.
New Orleans Bee, 1827–1830 and 1845–1850.
New Orleans Miscellany, 1847.
New York Herald, 1804.
The Southern Galaxy (Natchez), 1829–1830.
The Southern Quarterly Review (New Orleans), 1842–1851.
Tägliche Deutsche Zeitung (New Orleans), 1850–1858.
True American (New Orleans), 1835–1839.
Vicksburg Daily Sentinel, 1838–1850.
Vicksburg Register, 1831–1838.
War Eagle and Daily Evening Extra (Cairo), 1864–1865.
The Weekly Chronicle (Natchez), 1808–1810.
Weekly Picayune (New Orleans), December 17, 1838.

Primary Works

Abstract of the Returns of the Fifth Census. Washington, D.C.: Duff Green, 1832.

Actas de la Compania de Casadores de Orleans. Williams Research Center, The Historic New Orleans Collection, New Orleans, Louisiana.

"The African Slave Trade." *De Bow's Review* 1 (January 1855): 20.

Aggregate Amount of Each Description of Persons Within the United States of America in the Year 1810. Washington, D.C., 1811.

Alexander, James E. *Transatlantic Sketches*. Philadelphia: Key and Biddle, 1833.

Allen, Michael, ed. "Reminiscences of a Common Boatman (1849–1851)." *Gateway Heritage* 5 (Fall 1984): 36–49.

Allen, William Francis, Charles Pickard Ware, and Lucy McKim Garrison, eds. *Slave Songs of the United States*. New York: Simpson, 1867. Reprint, New York: Dover, 1995.

Anderson, John Q., ed. "Letter from a Yankee Bride in Ante-Bellum Louisiana." *Louisiana History* 1 (Summer 1960): 245–50.

"Art in China." *Dwight's Journal of Music* 3 (July 16, 1853): 116.

Ashe, Thomas. *Travels in America Performed in 1806*. Vol. 3. London: Richard Phillips, 1808.

Bailey, Ben E. "Music in the Life of a Free Black of Natchez." Manuscript. Mississippi Department of Archives and History, Jackson, Mississippi.

Baird, Robert. *View of the Valley of the Mississippi*. Philadelphia: H. S. Tanner, 1832. John Mason Peck Collection, St. Louis Mercantile Library, St. Louis, Missouri.

Barrow, Bennet H. *Plantation Life in the Florida Parishes of Louisiana 1836–1846, as Reflected in the Diary of Bennet H. Barrow*. Edited by Edwin Adams Davis. New York: AMS, 1967.

Bell, Horace. *Reminiscences of a Ranger*. Los Angeles: Yarnell, Caystile and Mathes, 1881.

Bernhard, duke of Saxe-Weimar-Eisenach. *Travels through North America during the Years 1825 and 1826*. Vol. 2. Philadelphia: Corey, Lea and Carey, 1828.

Berquin-Duvallon, Pierre-Louis. *Travels in Louisiana and the Floridas in the Year 1802*. Translated by John Davis. New York: I. Riley and Co., 1806.

Bispham, David. "Music as a Factor in National Life." *North American Review* 175 (December 1902).

Bremer, Fredrika. *America of the Fifties: Letters of Fredrika Bremer*. Edited by Adolph B. Benson. New York: American-Scandinavian Foundation, 1924.

———. *The Homes of the New World: Impressions of America*. Vol. 2. New York: Harper and Brothers, 1853.

Bromwell, William J. *History of Immigration to the United States*. New York: Redfield, 1856. Reprint, New York: Arno Press, 1969.

Brown, William Wells. *My Southern Home*. Boston: A. G. Brown, 1880.

———. *Narrative of William Wells Brown*. Boston: Anti-Slavery Office, 1848.

2nd ed. In *Four Fugitive Slave Narratives*, edited by Robin W. Winks. Reading, Mass.: Addison-Wesley, 1969.

Bound Sheet Music Collection. St. Louis Mercantile Library, University of Missouri St. Louis, St. Louis, Missouri.

Buckingham, James S. *America: Historical, Statistic, and Descriptive*. London: Fisher, Son and Co., 1841.

Bureau of the Census. *Population Schedule of the Seventh Census of the United States*, Louisiana, 1850.

Busch, Moritz. *Travels Between the Hudson and the Mississippi, 1851–1852*. Translated and edited by Norman H. Binger. Lexington: University Press of Kentucky, 1971.

Cable, George Washington. "Creole Slave Songs." *Century Illustrated Magazine* 31 (April 1886): 807–28.

———. "Dance in Place Congo." *Century Illustrated Magazine* 31 (February 1886): 517–31.

———. *Stories of Old Louisiana*. Edited by Arlene Turner. Gloucester, Mass.: Peter Smith, 1965.

Campaign Songbooks. John Mason Peck Collection. St. Louis Mercantile Library, University of Missouri St. Louis, St. Louis, Missouri.

Carter, Clarence E., comp., ed. *The Territorial Papers of the United States*. Vol. 9. Washington, D.C.: Government Printing Office, 1940.

Casey, Charles. *Two Years on the Farm of Uncle Sam*. London: R. Bentley, 1852.

Castellanos, Henry C. *New Orleans as It Was: Episodes of Louisiana Life*. Edited by George F. Reinecke. New Orleans: L. Graham and Son, 1895. Reprint, Baton Rouge: Louisiana State University Press, 1978.

Chahta, uba isht taloa holisso or Choctaw Hymn Book. 2nd ed. Boston: Crocker and Brewster, 1833. Mississippi Department of Archives and History, Jackson, Mississippi.

Chahta, uba isht taloa holisso or Choctaw Hymn Book. 3rd ed. Boston: Press of T. R. Marvin, 1844. Mississippi Department of Archives and History, Jackson, Mississippi.

"Character of the American People." *Southern Quarterly* (February 1857): 393–408.

"Chinese and Scotch Music." *Family Minstrel: A Musical and Literary Journal* (June 1835).

Claiborne, W. C. C. *Official Letter Books of W. C. C. Claiborne, 1801–1816*. Edited by Dunbar Rowland. Jackson, Miss.: State Department of Archives and History, 1917.

Clard, H. C. *City Directory*. Vicksburg, 1860. Mississippi Department of Archives and History, Jackson, Mississippi.

Clark, Robert T., Jr., ed. "Bavarian Organist Comes to New Orleans." *Louisiana Historical Quarterly* 29 (January 1946): 356–58.

Clemens, Samuel. *Mark Twain's Letters*. Vol. 1. Edited by Edgar M. Branch, Michael B. Frank, and Kenneth M. Sanderson. Berkeley: University of California Press, 1988.

Coffin, Levi. *Reminiscences of Levi Coffin.* Cincinnati: Robert Clark, 1898. Reprint, New York: Arno, 1968.

Cohen's New Orleans and Lafayette City Directory for 1850. New Orleans: Printed at the Job Office of the Delta, 1849. Louisiana Collection, Tulane University, New Orleans, Louisiana.

Collection of Miscellaneous Librettos, 1847–1855. Louisiana Collection, Tulane University, New Orleans, Louisiana.

The Collection of Sacred Songs for the Use of the Baptist Native Christians of the Six Nations. Revised by James Cusick. Philadelphia: American Baptist Publication Society, 1846. John Mason Peck Collection. St. Louis Mercantile Library, University of Missouri St. Louis, St. Louis, Missouri.

Collins, Tom. *The Adventures of T. C. Collins—Boatman: Twenty-Four Years on the Western Waters, 1849–1873.* Edited by Herbert L. Roush. Baltimore: Gateway, 1985.

"A Complaint on Behalf of Native Composers." *Dwight's Journal of Music* 5 (June 24, 1854): 94.

Conclin, George. *Conclin's New River Guide.* Cincinnati: G. Conclin, 1849.

Conner, Lemuel Parker. Family Papers. Louisiana and Lower Mississippi Valley Collections, Louisiana State University Libraries, Baton Rouge, Louisiana.

"Copy of the Telegraphe." *Louisiana Historical Quarterly* 2 (January 1919): 293–302.

Cox, Anna B. Letter. May 1, 1819. Cox Family Papers. Missouri History Museum, Library and Research Center, St. Louis, Missouri.

Creecy, James R. *Scenes in the South.* Philadelphia: J. B. Lippincott, 1860.

Creole Songs Box. Music Collection. Missouri History Museum, Library and Research Center, St. Louis, Missouri.

Cripps, Thomas. Papers. Williams Research Center, The Historic New Orleans Collection, New Orleans, Louisiana.

Cuming, Fortescue. *Sketches of a Tour to the Western Country.* Edited by Reuben Gold Thwaites. Pittsburgh: Cramer, Spear and Eichbaum, 1810. Reprint, Cleveland: Arthur H. Clark, 1904.

Davies, Ebenezer. *American Scenes and Christian Slavery.* London: J. Snow, 1849.

Davis, Reuben. *Recollections of Mississippi and Mississippians.* Boston: Houghton Mifflin, 1890.

Davis, William E., and F. Mark McKiernan, eds. "The Mighty Mississippi: Two Nineteenth-Century Accounts." *Louisiana History* 18 (Summer 1977): 338–48.

De Bow, J. D. B. *Statistical View of the United States: Being a Compendium of the Seventh Census.* Washington, D.C.: Beverly Tucker, 1854.

Delany, Martin Robison. *Blake; or, The Huts of America, a Novel.* Boston: Beacon Press, 1970.

"A Description of New Orleans." *Literary Magazine, and American Register* 4 (July 1805): 39–42.

"Editor's Address." *Family Minstrel: A Musical and Literary Journal* (January 1835).

Emerson, Ralph Waldo. "The American Scholar." In *Selected Works: Essays, Poems, and Dispatches,* edited by John Carlos Rowe. Boston: Houghton Mifflin, 2003.

———. "Nature." In *Selected Works: Essays, Poems, and Dispatches,* edited by Jon Carlos Rowe. Boston: Houghton Mifflin, 2003.

"Every Day Commerce." *Dollar Magazine* 8 (July 1851).

Fearon, Henry. *Sketches of America.* London: Longman, Hurst, Reese, Orme and Brown, 1818. Reprint, New York: Benjamin Blom, 1969.

"The Fields of June." *Southern Literary Messenger* 21 (August 1855).

"Fillmore and Donaldson: Songs for the Campaign." 1856. Peck Collection. St. Louis Mercantile Library, St. Louis, Missouri.

Finiels, Nicolas de. *An Account of Upper Louisiana.* Edited by Carl J. Ekberg and William E. Foley. Translated by Carl J. Ekberg. Columbia: University of Missouri Press, 1989.

Flint, Timothy. *The History and Geography of the Mississippi Valley.* 2nd ed. Cincinnati, Ohio: E. H. Flint and L. R. Lincoln, 1832.

———. *Recollections of the Last Ten Years.* Boston: Cummings, Hillard, 1826. Reprint, New York: Da Capo Press, 1968.

Flugel, Felix, ed. "Pages from a Journal of a Voyage Down the Mississippi to New Orleans in 1817." *Louisiana Historical Quarterly* 7 (July 1924): 414–35.

Fontenay, Marie. *L'Autre Monde.* Paris: Librairie Nouvelle, 1855.

Forest, P. "Forest's *Voyage aux Etats-Unis de l'Amerique en 1831.*" Edited by Georges J. Joyaux. *Louisiana Historical Quarterly* 39 (October 1956): 457–72.

Foster, Walter. Diary. Missouri History Museum, Library and Research Center, St. Louis, Missouri.

French Opera Programs. Albert L. Voss Collection. Manuscripts Department, Tulane University, New Orleans, Louisiana.

Fuller, Margaret. "American Facts." In *Margaret Fuller, Critic: Writings from the New-York Tribune, 1844–1846,* edited by Judith Mattson Bean and Joel Myerson. New York: Columbia University Press, 2000.

———. "The Celestial Empire." In *Margaret Fuller, Critic: Writings from the New-York Tribune, 1844–1846,* edited by Judith Mattson Bean and Joel Myerson. New York: Columbia University Press, 2000.

———. "Dispatch 18, New and Old World Democracy." In *Selected Works: Essays, Poems, and Dispatches,* edited by John Carlos Rowe. Boston: Houghton Mifflin, 2003.

———. "Ole Bull." In *Margaret Fuller, Critic: Writings from the* New York-Tribune, *1844–1846,* edited by Judith Mattson Bean and Joel Myerson. New York: Columbia University Press, 2000.

"German Literature." *De Bow's Review* 6 (September 1860): 280–90.

Gerstäcker, Friedrich. *Wild Sports in the Far West: The Narrative of a German Wanderer Beyond the Mississippi, 1837–1843.* Edited by E. L. and H. R. Steeves. London: Geo. Routledge, 1854. Reprint, Durham, N.C.: Duke University Press, 1969.

Gilman, Caroline. *Recollections of a Southern Matron.* New York: Harper Brothers, 1838.

Gilpin, William. Letter from New Barracks, New Orleans, February 18, 1837. "Dragoon Letters from the Western Frontier." Missouri History Museum, Library and Research Center, St. Louis, Missouri.

Girault, Auguste. Papers. Louisiana and Lower Mississippi Valley Collections, Louisiana State University Libraries, Baton Rouge, Louisiana.

Gottschalk, Louis Moreau. *Notes of a Pianist.* Edited by Jeanne Behrend. New York: A. A. Knopf, 1964.

Hall, A. Oakey. *The Manhattaner in New Orleans.* Edited by Henry Kmen. Baton Rouge: Louisiana State University, 1976.

Hall, Basil. *Travels in North America in the Years 1827 and 1828.* Vol. 2. Philadelphia: Carey, Lea and Carey, 1829.

Hall, Baynard R. *Frank Freeman's Barber Shop: A Tale.* New York: Charles Scribner, 1852.

Hall, James T. *Letters From the West.* London: Henry Colburn, 1828. Reprint, Gainesville, Fla.: Scholars' Fascimiles and Reprints, 1967.

Harris, William Tell. *Remarks Made During a Tour Through the United States of America in the Years 1817, 1818, and 1819.* London: Sherwood, Neely and Jones, 1821.

Hastings, Thomas. *Dissertation on Musical Taste; or, General Principles of Taste Applied to the Art of Music.* Albany, N.Y.: Websters and Skinners, 1822. Reprint, New York: Da Capo Press, 1974.

Hawes, G. W. *G. W. Hawes' Commercial Gazetteer and Business Directory of the Ohio River.* Indianapolis: G. W. Hawes, 1861.

Hawthorne, Nathaniel. *The Marble Faun; or, The Romance of Monti Beni.* Vol. 1. Boston: Ticknor and Fields, 1860.

Heine, Rosa Eugene. Bound Collection of Sheet Music. Mississippi Department of Archives and History, Jackson, Mississippi.

Heinrich, Anthony Philip. *The Dawning of Music in Kentucky; or, The Pleasures of Harmony in the Solitudes of Nature (Opera Prima), The Western Minstrel (Opera Seconda).* Introduction by H. Wiley Hitchcock. Philadelphia: Bacon and Hart, 1820. Reprint, New York: Da Capo, 1972.

"Histoire de la Louisiane par Charles Gayarré." *Southern Quarterly Review* 9 (April 1846): 362–63.

"A History of the Proceedings in the City of New Orleans on the Occasion of the Funeral Ceremonies in Honor of Calhoun, Clay and Webster." New Orleans: Office of the Picayune, 1853. Online Pamphlet Collection, Special

Collections, Louisiana Division, New Orleans Public Library, New Orleans, Louisiana.

Hodgson, Adam. *Remarks during a Journey through North America.* New York: J. Seymour, 1823.

Holcombe, William Henry. "Sketches of Plantation Life." *The Knickerbocker; or, New York Monthly Magazine* 57 (June 1861): 619–33.

Holmes, Isaac. *An Account of the United States of America.* London: Caxton Press, 1823. Reprint, New York: Arno Press, 1974.

Houstoun, Matilda. *Hesperos; or, Travels in the West.* Vol. 2. London: J. W. Parker, 1850.

———. *Texas and the Gulf of Mexico; or, Yachting in the New World.* Philadelphia: G. B. Zieber, 1845.

Hubar, Leonard V., comp. *Advertisements of Lower Mississippi River Steamboats, 1812–1920.* West Barrington, R.I.: Steamship Historical Society of America, 1959.

Hundley, Daniel R. *Social Relations in Our Southern States.* New York: Henry B. Price, 1860. Reprint, New York: Arno Press, 1973.

"The Hungarian Orchestra." *Dwight's Journal of Music* 1 (April 24, 1852): 19.

Ingersoll, Charles Jared. *A Discourse Concerning the Influence of America on the Mind.* London: Printed for James Ridgeway, 1824.

———. *Inchiquin, the Jesuit's Letters, During a Late Residence in the United States of America.* New York: I. Riley, 1810.

Ingraham, Joseph Holt. *The South-West, By a Yankee.* Vol. 1. New York: Harper and Brothers, 1835. Reprint, Ann Arbor, Mich.: University Microfilms, Inc., 1966.

"Interview With Ben Cotton." *New York Dramatic Mirror* (July 1897).

Invitations Collection, Missouri History Museum, Library and Research Center, St. Louis, Missouri.

Jefferson, Thomas. Letter to unknown (possibly Francis Alberti). June 8, 1778. In *The Life and Selected Writings of Thomas Jefferson*, edited by Adrian Koch and William Peden. New York: Random House, 1944.

———. *Notes on the State of Virginia.* Edited by Frank Shuffelton. New York: Penguin Books, 1999.

Jenkins, Thomas F. Letter. July 11, 1842. James Emile Armor Papers. Manuscripts Collection, Louisiana Division, New Orleans Public Library, New Orleans, Louisiana.

Johnson, William. *William Johnson's Natchez: The Antebellum Diary of a Free Negro.* Edited by William Ransom Hogan and Edwin Adams Davis. Baton Rouge: Louisiana State University Press, 1951.

Johnson, William T. Memorial Collection. Louisiana and Lower Mississippi Valley Collections, Louisiana State University Libraries, Baton Rouge, Louisiana.

Keeler, Ralph. "Three Years as a Negro Minstrel." *Atlantic Monthly* 24 (July 1869): 71–85.

———. *Vagabond Adventures*. Boston: Fields, Osgood, 1870.

Kemble, Frances. *Records of Later Life*. New York: H. Holt, 1882.

Ker, Henry. *Travels Through the Western Interior of the United States*. Elizabethtown, N.J.: printed for the author, 1816.

Kohn, Carl. Letterbook. Williams Research Center, The Historic New Orleans Collection, New Orleans, Louisiana.

La Hache, Theodore von. "The Musical Album for 1855." Louisiana Collection, Tulane University, New Orleans, Louisiana.

Lange, Torbau. Diary. Missouri History Museum, Library and Research Center, St. Louis, Missouri.

Latrobe, Benjamin Henry. *The Journal of Latrobe*. New York: D. Appleton, 1905. Reprint, New York: Burt Franklin, 1971.

Laussat, Pierre-Clément de. *Memoirs of My Life*. Translated by Sister Agnes-Josephine Pastwa, O.S.F., and edited by Robert D. Bush. Baton Rouge: Louisiana State University Press, 1978.

Lavasseur, A. *Lafayette in America in 1824 and 1825*. Philadelphia: Carey and Lea, 1829. Reprint, New York: Research Reprints, 1970.

Leovy, Henry J. *The Laws and General Ordinances of the City of New Orleans*. New Orleans: E. C. Wharton, 1857. Williams Research Center, The Historic New Orleans Collection, New Orleans, Louisiana.

"A Letter from A.W.T. on Oratorio Practice, American Voices, &c." *Dwight's Journal of Music* 1 (September 11, 1852): 170.

"Letters of Nathaniel Cox to Gabriel Lewis." *Louisiana Historical Quarterly* 2 (April 1919): 179–92.

"The Levee at New Orleans." *Illustrated London Daily News* (June 1858).

Lewis, Henry. *The Valley of the Mississippi Illustrated*. Translated by A. Hermina Poatgieter. Edited by Bertha L. Heilbron. St. Paul: Minnesota Historical Society, 1967.

Ludlow, Noah M. *Dramatic Life as I Found It*. St. Louis: G. I. Jones, 1880. Reprint, New York: Benjamin Blom, 1966.

Lyell, Charles. *A Second Visit to the United States of North America*. Vol. 1. New York: Harper Brothers, 1868.

Macartney, George. *An Embassy to China: Lord Macartney's Journal*. Edited by J. L. Cranmer-Byng. Reprint, New York: Routledge, 2000.

Marigny, Bernard. "Reflections on the Campaign of General Andrew Jackson in Louisiana in 1814 and '15." Translated by Grace King. *Louisiana Historical Quarterly* 6 (January 1923): 61–85.

Martin, François-Xavier. *The History of Louisiana from the Earliest Period*. New Orleans: A. T. Penniman, 1829. Reprint, New Orleans: J. A. Gresham, 1882.

Martineau, Harriet. *Retrospect of Western Travel*. Vol. 2. Cincinnati: U. P. James, 1836.

Mathews, Anne. *Memoirs of Charles Mathews, Comedian*. Vol. 3. London: Samuel Bentley, 1838.

McCollam, Ellen. Diary. Louisiana and Lower Mississippi Valley Collections, Louisiana State University Libraries, Baton Rouge, Louisiana.

McDermott, John Francis, ed. *Before Mark Twain: A Sampler of Old, Old Times on the Mississippi.* Carbondale: Southern Illinois University Press, 1998.

Meeker, Nathan Cook. *Life in the West; or, Stories of the Mississippi Valley.* New York: S. R. Wells, 1968.

Merrick, George Byron. *Old Times on the Upper Mississippi: The Recollections of a Steamboat Pilot from 1854–1863.* Cleveland, Ohio: Arthur H. Clark, 1909.

Miller, Henry. "The Journal of Henry Miller." Edited by Thomas Marshall Martland. *Missouri Historical Society Collections* 6 (1931): 213–86.

Miller, Henry B. Journal. Missouri History Museum, Library and Research Center, St. Louis, Missouri.

Monette, John W. *History of the Discovery and Settlement of the Valley of the Mississippi.* Vol. 2. New York: Harper and Brothers, 1846.

Murray, Charles Augustus. *Travels in North America During the Years 1834, 1835 and 1836.* Vol. 2. London: Richard Bentley, 1839.

"Music in America." *North American Review* (April 1841).

"Music in Boston." *Musical Magazine* (April 1824).

"Musical Authors and Publications of the United States." *Musical Magazine* (July 1835).

"Musical Talent of the Americans." *Dwight's Journal of Music* 7 (June 16, 1855): 82.

Mygatt's New Orleans Business Directory. New Orleans: Mygatt, 1857. Mississippi Department of Archives and History, Jackson, Mississippi.

"Nathaniel Phillips: The First Music Publisher in St. Louis." Ernest C. Krohn Collection. Missouri History Museum, Library and Research Center, St. Louis, Missouri.

"National Music." *American Quarterly Review* (June 1835).

"National Music." *Dwight's Journal of Music* 6 (February 3, 1855).

"National Music." *North American Review* (January 1840).

"Negro Minstrelsy—Ancient and Modern." *Putnam's Monthly Magazine* 5 (January 1855).

New Orleans Annual and Commercial Register for 1846. New Orleans: E. A. Michel, 1845. Louisiana and Lower Mississippi Valley Collections, Louisiana State University Libraries, Baton Rouge, Louisiana.

New Orleans Directory for 1841. New Orleans: Michel, 1840. Louisiana Collection, Tulane University, New Orleans, Louisiana.

Nichols, Thomas L. *Forty Years of American Life.* London: J. Maxwell, 1864. Reprint, New York: Negro Universities Press, 1968.

Noble, Jordan B. Manuscript Collection. Williams Research Center, The Historic New Orleans Collection, New Orleans, Louisiana.

Norman, Benjamin Moore. *Norman's New Orleans and Environs.* New Orleans: B. M. Norman, 1845. Reprint, Baton Rouge: Louisiana State University Press, 1976.

Northup, Solomon. *Twelve Years a Slave.* Edited by Sue Eakin and Joseph Logsdon. Auburn, N.Y.: Derby and Miller, 1853. Reprint, Baton Rouge: Louisiana State University Press, 1968.

Nuebling, Max. Letterbook. Louisiana and Lower Mississippi Valley Collections, Louisiana State University Libraries, Baton Rouge, Louisiana.

Nuttall, Thomas. *A Journal of Travels into the Arkansas Territory During the Year 1819.* Philadelphia: Thomas H. Palmer, 1821. Reprint, Norman: University of Oklahoma Press, 1980.

"Office of the Mayor Complaint Book." Louisiana Division, New Orleans Public Library, New Orleans, Louisiana.

Olmsted, Frederick Law. *A Journey in the Back Country.* New York: Mason, 1860. Reprint, New York: Burt Franklin, 1970.

———. *A Journey in the Seaboard Slave States.* New York: Dix and Edwards, 1856.

Olshausen, Theodore. *Forty Years Ago: Annals of the Mercantile Library Association and Its Public Hall, 1846–1886.* Rare Books Reading Room, St. Louis Mercantile Library, St. Louis, Missouri.

"On Singing in Sabbath Schools." *Musical Magazine* (January 1840).

The Opera Box, La Loge Opera: A Literary Journal (November–May 1856–1857). Williams Research Center, The Historic New Orleans Collection, New Orleans, Louisiana.

Opera Librettos. Collection of Miscellaneous Librettos, 1847–1855. Louisiana Collection, Tulane University, New Orleans, Louisiana.

"Original Communication." *Family Minstrel: A Musical and Literary Journal* (May 1835).

Paxton, John Adams. *The New Orleans Directory and Register.* New Orleans: Benjamin Levy, 1822. Louisiana Collection, Tulane University, New Orleans, Louisiana.

———. *Supplement to the New Orleans Directory for Last Year.* New Orleans: Benjamin Levy, 1822. Louisiana Collection, Tulane University, New Orleans, Louisiana.

Peck, John Mason. Papers. St. Louis Mercantile Library, University of Missouri St. Louis, St. Louis, Missouri.

Perin du Lac, François-Marie. *Travels through the Two Louisianas.* London: J. G. Barnard, 1807.

Poole, Caroline B. "A Yankee School Teacher in Louisiana, 1835–1837: The Diary of Caroline B. Poole." Edited by James A. Padgett. *Louisiana Historical Quarterly* 20 (July 1937): 650–79.

"Popular Amusements." *Dwight's Journal of Music* 7 (July 14, 1855): 117.

Power, Tyrone. *Impressions of America During the Years 1833, 1834, and 1835.* London: Richard Bentley, 1836. Reprint, New York: Benjamin Blom, 1971.

"The Present and Future of American Art." *North American Review* (July 1856).

"Prospects for a National Music in America." *Musical Magazine* (January 1840).

Pulszky, Francis, and Theresa Pulszky. *White, Red, Black: Sketches of Society in the United States.* Vol. 2. New York: Redfield, 1853. Reprint, New York: Negro Universities Press, 1968.

Randall, Lizzie. Letter. Louisiana and Lower Mississippi Valley Collections, Louisiana State University Libraries, Baton Rouge, Louisiana.

Rawick, George P., ed. *The American Slave: A Composite Autobiography.* Westport, Conn.: Greenwood, 1972.

Regan, John. *The Emigrant's Guide to the Western States of America.* Edinburgh: Oliver and Boyd, 1852.

Reiff, Anton. Journal. Louisiana and Lower Mississippi Valley Collections, Louisiana State University Libraries, Baton Rouge, Louisiana.

Reinecke, George, trans., ed. "Early Louisiana French Life and Folklore: From the Anonymous Breaux Manuscript." *Louisiana Folklore Miscellany* 2 (1966): 1–58.

Report of the Superintendent of the Census. Washington, D.C.: Robert Armstrong, 1853.

"Review 10." *Southern Quarterly Review* (July 1842).

Ripley, Eliza. *Social Life in New Orleans Being Recollections of My Girlhood.* New York: D. Appleton, 1912.

Rittenhouse, Maud. *Maud.* Edited by Richard Lee Strout. New York: Macmillan, 1939.

Rosenberg, Charles G. *Jenny Lind in America.* New York: Stringer and Townsend, 1851.

Rossiter, Harold. *How to Put on a Minstrel Show.* Chicago: Max Stein, 1921.

Russell, William Howard. *My Diary North and South.* Edited by Eugene H. Berwanger. Philadelphia: Temple University Press, 1988.

Schultz, Christian. *Travels on an Inland Voyage.* Vol. 2. New York: Isaac Riley, 1810. Reprint, Ridgewood, N.J.: Gregg Press, 1968.

Shaw, James. *Twelve Years in America.* Chicago: Poe and Hitchcock, 1867.

Sheet Music. Ste. Genevieve Collection. Western Historical Society Manuscript Collection. Missouri University of Science and Technology, Rolla, Missouri.

Sheet Music and Broadsides Collections. Center for Popular Music, Middle Tennessee State University, Murfreesboro, Tennessee.

Sheet Music Collection. Missouri History Museum, Library and Research Center, St. Louis, Missouri.

Simpson, Sarah. Letter. Louisiana and Lower Mississippi Valley Collections, Louisiana State University Libraries, Baton Rouge, Louisiana.

Singleton, Arthur. *Letters from the South and West.* Boston: Richardson and Lord, 1824.

Smith, Sol. Theatre Collection. Missouri History Museum, Library and Research Center, St. Louis, Missouri.

———. *Theatrical Management in the West and South for Thirty Years.* New York: Harper and Brothers, 1868. Reprint, New York: Benjamin Blom, 1968.

Songs for the Campaign; Union and Peace. New York: Robert M. De Witt, 1856. Peck Collection. St. Louis Mercantile Library, St. Louis, Missouri.

Spence, Thomas. *The Settler's Guide in the United States.* New York: Davis and Kent, 1862.

Stoddard, Amos. *Sketches, Historical and Descriptive, of Louisiana.* Philadelphia: Mathew Carey, 1812.

Stuart, James. *Three Years in North America.* Edinburgh: R. Cadell, 1833.

Sullivan, Edward Robert. *Rambles and Scrambles in North America.* London: Richard Bentley, 1852.

Sydnor, Charles S. *A Gentleman of the Old Natchez Region, Benjamin L. C. Wailes.* Durham, N.C.: Duke University Press, 1938.

Thomas, James. *From Tennessee Slave to St. Louis Entrepreneur: The Autobiography of James Thomas.* Edited by Loren Schweninger. Columbia: University of Missouri Press, 1984.

Thorpe, T. B. "Remembrances of the Mississippi." *Harper's New Monthly Magazine* 12 (December–May 1855–1856).

Thwaites, Reuben Gold. *Afloat on the Ohio: An Historical Pilgrimage of a Thousand Miles in a Skiff, from Redstone to Cairo.* Chicago: Way and Williams, 1897. Carbondale: Southern Illinois University Press, 1999.

———. *Early Western Travels, 1748–1846.* 32 vols. Cleveland: A. H. Clark, 1904–7.

Tocqueville, Alexis de. *Democracy in America and Two Essays on America.* Translated by Gerald E. Bevan. Vol. 2. New York: Penguin Books, 2003.

Tower, Luther Field. Diary. Louisiana and Lower Mississippi Valley Collections, Louisiana State University Libraries, Baton Rouge, Louisiana.

Trollope, Frances. *Domestic Manners of the Americans.* Edited by Donald Smalley. New York: Alfred A. Knopf, 1949.

Turnbull, Jane, and Marion Turnbull. *American Photographs.* Vol. 2. London: T. C. Newby, 1859.

"Typed Autobiography." Robyn Family Papers. Missouri History Museum, Library and Research Center, St. Louis, Missouri.

"The United States, Her Past and Her Future." *De Bow's Review* 2 (June 1852).

Vallé, Zoé. Sheet Music. Ste. Genevieve Collection, Western Historical Society Manuscript Collection, Missouri University of Science and Technology, Rolla, Missouri.

Vandenhoff, George. *Leaves from an Actor's Note-book.* New York: D. Appleton, 1860.

Varieties Theater Programs. Theater and Minnie Milne Collection. St. Louis Mercantile Library, University of Missouri St. Louis, St. Louis, Missouri.

Walker, Elijah. *A Bachelor's Life in Antebellum Mississippi: The Diary of Dr. Elijah Millington Walker, 1849–1852.* Edited by Lynette Boney Wrenn. Knoxville: University of Tennessee Press, 2004.

Walker, Enna Massey. Piano Lesson Book. Mississippi Department of Archives and History, Jackson, Mississippi.

Walker, James Barr. *Experiences of Pioneer Life in the Early Settlements and Cities of the West.* Chicago: Sumner, 1881.

"War Song of the Natives." Antebellum Period Collection. Louisiana Digital Library, Louisiana State Museum, New Orleans, Louisiana.

Water Related Sheet Music Collection. St. Louis Mercantile Library, University of Missouri St. Louis, St. Louis, Missouri.

Webster, Noah. "On the Education of Youth in America." In *Essays on Education in the Early Republic,* edited by Frederick Rudolph. Cambridge, Mass.: Harvard University Press, 1965.

Wemyss, Francis Courtney. *Twenty-Six Years of the Life of an Actor and Manager.* New York: Burgess, Stringer, 1847.

"Western Music Convention Announcement." Music Collection. Missouri History Museum Library and Research Center, St. Louis, Missouri.

Whipple, Henry Benjamin. *Bishop Whipple's Southern Diary, 1843–1844.* Edited by Lester B. Shippee. Minneapolis: University of Minnesota Press, 1937. Reprint, New York: Da Capo Press, 1968.

Whitman, Walt. "American Music, New and True." In *The Collected Writings of Walt Whitman: The Journalism, 1834–1846,* edited by Herbert Bergman. Vol. 1. New York: Peter Lang, 1998.

———. "Art-Singing and Heart-Singing." In *The Collected Writings of Walt Whitman: The Journalism, 1834–1846,* edited by Herbert Bergman. Vol. 1. New York: Peter Lang, 1998.

———. "The Hutchinson Family." In *The Collected Writings of Walt Whitman: The Journalism, 1834–1846,* edited by Herbert Bergman. Vol. 1. New York: Peter Lang, 1998.

———. "Music That IS Music." In *The Collected Writings of Walt Whitman: The Journalism, 1846–1848,* edited by Herbert Bergman. Vol. 2. New York: Peter Lang, 1998.

———. "Templeton the Singer." In *The Collected Writings of Walt Whitman: The Journalism, 1834–1846,* edited by Herbert Bergman. Vol. 1. New York: Peter Lang, 1998.

———. "A Thought of Ours about Music in the United States." In *The Collected Writings of Walt Whitman: The Journalism, 1846–1848,* edited by Herbert Bergman. Vol. 2. New York: Peter Lang, 1998.

"Who Are Our National Poets?" *Knickerbocker; or, New York Monthly Magazine* 26 (October 1845).

Wilhelm, Paul, duke of Württemberg. *Travels in North America, 1822–1824.* Edited by Savoie Lottinville. Translated by W. Robert Ninske. Norman: University of Oklahoma Press, 1973.

Wilkinson, James. *Memoirs of My Own Times.* Vol. 2. Philadelphia: Abraham Small, 1816. Reprint, New York: AMS Press, 1973.

Worley, Ted R., ed. "A Letter of Governor Miller to His Wife." *Arkansas Historical Quarterly* 13 (1954): 389–90.

Secondary Works

Abrahams, Roger D. *Deep the Water, Shallow the Shore: Three Essays on Shanty-ing in the West Indies.* Austin: University of Texas Press, 1974.

———. *Singing the Master: The Emergence of African-American Culture in the Plantation South.* New York: Penguin Books, 1993.

Abrahams, Roger D., Nick Spitzer, John F. Szwed, and Robert Farris Thompson. *Blues for New Orleans: Mardi Gras and America's Creole Soul.* Philadelphia: University of Pennsylvania Press, 2006.

Allain, Mathé, and Adele Cornay St. Martin. "French Theatre in Louisiana." In *Ethnic Theatre in the United States,* edited by Maxine Schwartz Seller. Westport, Conn.: Greenwood Press, 1983.

Allen, Michael. "'Row Boatmen Row!' Songs of the Early Ohio and Mississippi Rivermen." *Gateway Heritage* 14 (Winter 1993–94): 46–59.

———. *Western Rivermen, 1763–1861: Ohio and Mississippi Boatmen and the Myth of the Alligator Horse.* Baton Rouge: Louisiana State University Press, 1990.

Ancelet, Barry Jean. *Cajun Music: Its Origins and Development.* Lafayette, La.: Center for Louisiana Studies, University of Southwest Louisiana, 1989.

Anderson, Benedict. *Imagined Communities: Reflections on the Origin and Spread of Nationalism.* Rev. ed. New York: Verso, 1991.

Appleby, Joyce. *Inheriting the Revolution: The First Generation of Americans.* Cambridge, Mass.: Harvard University Press, 2000.

Arnold, Morris S. *Colonial Arkansas, 1686–1804: A Social and Cultural History.* Fayetteville: University of Arkansas Press, 1991.

———. *The Rumble of a Distant Drum: The Quapaws and Old World Newcomers, 1673–1804.* Fayetteville: University of Arkansas Press, 2000.

Aron, Stephen. *American Confluence: The Missouri Frontier from Borderland to Border State.* Bloomington: Indiana University Press, 2006.

Arrington, Golden Alwyn. "Nationalism and American Music, 1790–1815." Ph.D. diss., University of Texas Austin, 1969.

Austin, William W. *"Susanna," "Jeanie," and "The Old Folks at Home": The Songs of Stephen C. Foster from His Time to Ours.* New York: Macmillan, 1975.

Ayers, Edward L., Patricia Nelson Limerick, Stephen Nissenbaum, and Peter S. Onuf. *All Over the Map: Rethinking American Regions.* Baltimore: Johns Hopkins University Press, 1996.

Baer, Friederike. *The Trial of Frederick Eberle: Language, Patriotism, and Citizenship in Philadelphia's German Community, 1790–1830.* New York: New York University Press, 2008.

Bailey, Ben E. "Music in Slave Era Mississippi." *Journal of Mississippi History* 54 (February 1992): 29–58.

Bailey, Richard W. "The Foundation of English in the Louisiana Purchase: New Orleans, 1800–1850." *American Speech* 78 (Winter 2003): 363–84.

Baldwin, Leland D. *The Keelboat Age on Western Waters*. Pittsburgh: University of Pittsburgh Press, 1941.

Bank, Rosemarie K. *Theatre Culture in America, 1825–1860*. Cambridge, Mass.: Cambridge University Press, 1997.

Baron, John H. "Paul Emile Johns of New Orleans: Tycoon, Musician, and Friend of Chopin." *Report of the Congress of the International Musicological Society* 11 (1972): 246–50.

Barrett, James R. "Americanization from the Bottom Up: Immigration and the Remaking of the Working Class in the United States, 1880–1930." *Journal of American History* 79 (December 1992): 996–1020.

Barth, Fredrik. *Ethnic Groups and Boundaries: The Social Organization of Cultural Difference*. Boston: Little, Brown, 1969.

Bassett, T. D. Seymour. "Minstrels, Musicians, and Melodeons: A Study in the Social History of Music in Vermont, 1848–1872." *New England Quarterly* 19 (March 1946): 32–49.

Bauer, Ralph, and José Antonio Mazzotti, eds. *Creole Subjects in the Colonial Americas: Empires, Texts, Identities*. Chapel Hill: University of North Carolina Press, 2009.

Baughman, James P. "A Southern Spa: Ante-Bellum Lake Pontchartrain." *Louisiana History* 3 (Winter 1962): 5–32.

Bauman, Richard, Roger D. Abrahams, and Susan Kalcik. "American Folklore and American Studies." *American Quarterly* 28 (1976): 360–77.

Bean, Annemarie, James V. Hatch, and Brooks McNamara, eds. *Inside the Minstrel Mask: Readings in Nineteenth-Century Blackface Minstrelsy*. Hanover, N.H.: Wesleyan University Press, 1996.

Béhague, Gerard H., ed. *Music and Black Ethnicity: The Caribbean and South America*. Coral Gables, Fla.: North-South Center Press, 1994.

Bell, Caryn Cossé. *Revolution, Romanticism, and the Afro-Creole Protest Tradition in Louisiana, 1718–1868*. Baton Rouge: Louisiana State University Press, 1997.

Bendix, Regina. *In Search of Authenticity: The Formation of Folklore Studies*. Madison: University of Wisconsin Press, 1997.

Benes, Peter, ed. *New England Music: The Public Sphere, 1600–1900*. Boston: Boston University, 1998.

Bennett, Michael J. "'Frictions': Shipboard Relations between White and Contraband Sailors." *Civil War History* 47 (June 2001): 118–45.

Bercovitch, Sacvan. *The Rites of Assent: Transformations in the Symbolic Construction of America*. New York: Routledge, 1993.

Bergeron, Paul H., Stephen V. Ash, and Jeanette Keith. *Tennesseans and Their History*. Knoxville: University of Tennessee Press, 1999.

Berkeley, Kathleen C. *"Like a Plague of Locusts": From an Antebellum Town to a New South City, Memphis Tennessee, 1850–1880*. New York: Garland, 1991.

Berlin, Ira, and Herbert Gutman. "Natives and Immigrants, Free Men and

Slaves: Urban Workingmen in the Antebellum South." *American Historical Review* 88 (December 1983): 1175–1200.

Bernard, Kenneth. *Lincoln and the Music of the Civil War*. Caldwell, Id.: Caxton, 1966.

Bernard, Shane, and Julia Girouard. "'Colinda': Mysterious Origins of a Cajun Folksong." *Journal of Folklore Research* 29 (1992): 37–52.

Berthold, Dennis. "Class Act: The Astor Place Riots and Melville's 'The Two Temples.'" *American Literature* 71 (September 1999): 429–61.

Berwanger, Eugene H. *The Frontier against Slavery: Western Anti-Negro Prejudice and the Slavery Extension Controversy*. Urbana: University of Illinois Press, 1967.

Beveridge, Albert J. *Abraham Lincoln, 1809–1858*. Vol. 1. New York: Houghton Mifflin, 1928.

Biddle, Ian, and Vanessa Knights, eds. *Music, National Identity, and the Politics of Location: Between the Global and the Local*. Burlington, Vt.: Ashgate, 2007.

Bigham, Darrel. *On Jordan's Banks: Emancipation and Its Aftermath in the Ohio River Valley*. Lexington: University Press of Kentucky, 2006.

———. *Towns and Villages of the Lower Ohio*. Lexington: University Press of Kentucky, 1998.

Biles, Roger. *Illinois: A History of the Land and Its People*. DeKalb: Northern Illinois University Press, 2005.

Blair, Walter, and Franklin J. Meine. *Mink Fink: King of the Mississippi Keelboatmen*. New York: Henry Holt and Company, 1933.

Blassingame, John W. *Black New Orleans, 1860–1880*. Chicago: University of Chicago Press, 1973.

Blume, Helmut. *The German Coast during the Colonial Era, 1772–1803*. Translated and edited by Ellen C. Merrill. Destrehan, La.: German and Acadian Coast Historical and Genealogical Society, 1990.

Bode, Carl. *The Anatomy of Popular Culture, 1840–1861*. Berkeley: University of California Press, 1959.

Bogner, Harold F. "Sir Walter Scott in New Orleans, 1818–1832." *Louisiana Historical Quarterly* 21 (January 1938): 443–56.

Bolster, W. Jeffrey. *Black Jacks: African American Seamen in the Age of Sail*. Cambridge, Mass.: Harvard University Press, 1997.

Bolton, S. Charles. *Arkansas, 1800–1860: Remote and Restless*. Fayetteville: University of Arkansas Press, 1998.

Borders, Florence E. "Researching Creole and Cajun Musics in New Orleans." *Black Music Research Journal* 8 (1988): 15–31.

Botkin, B. A., ed. *A Treasury of Mississippi River Folklore*. New York: Crown, 1955.

Boudreaux, Peggy C. "Music Publishing in New Orleans in the Nineteenth Century." Master's thesis, Louisiana State University, 1977.

Brady, Joe. "The Irish Community in Antebellum Memphis." *West Tennessee Historical Society Papers* 40 (1986): 45–54.

Brandon, Elizabeth. "The Socio-Cultural Traits of the French Folksong in Louisiana." *Revue de Louisiane* 1 (1972): 19–52.

Brasseaux, Carl A. *Acadian to Cajun: Transformation of a People, 1803–1877.* Jackson: University Press of Mississippi, 1992.

———. *The Founding of New Acadia: The Beginnings of Acadian Life in Louisiana, 1765–1803.* Baton Rouge: Louisiana State University Press, 1987.

———. *French, Cajun, Creole, Houma: A Primer on Francophone Louisiana.* Baton Rouge: Louisiana State University Press, 2005.

———, comp. *The "Foreign French": Nineteenth Century French Immigration into Louisiana.* Lafayette: Center for Louisiana Studies, 1990.

Brasseaux, Carl A., and Glenn R. Conrad, eds. *The Road to Louisiana: The Saint-Domingue Refugees, 1792–1809.* Lafayette: Center for Louisiana Studies, University of Southwestern Louisiana, 1992.

Brasseaux, Carl A., and Keith P. Fontenot. *Steamboats on Louisiana's Bayous: A History and Directory.* Baton Rouge: Louisiana State University Press, 2004.

Brasseaux, Carl A., Keith P. Fontenot, and Claude F. Oubre. *Creoles of Color in the Bayou Country.* Jackson: University Press of Mississippi, 1994.

Briggs, Harold E. "Entertainment and Amusement in Cairo, 1848–1858." *Journal of the Illinois State Historical Society* 47 (Autumn 1954): 231–51.

———. "Lawlessness in Cairo, Illinois 1848–1858." *Mid-America: An Historical Review* 33 (April 1951): 67–88.

Brinkley, Douglas, and Stephen Ambrose. *The Mississippi and the Making of a Nation: From the Louisiana Purchase to Today.* Washington, D.C.: National Geographic, 2002.

Broven, John. *South to Louisiana: The Music of the Cajun Bayous.* Gretna, La.: Pelican, 1983.

Brown, Cecil. *Stagolee Shot Billy.* Cambridge, Mass.: Harvard University Press, 2003.

Brown, Sterling. "Negro Folk Expression: Spirituals, Seculars, Ballads, and Work Songs." *Phylon* 14 (1953): 45–61.

Bryant, James C. "The Fallen World in *Nick of the Woods*." *American Literature* 38 (November 1966): 352–64.

Buchanan, Thomas C. *Black Life on the Mississippi: Slaves, Free Blacks, and the Western Steamboat World.* Chapel Hill: University of North Carolina Press, 2004.

———. "Rascals on the Antebellum Mississippi: African American Steamboat Workers and the St. Louis Hanging of 1841." *Journal of Social History* 34 (Summer 2001): 797–816.

Budick, Emily Miller. *Nineteenth-Century American Romance: Genre and the Construction of Democratic Culture.* New York: Twayne, 1996.

Buisseret, David, and Steven G. Reinhardt, eds. *Creolization in the Americas.* College Station: Texas A&M University Press, 2000.

Busch, Jason T., Christopher P. Monkhouse, and Janet L. Whitmore. *Currents of Change: Art and Life along the Mississippi River, 1850–1861.* Minneapolis: Minneapolis Institute of Arts, 2004.

Butler, Ben E. "Music in Slave Era Mississippi." *Journal of Mississippi History* 54 (February 1992): 29–58.

Butsch, Richard. "Bowery B'hoys and Matinee Lades: The Re-Gendering of Nineteenth-Century American Theater Audiences." *American Quarterly* 46 (September 1994): 374–405.

Cade, John B. "Out of the Mouths of Ex-Slaves." *Journal of Negro History* 20 (July 1935): 294–337.

Cale, John Gustav. "French Secular Music in Saint-Domingue, 1750–1795: Viewed as a Factor in America's Musical Growth." Ph.D. diss., Louisiana State University, 1971.

Callahan, Richard, ed. *New Territories, New Perspectives: The Religious Impact of the Louisiana Purchase.* Columbia: University of Missouri Press, 2008.

Capers, Gerald M., Jr. *The Biography of a River Town, Memphis: Its Heroic Age.* Chapel Hill: University of North Carolina Press, 1939.

Carlyon, David. *Dan Rice: The Most Famous Man You've Never Heard Of.* New York: Public Affairs, 2001.

Carmer, Carl, ed. *Songs of the Rivers of America.* New York: Farrar and Rinehart, 1942.

Carney, George O., ed. *The Sounds of People and Places: Readings in the Geography of Music.* Washington, D.C.: University Press of America, 1978.

Carson, James Taylor. *Searching for the Bright Path: The Mississippi Choctaws from Prehistory to Removal.* Lincoln: University of Nebraska Press, 1999.

Carter, Hodding. *Lower Mississippi.* New York: Farrar and Rinehart, 1942.

Cayton, Andrew R. L. Review of *In the Midst of Perpetual Fetes: The Making of American Nationalism, 1776–1820,* by David Waldstreicher. *Journal of the Early Republic* 1 (Fall 1998): 521–28.

Cecelski, David S. *The Waterman's Song: Slavery and Freedom in Maritime North Carolina.* Chapel Hill: University of North Carolina Press, 2001.

Chapman, Margaret Sue. "Literature and the Drama in Memphis, Tennessee, to 1860." Master's thesis, Duke University, 1942.

Charosh, Paul. "'Popular' and 'Classical' in the Mid-Nineteenth Century." *American Music* 10 (Summer 1992): 117–35.

———. "Studying Nineteenth-Century Popular Song." *American Music* 15 (Winter 1997): 459–92.

Chase, Gilbert. *America's Music, from the Pilgrims to the Present.* 3rd ed. Urbana: University of Illinois Press, 1987.

———. "American Music and American Musicology." *Journal of Musicology* 1 (January 1982): 59–62.

Chindahl, George L. *A History of the Circus in America.* Caldwell, Id.: Caxton, 1959.

Chmaj, Betty E. "Fry Versus Dwight: American Music's Debate over Nationality." *American Music* 3 (Spring 1985): 63–84.

Cimbala, Paul A. "Black Musicians from Slavery to Freedom: An Exploration of an African-American Folk Elite and Cultural Continuity in the Nineteenth-Century Rural South." *Journal of Negro History* 80 (Winter 1995): 15–29.

Clark, Robert T. "The German Liberals in New Orleans." *Louisiana Historical Quarterly* 20 (January 1937): 137–51.

Cliff, Nigel. *The Shakespeare Riots: Revenge, Drama, and Death in Nineteenth-Century America.* New York: Random House, 2007.

Clifford, James. *The Predicament of Culture: Twentieth-Century Ethnography, Literature, and Art.* Cambridge, Mass.: Harvard University Press, 1988.

Clifford, James, and George E. Marcus, eds. *Writing Culture: The Poetics and Politics of Ethnography.* Berkeley: University of California Press, 1986.

Cobb, James C. *Away Down South: A History of Southern Identity.* New York: Oxford University Press, 2005.

——. *The Most Southern Place on Earth: The Mississippi Delta and the Roots of Regional Identity.* New York: Oxford University Press, 1992.

Cockrell, Dale. "Callithumpians, Mummers, Maskers, and Minstrels: Blackface in the Streets of Jacksonian America." *Theatre Annual* 49 (1996): 1–20.

——. "Jim Crow, Demon of Disorder." *American Music* 14 (Summer 1996): 161–84.

Cohen, David, and Ben Greenwood. *The Buskers: A History of Street Entertainment.* North Pomfret, Vt.: David and Charles, 1981.

Cohen, Lester H. *The Revolutionary Histories: Contemporary Narratives of the American Revolution.* Ithaca, N.Y.: Cornell University Press, 1980.

Cohen, Norm. *Folk Music: A Regional Exploration.* Westport, Conn.: Greenwood Press, 2005.

——, ed. *Ethnic and Border Music: A Regional Exploration.* Westport, Conn.: Greenwood Press, 2007.

Colcord, Joanna Carver, comp. *Songs of American Sailormen.* New York: W. W. Norton, 1938.

Colley, Linda. *Britons: Forging the Nation, 1707–1837.* New Haven, Conn.: Yale University Press, 2005.

Comeaux, Malcolm L. "Impact of Transportation Activities upon the Historical Development of Cairo, Illinois." Master's thesis, Southern Illinois University, 1966.

Conrad, Glenn R., ed. *A Dictionary of Louisiana Biography.* New Orleans: Louisiana Historical Association, 1988.

Conzen, Michael P. "American Homelands: A Dissenting View." In *Homelands: A Geography of Culture and Place across America*, edited by Richard L. Nostrand and Lawrence E. Estaville. Baltimore: Johns Hopkins University Press, 2001.

Coolen, Michael Theodore. "The Fodet: A Senegambian Origin for the Blues?" *Black Perspective in Music* 10 (Spring 1982): 69–81.

Cornelius, Janet Duitsman. *Slave Missions and the Black Church in the Antebellum South*. Columbia: University of South Carolina Press, 1999.

Cornelius, Steven. *Music of the Civil War Era*. Westport, Conn.: Greenwood Press, 2004.

Costonis, Maureen Needham. "The American Career of Jean Baptiste Francisqui, 1793–1808." *Bulletin of Research in the Humanities* 85 (Winter 1982): 430–42.

———. "Ballet Comes to America, 1792–1842: French Contributions to the Establishment of Theatrical Dance in New Orleans and Philadelphia." Ph.D. diss., New York University, 1989.

———. "The War of the Quadrilles: Creoles vs. Americans, 1804." *Bulletin of Research in the Humanities* 87 (1986–87): 63–81.

Cox, John D. *Traveling South: Travel Narratives and the Construction of American Identity*. Athens: University of Georgia Press, 2005.

Crawford, Richard. *The American Musical Landscape*. Berkeley: University of California Press, 1993.

———. *America's Musical Life: A History*. New York: W. W. Norton, 2001.

———. "Musical Learning in Nineteenth-Century America." *American Music* 1 (Spring 1983): 1–11.

Cremin, Lawrence A. *American Education: The National Experience, 1783–1876*. New York: Harper and Row, 1980.

Crété, Lilian. *Daily Life in Louisiana, 1815–1830*. Translated by Patrick Gregory. Baton Rouge: Louisiana State University Press, 1981.

Crew, Danny O. *Ku Klux Klan Sheet Music: An Illustrated Catalogue of Published Music, 1867–2002*. Jefferson, N.C.: McFarland, 2003.

Cripe, Helen. *Thomas Jefferson and Music*. Charlottesville: University Press of Virginia, 1974.

Cruz, Jon. *Culture on the Margins: The Black Spiritual and the Rise of American Cultural Interpretation*. Princeton, N.J.: Princeton University Press, 1999.

Cummins, Light Townsend, and Glen Jeansonne, eds. *A Guide to the History of Louisiana*. Westport, Conn.: Greenwood Press, 1982.

Curran, Thomas. "Assimilation and Nativism." *International Migration Digest* 3 (Spring 1966): 15–25.

Curry, Leonard P. *The Free Black in Urban America, 1800–1850: The Shadow of a Dream*. Chicago: University of Chicago Press, 1981.

———. "Urbanization and Urbanism in the Old South: A Comparative View." *Journal of Southern History* 40 (February 1974): 43–60.

Curtis, Robert R. "Enterprise and Life in Early Cairo." Master's thesis, Southern Illinois University, 1950.

Dahl, Curtis. "Artemus Ward: Comic Panoramist." *New England Quarterly* 32 (December 1959): 476–85.

———. "Mark Twain and Moving Panoramas." *American Quarterly* 13 (Spring 1961): 20–32.

Dain, Bruce. *A Hideous Monster of the Mind: American Race Theory in the Early Republic.* Cambridge, Mass.: Harvard University Press, 2002.

Davenport, F. Garvin. "Cultural Life in Nashville on the Eve of the Civil War." *Journal of Southern History* 3 (August 1937): 326–47.

Davis, Alva L., and Raven I. McDavid, Jr. "'Shivaree': An Example of Cultural Diffusion." *American Speech* 24 (December 1949): 249–55.

Davis, Janet M. *The Circus Age: Culture and Society under the American Big Top.* Chapel Hill: University of North Carolina Press, 2002.

Davis, Natalie Zemon. "Printing and the People." In *Rethinking Popular Culture: Contemporary Perspectives in Cultural Studies,* edited by Chandra Mukerji and Michael Schudson. Berkeley: University of California Press, 1991.

Davis, Susan G. *Parades and Power: Street Theatre in Nineteenth-Century Philadelphia.* Philadelphia: Temple University Press, 1986.

Dawdy, Shannon Lee. *Building the Devil's Empire: French Colonial New Orleans.* Chicago: University of Chicago Press, 2008.

Deiler, J. Hanno. *A History of the German Churches in Louisiana, (1823–1893).* Edited and translated by Marie Stella Condon. Lafayette: Center for Louisiana Studies, University of Southwestern Louisiana, 1983.

———. *The Settlement of the German Coast of Louisiana and the Creoles of German Descent.* Philadelphia: Americana Germanica Press, 1909.

Dennis, Matthew. *Red, White, and Blue Letter Days: An American Calendar.* Ithaca, N.Y.: Cornell University Press, 2002.

Dennison, Sam. *Scandalize My Name: Black Imagery in American Popular Music.* New York: Garland, 1982.

Desdunes, Rodolphe Lucien. *Our People and Our History.* Translated and edited by Sister Dorothea Olga McCants. Baton Rouge: Louisiana State University Press, 1973.

Dessens, Nathalie. *From Saint-Domingue to New Orleans: Migration and Influences.* Gainesville: University Press of Florida, 2007.

Deyle, Steven. *Carry Me Back: The Domestic Slave Trade in American Life.* New York: Oxford University Press, 2005.

Dichter, Harry, and Elliot Shapiro. *Early American Sheet Music: Its Lure and Its Lore, 1768–1889.* New York: R. R. Bowker, 1941.

Dick, Everett. *The Dixie Frontier: A Social History of the Southern Frontier.* New York: A. A. Knopf, 1949. Reprint, Norman: University of Oklahoma Press, 1993.

Dickey, Judy Ruth. "The Music of a Louisiana Plantation Family, 1814–1874." Master's thesis, Louisiana State University, 1968.

Dillard, J. L. *All-American English.* New York: Random House, 1975.

Dizikes, John. *Opera in America: A Cultural History.* New Haven, Conn.: Yale University Press, 1993.

Dominguez, Virginia R. *White by Definition: Social Classification in Creole Louisiana.* New Brunswick, N.J.: Rutgers University Press, 1986.

Donaldson, Gary A. "A Window on Slave Culture: Dances at Congo Square in New Orleans, 1800–1862." *Journal of Negro History* 69 (Spring 1984): 63–72.

Doorley, Michael. "Irish Catholics and French Creoles: Ethnic Struggles within the Catholic Church in New Orleans, 1835–1920." *Catholic Historical Review* 87 (January 2001): 34–54.

Dormon, James H. "The Persistent Specter: Slave Rebellion in Territorial Louisiana." *Louisiana History* 18 (Fall 1977): 389–404.

———. *Theater in the Ante Bellum South, 1815–1861.* Chapel Hill: University of North Carolina Press, 1967.

———, ed. *Creoles of Color of the Gulf South.* Knoxville: University of Tennessee Press, 1996.

Dorson, Richard M. "American Folklore vs. Folklore in America." *Journal of Folklore Institute* 15 (May 1978): 97–111.

Dougherty, James P. Review of *Literary Democracy: The Declaration of Cultural Independence in America*, by Larzer Ziff. *Review of Politics* 45 (July 1983): 472–75.

Draper, David E. "Abba isht tuluwa: The Christian Hymns of the Mississippi Choctaw." *American Indian Culture and Research Journal* 6 (1982): 43–61.

Dunbar, Tony. *Delta Time: A Journey through Mississippi.* New York: Pantheon Books, 1990.

Dunbar-Nelson, Alice Moore. "People of Color in Louisiana." In *Creole: The History and Legacy of Louisiana's Free People of Color*, edited by Sybil Kein. Baton Rouge: Louisiana State University Press, 2000.

During, Simon. *The Cultural Studies Reader.* New York: Routledge, 1993.

Dvorak, Katherine L. *An African-American Exodus: The Segregation of the Southern Churches.* Brooklyn, N.Y.: Carlson, 1991.

Eastman, Carolyn. *A Nation of Speechifiers: Making an American Public after the Revolution.* Chicago: University of Chicago Press, 2009.

Ekberg, Carl J. *Colonial Ste. Genevieve: An Adventure on the Mississippi Frontier.* Gerald, Mo.: Patrice Press, 1985.

Elson, Louis Charles. *The National Music of America and Its Sources.* Rev. ed. Boston: L. C. Page, 1924.

Emerson, Ken. *Doo Dah! Stephen Foster and the Rise of American Popular Culture.* New York: Simon and Schuster, 1997.

Emery, Lynn Fauley. *Black Dance in the United States from 1619 to 1970.* Palo Alto, Calif.: National Press Books, 1972.

Epstein, Dena J. "African Music in British and French America." *Musical Quarterly* 59 (January 1973): 61–91.

———. "The Folk Banjo: A Documentary History." *Ethnomusicology* 19 (September 1975): 347–71.

———. *Sinful Tunes and Spirituals: Black Folk Music to the Civil War.* Urbana: University of Illinois Press, 1977.

———. "Slave Music in the United States Before 1860: A Survey of Sources (Part I)." *Music Library Association Notes* 20 (Spring 1963): 195–212.

———. "Slave Music in the United States Before 1860: A Survey of Sources (Part 2)." *Music Library Association Notes* 20 (Summer 1963): 377–90.

Eskew, Harry. "German Contributions to the Musical Culture of New Orleans." *Southern Quarterly* 27 (Winter 1989): 25–39.

Etzkorn, K. Peter. "Georg Simmel and the Sociology of Music." *Social Forces* 43 (October 1964): 101–7.

Everett, Donald E. "Ben Butler and the Louisiana Native Guards, 1861–1862." *Journal of Southern History* 24 (May 1958): 202–17.

Fahs, Alice. *The Imagined Civil War: Popular Literature of the North and South, 1861–1865*. Chapel Hill: University of North Carolina Press, 2001.

Feldman, Jay. *When the Mississippi Ran Backwards: Empire, Intrigue, Murder, and the New Madrid Earthquakes*. New York: Free Press, 2005.

Ferguson, James Smith. "A History of Music in Vicksburg, Mississippi, 1820–1900." Ph.D. diss., University of Michigan, 1970.

Ferris, William, and Mary L. Hart, eds. *Folk Music and Modern Sound*. Jackson: University Press of Mississippi, 1982.

Fiehrer, Thomas. "From Quadrille to Stomp: The Creole Origins of Jazz." *Popular Music* 10 (January 1991): 21–38.

Finson, Jon W. "The Romantic Savage: American Indians in the Parlor." *Journal of Musicological Research* 13 (1993): 203–33.

———. *The Voices That Are Gone: Themes in Nineteenth-Century American Popular Song*. New York: Oxford University Press, 1994.

Foote, Stephanie. *Regional Fictions: Culture and Identity in Nineteenth-Century American Literature*. Madison: University of Wisconsin Press, 2001.

Foster, A. Kristen. *Moral Visions and Material Ambitions: Philadelphia Struggles to Define the Republic, 1776–1836*. Lanham, Md.: Lexington Books, 2004.

Fouchard, Jean. *Le Théâtre a Saint-Domingue*. Port-au-Prince, Haiti: H. Deschamps, 1988.

Free, Joseph Miller. "The Theatre of Southwestern Mississippi to 1840." Ph.D. diss., State University of Iowa, 1941.

Frink, Sandra Margaret. "Spectacles of the Street: Performance, Power, and Public Space in Antebellum New Orleans." Ph.D. diss., University of Texas, Austin, 2004.

Frith, Simon. *Sound Effects: Youth, Leisure, and the Politics of Rock 'n' Roll*. New York: Pantheon Books, 1981.

Frost, Linda. *Never One Nation: Freaks, Savages, and Whiteness in U.S. Popular Culture, 1850–1877*. Minneapolis: University of Minnesota Press, 2005.

Furstenberg, François. "The Significance of the Trans-Appalachian Frontier in Atlantic History." *American Historical Review* (June 2008): 647–77.

Gabacia, Donna R. "Is Everywhere Nowhere? Nomads, Nations, and the Immigrant Paradigm of United States History." *Journal of American History* (December 1999): 1115–34.

Gac, Scott. *Singing for Freedom: The Hutchinson Family Singers and the Nineteenth-Century Culture of Reform.* New Haven, Conn.: Yale University Press, 2007.

Garrett, Charles Hiroshi. *Struggling to Define a Nation: American Music and the Twentieth Century.* Berkeley: University of California Press, 2008.

Gayarré, Charles. *History of Louisiana.* 4th ed. New Orleans: F. F. Hansell and Brothers, 1903.

Geertz, Clifford. *The Interpretation of Cultures: Selected Essays.* New York: Basic Books, 1973.

Gillespie, Michael. *Come Hell or High Water: A Lively History of Steamboating on the Mississippi and Ohio Rivers.* Stoddard, Wisc.: Heritage Press, 2001.

Gilroy, Paul. *The Black Atlantic: Modernity and Double Consciousness.* Cambridge, Mass.: Harvard University Press, 1993.

———. "Sounds Authentic: Black Music, Ethnicity, and the Challenge of a *Changing* Same." *Black Music Research Journal* 11 (Fall 1991): 111–36.

Glass, Barbara S. *African American Dance: An Illustrated History.* Jefferson, N.C.: McFarland, 2007.

Glazer, Nathan. "Is Assimilation Dead?" *Annals of the American Academy of Political and Social Science* 530 (November 1993): 122–36.

Gleeson, David T. *The Irish in the South, 1815–1877.* Chapel Hill: University of North Carolina Press, 2001.

Goldfield, David R. "The Urban South: A Regional Framework." *American Historical Review* 86 (December 1981): 1009–34.

Gomez, Michael A. *Exchanging Our Country Marks: The Transformation of African Identities in the Colonial and Antebellum South.* Chapel Hill: University of North Carolina Press, 1998.

Gould, E. W. *Fifty Years on the Mississippi; or, Gould's History of River Navigation.* St. Louis: Nixon Jones, 1889. Reprint, Columbus, Ohio: Long's College Book Co., 1951.

Gould, Virginia Meacham. *Chained to the Rock of Adversity: To Be Free, Black and Female in the Old South.* Athens: University of Georgia Press, 1998.

———. "In Full Enjoyment of Their Liberty: The Free Women of Color of the Gulf Ports of New Orleans, Mobile, and Pensacola, 1769–1860." Ph.D. diss., Emory University, 1991.

Graham, Philip. *Showboats: The History of an American Institution.* Austin: University of Texas Press, 1951.

Gramsci, Antonio. *Selections from Cultural Writings.* Edited by David Forgacs and Geoffrey Nowell-Smith. Translated by William Boelhower. Cambridge, Mass.: Harvard University Press, 1985.

Grant, Susan-Mary. *North Over South: Northern Nationalism and American Identity in the Antebellum Era.* Lawrence: University Press of Kansas, 2000.

Greene, Victor. *A Singing Ambivalence: American Immigrants between Old World and New, 1830–1930*. Kent, Ohio: Kent State University Press, 2004.

Greenfeld, Liah. "The Origins and Nature of American Nationalism in Comparative Perspective." In *The American Nation, National Identity, Nationalism*, edited by Knud Krakau. New Brunswick, N.J.: Transaction, 1997.

Grimes, Robert R. *How Shall We Sing in a Foreign Land? Music of Irish Catholic Immigrants in the Antebellum United States*. Notre Dame, Ind.: University of Notre Dame, 1996.

Grimsted, David. *Melodrama Unveiled: American Theater and Culture, 1800–1850*. Chicago: University of Chicago Press, 1968.

Grob, Gerald N., and George Athan Billias, eds. *Interpretations of American History: Patterns and Perspectives*. Vol. 1. New York: Free Press, 1992.

Gruver, Rebecca Brooks, comp. *American Nationalism, 1783–1830: A Self Portrait*. New York: G. P. Putnam's Sons, 1970.

Guice, John D. W. "Face to Face in Mississippi Territory, 1789–1817." In *The Choctaw before Removal*, edited by Carolyn Keller Reeves. Jackson: University of Mississippi Press, 1985.

Guion, David M. "Felippe Cioffi: A Trombonist in Antebellum America." *American Music* 14 (Spring 1996): 1–41.

Gushee, Lawrence. "Black Professional Musicians in New Orleans c. 1880." *Inter-American Music Review* 11 (1991): 53–63.

———. "The Nineteenth-Century Origins of Jazz." *Black Music Research Journal* 14 (Spring 1994): 1–24.

Hackett, Mary A., ed. *The Papers of James Madison*. Vol. 8. Charlottesville: University of Virginia Press, 2007.

Hall, Gwendolyn Midlo. *Africans in Colonial Louisiana: The Development of Afro-Creole Culture in the Eighteenth Century*. Baton Rouge: Louisiana State University Press, 1992.

———. *Slavery and African Ethnicities in the Americas: Restoring the Links*. Chapel Hill: University of North Carolina Press, 2005.

Hamilton, William B. "The Southwestern Frontier, 1795–1817: An Essay in Social History." *Journal of Southern History* 10 (November 1944): 389–403.

———. "The Theater in the Old Southwest the First Decade at Natchez." *American Literature* 12 (January 1941): 471–85.

Hamm, Charles. *Yesterdays: Popular Song in America*. New York: Norton, 1979.

Hanger, Kimberly S. *Bounded Lives, Bounded Places: Free Black Society in Colonial New Orleans, 1769–1803*. Durham, N.C.: Duke University Press, 1997.

Hanley, Miles. "Charivaria: Serenade in New England." *American Speech* 8 (1933): 24–26.

Harrison, Lowell H. *Kentucky's Road to Statehood*. Lexington: University Press of Kentucky, 1992.

Hatch, Christopher. "Music for America: A Critical Controversy of the 1850s." *American Quarterly* 14 (Winter 1962): 578–86.

Hatfield, Joseph T. *William Claiborne: Jeffersonian Centurion in the American Southwest.* Lafayette: University of Southwestern Louisiana, 1976.

Havinghurst, Walter. *River to the West: Three Centuries of the Ohio.* New York: G. P. Putnam's Sons, 1970.

Hays, Christopher. "The Afro-American Struggle for Equality and Justice in Cairo, Illinois, 1865–1900." *Illinois Historical Journal* 90 (Winter 1997): 265–84.

———. "Way Down in Egypt Land: Conflict and Community in Cairo Illinois, 1850–1910." Ph.D. diss., University of Missouri, Columbia, 1996.

Hearn, Lafcadio. *Children of the Levee.* Lexington: University of Kentucky Press, 1957.

Heintze, James R. *Early American Music: A Research and Information Guide.* New York: Garland, 1990.

———, ed. *American Musical Life in Context and Practice to 1865.* New York: Garland, 1994.

Hill, Henry Bertram, and Larry Gara. "A French Traveler's View of Ante-Bellum New Orleans." *Louisiana History* 1 (Autumn 1960): 335–41.

Hitchcock, H. Wiley. *American Music before 1865 in Print and on Records: A Biblio-Discography.* Brooklyn: Institute for the Study of American Music, City University of New York, 1976.

Hobsbawm, Eric, and Terence Ranger, eds. *The Invention of Tradition.* New York: Cambridge University Press, 1983.

Hodge, Francis. *Yankee Theatre: The Image of America on the Stage, 1825–1850.* Austin: University of Texas Press, 1964.

Hoffman, Ronald, Mechal Sobel, and Fredrika J. Teute, eds. *Through a Glass Darkly: Reflections on Personal Identity in Early America.* Chapel Hill: University of North Carolina Press, 1997.

Holmberg, Carl Bryan, and Gilbert D. Schneider. "Daniel Decatur Emmett's Stump Sermons: Genuine Afro-American Culture, Language and Rhetoric in the Negro Minstrel Show." *Journal of Popular Culture* 19 (Spring 1986): 27–38.

Holmes, Jack D. L. *Gayoso: The Life of a Spanish Governor in the Mississippi Valley, 1789–1799.* Baton Rouge: Louisiana State University Press, 1965.

Horn, David. *The Literature of American Music in Books and Folk Music Collections: A Fully Annotated Bibliography.* Metuchen, N.J.: Scarecrow Press, 1977.

Housewright, Wiley L. *A History of Music and Dance in Florida, 1565–1865.* Tuscaloosa: University of Alabama Press, 1991.

Howard, John Tasker. *Our American Music: Three Hundred Years of It.* Rev. 3rd ed. New York: Thomas Y. Crowell, 1946.

Hudson, Arthur Palmer. *Folksongs of the Mississippi and Their Background: A Study with Texts.* Chapel Hill: University of North Carolina Press, 1936.

Hurt, R. Douglas. *The Indian Frontier, 1763-1846*. Albuquerque: University of New Mexico Press, 2002.

Ignatiev, Noel. *How the Irish Became White*. New York: Routledge, 1995.

Jacobson, Matthew Frye. *Whiteness of a Different Color: European Immigrants and the Alchemy of Race*. Cambridge, Mass.: Harvard University Press, 1998.

James, D. Clayton. *Antebellum Natchez*. Baton Rouge: Louisiana State University Press, 1968.

James, Larry M. "Biracial Fellowship in Antebellum Baptist Churches." In *Masters and Slaves in the House of the Lord: Race and Religion in the American South, 1740-1870*, edited by John B. Boles. Lexington: University Press of Kentucky, 1988.

Jerde, Curtis D. "Black Music in New Orleans: A Historical Overview." *Black Music Research Journal* 10 (Spring 1990): 18-24.

Johnson, Charles. "The Frontier Camp Meeting: Contemporary and Historical Appraisals, 1805-1840." *Mississippi Valley Historical Review* 37 (June 1950): 91-110.

Johnson, Jerah. "Colonial New Orleans: A Fragment of the Eighteenth-Century French Ethos." In *Creole New Orleans: Race and Americanization*, edited by Arnold R. Hirsch and Joseph Logsdon. Baton Rouge: Louisiana State University Press, 1992.

———. "New Orleans's Congo Square: An Urban Setting for Early Afro-American Cultural Formation." *Louisiana History* 32 (Spring 1991): 117-57.

Johnson, Loretta. "Charivari/Shivaree: A European Folk Ritual on the American Plains." *Journal of Interdisciplinary History* 20 (Winter 1990): 371-87.

Jones, Howard Mumford. *America and French Culture, 1750-1848*. Chapel Hill: University of North Carolina Press, 1927.

Jordan, Phillip D. "Humor of the Backwoods, 1820-1840." *Mississippi Valley Historical Review* 25 (June 1938): 25-38.

Jordan-Bychkov, Terry G. "The Creole Coast: Homeland to Substrate." In *Homelands: A Geography of Culture and Place across America*, edited by Richard L. Nostrand and Lawrence E. Estaville. Baltimore: Johns Hopkins University Press, 2001.

Joyner, Charles. *Shared Traditions: Southern History and Folk Culture*. Urbana: University of Illinois Press, 1999.

Jumonville, Florence M. *Louisiana History: An Annotated Bibliography*. Westport, Conn.: Greenwood Press, 2002.

Kammen, Michael. *Mystic Chords of Memory: The Transformation of Tradition in American Culture*. New York: Alfred A. Knopf, 1991.

———. *A Season of Youth: The American Revolution and the Historical Imagination*. New York: Alfred A. Knopf, 1978.

Kamphoefner, Walter D. *The Westfalians: From Germany to Missouri*. Princeton, N.J.: Princeton University Press, 1987.

Kane, Harnett Thomas. *Natchez on the Mississippi*. New York: William Morrow, 1947.

Kartomi, Margaret J. "The Process and Results of Musical Culture Contact: A Discussion of Terminology and Concepts." *Ethnomusicology* 25 (May 1981): 227–50.

Kastor, Peter J. *The Nation's Crucible: The Louisiana Purchase and the Creation of America*. New Haven, Conn.: Yale University Press, 2004.

Katz, Bernard, ed. *The Social Implications of Early Negro Music in the United States*. New York: Arno Press, 1969.

Kelley, Laura D. "Erin's Enterprise: Immigration by Appropriation. The Irish in Antebellum New Orleans." Ph.D. diss., Tulane University, 2004.

Kelman, Ari. "Boundary Issues: Clarifying New Orleans's Murky Edges." *Journal of American History* 94 (December 2007): 695–703.

Kenney, William Howland. *Jazz on the River*. Chicago: University of Chicago Press, 2005.

Kerber, Linda. "The Revolutionary Generation: Ideology, Politics, and Culture in the Early Republic." In *The New American History*, edited by Eric Foner. Philadelphia: Temple University Press, 1997.

Kermes, Stephanie. *Creating an American Identity: New England, 1789–1825*. New York: Palgrave Macmillan, 2008.

Kersh, Rogan. *Dreams of a More Perfect Union*. Ithaca, N.Y.: Cornell University Press, 2001.

Key, Susan. "Sound and Sentimentality: Nostalgia in the Song of Stephen Foster." *American Music* 13 (Summer 1995): 145–66.

Kinnaird, Lawrence. "American Penetration into Spanish Louisiana." In *New Spain and the Anglo-American West*, edited by Charles W. Hackett, George P. Hammond, and J. Lloyd Mecham. Los Angeles: privately printed, 1932.

Kinser, Samuel. *Carnival American Style: Mardi Gras at New Orleans and Mobile*. Chicago: University of Chicago Press, 1990.

Kinzer, Charles E. "The Band of Music of the First Battalion of Free Men of Color and the Siege of New Orleans, 1814–1815." *American Music* 10 (Fall 1992): 348–69.

———. "The Tio Family: Four Generations of New Orleans Musicians, 1814–1933." Ph.D. diss., Louisiana State University, 1993.

Kleber, John E., ed. *The Kentucky Encyclopedia*. Lexington: University Press of Kentucky, 1992.

Kmen, Henry A. *Music in New Orleans: The Formative Years, 1791–1841*. Baton Rouge: Louisiana State University Press, 1966.

———. "Old Corn Meal: A Forgotten Urban Negro Folksinger." *Journal of American Folklore* 75 (January–March 1962): 29–34.

———. "Singing and Dancing in New Orleans: A Social History of the Birth and Growth of Balls and Operas, 1791–1841." Ph.D. diss., Tulane University, 1961.

Knight, Larry. "The Cart War: Defining American in San Antonio in the 1850's." *Southwestern Historical Quarterly* 109 (January 2006): 318–35.

Knobel, Dale T. *Paddy and the Republic: Ethnicity and Nationality in Antebellum America.* Middletown, Conn.: Wesleyan University Press, 1986.

Knoper, Randall. *Acting Naturally: Mark Twain and the Culture of Performance.* Berkeley: University of California Press, 1995.

Knowles, Horace, ed. *Gentlemen, Scholars, and Scoundrels: A Treasury of the Best of Harpers Magazine from 1850 to the Present.* New York: Harper and Brothers, 1959.

Kohn, Hans. *American Nationalism: An Interpretative Essay.* New York: Macmillan, 1957.

Kondert, Reinhart. *The Germans of Colonial Louisiana, 1720–1803.* Stuttgart, Germany: Academic Publishing House, 1990.

Konrad, William Robinson. "The Diminishing Influences of German Culture in New Orleans Life Since 1865." *Louisiana Historical Quarterly* 24 (January 1941): 127–67.

Kornfeld, Eve. *Creating an American Culture, 1775–1800: A Brief History with Documents.* New York: Palgrave, 2001.

Koskoff, Ellen. *Music Cultures in the United States.* New York: Routledge, 2005.

Kroeber, A. L., and Clyde Kluckhohn. *Culture: A Critical Review of Concepts and Definitions.* Cambridge, Mass.: Peabody Museum of American Archeology, 1952.

Kruger, Loren. "Our Theatre? Stages in an American Cultural History." *American Literary History* 8 (Winter 1996): 699–714.

Kulikoff, Allan. "Uprooted Peoples: Black Migrants in the Age of the American Revolution, 1790–1820." In *Slavery and Freedom in the Age of the American Revolution,* edited by Ira Berlin and Ronald Hoffman. Charlottesville: University Press of Virginia, 1983.

Kunzog, John C. *The One-Horse Show: The Life and Times of Dan Rice, Circus Jester and Philanthropist.* Jamestown, N.Y.: John C. Kunzog, 1962.

Lacey, Mary Frances. "Intellectual Activities of Vicksburg Prior to 1860." Master's thesis, Duke University, 1937.

Lachance, Paul F. "The 1809 Immigration of Saint-Domingue Refugees to New Orleans: Reception, Integration and Impact." *Louisiana History* 29 (Spring 1988): 109–41.

———. "The Foreign French." In *Creole New Orleans: Race and Americanization,* edited by Arnold R. Hirsch and Joseph Logsdon. Baton Rouge: Louisiana State University Press, 1992.

———. "The Growth of Free and Slave Populations of French Colonial Louisiana." In *French Colonial Louisiana and the Atlantic World,* edited by Bradley G. Bond. Baton Rouge: Louisiana State University Press, 2005.

Lapham, Lewis H., and Ellen Rosenbush, eds. *An American Album: One Hun-*

dred and Fifty Years of Harper's Magazine. New York: Franklin Square Press, 2000.

Larner, John P. "North American Hero? Christopher Columbus, 1702–2002." *Proceedings of the American Philosophical Society* 137 (March 1993): 46–63.

Laver, Harry S. "Rethinking the Social Role of the Militia: Community-Building in Antebellum Kentucky." *Journal of Southern History* 68 (November 2002): 777–816.

Lears, T. J. Jackson. "The Concept of Cultural Hegemony: Problems and Possibilities." *American Historical Review* 90 (June 1985): 567–93.

Leary-Warsaw, Jacqueline J. "Nineteenth-Century French Art Song of New Orleans: A Repertoire Study." Ph.D. diss., Johns Hopkins University, 2000.

Le Gardeur, René J., Jr. *The First New Orleans Theatre, 1792–1803.* New Orleans: Leeward Books, 1963.

LeMenager, Stephanie. "Floating Capital: The Trouble with Whiteness on Twain's Mississippi." *English Literary History* 71 (Summer 2004): 405–31.

Lemisch, Jesse. "Jack Tar in the Streets: Merchant Seamen in the Politics of Revolutionary America." *William and Mary Quarterly* 25 (July 1968): 371–407.

Levine, Lawrence. *Black Culture and Black Consciousness: Afro-American Folk Thought from Slavery to Freedom.* New York: Oxford University Press, 1978.

———. *Highbrow/Lowbrow: The Emergence of Cultural Hierarchy in America.* Cambridge, Mass.: Harvard University Press, 1988.

———. "Slave Songs and Slave Consciousness: An Exploration in Neglected Sources." In *African-American Religion: Interpretive Essays in History and Culture,* edited by Timothy A. Fulop and Albert J. Raboteau. New York: Routledge, 1997.

Levine, Victoria Lindsay. "American Indian Musics, Past and Present." In *The Cambridge History of American Music,* edited by David Nicholls. New York: Cambridge University Press, 1998.

Levy, Lester S. *Flashes of Merriment: A Century of Humorous Songs in America, 1805–1905.* Norman: University of Oklahoma Press, 1971.

———. *Grace Notes in American History: Popular Sheet Music from 1820–1900.* Norman: University of Oklahoma Press, 1967.

Libby, David J. *Slavery and Frontier Mississippi, 1720–1835.* Jackson: University Press of Mississippi, 2004.

Lichtenstien, Grace, and Laura Dankner. *Musical Gumbo: The Music of New Orleans.* New York: W. W. Norton, 1993.

Linebaugh, Peter, and Marcus Rediker. *The Many-Headed Hydra: Sailors, Slaves, Commoners, and the Hidden History of the Revolutionary Atlantic.* Boston: Beacon Press, 2000.

Loesser, Arthur. *Men, Women, and Pianos: A Social History.* New York: Simon and Schuster, 1954.

Logsdon, Joseph, and Caryn Cossé Bell. "The Americanization of Black New Orleans." In *Creole New Orleans: Race and Americanization,* edited by Arnold R. Hirsch and Joseph Logsdon. Baton Rouge: Louisiana State University Press, 1992.

Long, Alecia P. *The Great Southern Babylon: Sex, Race, and Respectability in New Orleans, 1865–1920*. Baton Rouge: Louisiana States University Press, 2004.

Lott, Eric. *Love and Theft: Blackface Minstrelsy and the American Working Class*. New York: Oxford University Press, 1993.

Lowe, John, ed. *Louisiana Culture from the Colonial Era to Katrina*. Baton Rouge: Louisiana State University Press, 2008.

Lowens, Irving. *A Bibliography of Songsters Printed in America before 1821*. Worcester, Mass.: American Antiquarian Society, 1976.

——. *Music and Musicians in Early America*. New York: W. W. Norton, 1964.

——. *Music in America and American Music: Two Views of the Scene*. Brooklyn: City University of New York, 1978.

Luconi, Stefano. *From Paesani to White Ethnics: The Italian Experience in Philadelphia*. Albany: State University of New York Press, 2001.

Mahar, William J. *Behind the Burnt Cork Mask: Early Blackface Minstrelsy and Antebellum American Popular Culture*. Urbana: University of Illinois Press, 1999.

Mali, Joseph. *Mythistory: The Making of Modern Historiography*. Chicago: University of Chicago Press, 2003.

Malone, Bill. "Neither Anglo-Saxon nor Celtic: The Music of the Southern Plain Folk." In *Plain Folk of the South Revisited*, edited by Samuel C. Hyde Jr. Baton Rouge: Louisiana State University Press, 1997.

——. *Southern Music, American Music*. Lexington: University Press of Kentucky, 1979.

Marrocco, W. Thomas, and Harold Gleason, eds. *Music in America: An Anthology from the Landing of the Pilgrims to the Close of the Civil War, 1620–1865*. New York: W. W. Norton, 1964.

Marsh, John L. "Drama and Spectacle by the Yard: The Panorama in America." *Journal of Popular Culture* 10 (Winter 1976): 581–93.

Martin, Joan M. "*Plaçage* and the Louisiana *Gens de Couleur Libre*." In *Creole: The History and Legacy of Louisiana's Free People of Color*, edited by Sybil Kein. Baton Rouge: Louisiana State University Press, 2000.

Martin, John M. "The People of New Orleans as Seen by Her Visitors, 1803–1860." *Louisiana Studies* 6 (Winter 1967): 361–75.

Mason, Laura. *Singing the French Revolution: Popular Culture and Politics, 1787–1799*. Ithaca, N.Y.: Cornell University Press, 1996.

Mates, Julian. *America's Musical Stage: Two Hundred Years of Musical Theatre*. Westport, Conn.: Greenwood Press, 1985.

Mattfeld, Julius. *Variety Music Cavalcade, 1620–1969: A Chronology of Vocal and Instrumental Music Popular in the United States*. 3rd ed. Englewood Cliffs, N.J.: Prentice Hall, 1971.

Matthias, Virginia P. "Natchez-Under-the-Hill as it Developed Under the Influence of the Mississippi River and the Natchez Trace." *Journal of Mississippi History* 7 (October 1945): 201–21.

Maurer, Heinrich H. "The Earlier German Nationalism in America." *American Journal of Sociology* 22 (January 1917): 519–43.

McDermott, John Francis. *The Lost Panoramas of the Mississippi*. Chicago: University of Chicago Press, 1958.

McIntosh, David S. *Folk Songs and Singing Games of the Illinois Ozarks*. Carbondale: Southern Illinois University Press, 1974.

McKinsey, Elizabeth R. *The Western Experiment: New England Transcendentalists in the Ohio Valley*. Cambridge, Mass.: Harvard University Press, 1973.

McKinstry, E. Richard, comp. *Personal Accounts of Events, Travels, and Everyday Life in America: An Annotated Bibliography*. Winterthur, Del.: Henry Francis du Pont Winterthur Museum, 1997.

McKnight, Mark. "Charivaris, Cowbellions, and Sheet Iron Bands: Nineteenth-Century Rough Music in New Orleans." *American Music* 23 (Winter 2005): 407–25.

McMichael, F. Andrew. *Atlantic Loyalties: Americans in Spanish West Florida, 1785–1810*. Athens: University of Georgia Press, 2008.

McNally, Michael D. *Ojibwe Singers: Hymns of Grief, and a Native Culture in Motion*. New York: Oxford University Press, 2000.

———. "The Practice of Native American Christianity." *Church History* 69 (December 2000): 834–59.

McNamara, Brooks. *Step Right Up*. Garden City, N.Y.: Doubleday, 1976.

McNeilly, Donald. *The Old South Frontier: Cotton Plantations and the Formation of Arkansas Society, 1819–1861*. Fayetteville: University of Arkansas Press, 2000.

McPherson, James. "Antebellum Southern Exceptionalism: A New Look at an Old Question." *Civil War History* 50 (December 2004): 418–33.

McWhiney, Grady. *Cracker Culture: Celtic Ways in the Old South*. Tuscaloosa: University of Alabama Press, 1988.

Meer, Sarah. *Uncle Tom Mania: Slavery, Minstrelsy, and Transatlantic Culture in the 1850s*. Athens: University of Georgia Press, 2005.

Mellers, Wilfrid. *Music in a New Found Land: Themes and Developments in the History of American Music*. New York: Alfred Knopf, 1965.

Melton, Buckner F. *Aaron Burr: Conspiracy to Treason*. New York: Wiley, 2001.

Melton, Jeffrey Allen. *Mark Twain, Travel Books, and Tourism: The Tide of a Great Popular Movement*. Tuscaloosa: University of Alabama Press, 2002.

Merchant, Carolyn. *American Environmental History: An Introduction*. New York: Columbia University Press, 2007.

Merrill, Ellen C. *Germans of Louisiana*. Gretna, La.: Pelican, 2005.

Miller, Angela. *The Empire of the Eye: Landscape Representation and American Cultural Politics, 1825–1875*. Ithaca, N.Y.: Cornell University Press, 1993.

Miller, James M. *The Genesis of Western Culture: The Upper Ohio Valley, 1800–1825.* New York: Da Capo Press, 1969.

Miller, Randall M. "A Church in Cultural Captivity: Some Speculations on Catholic Identity in the Old South." In *Catholics in the Old South: Essays on Church and Culture,* edited by Randall M. Miller and Jon L. Wakelyn. Macon, Ga.: Mercer University Press, 1983.

———. "Slaves and Southern Catholicism." In *Masters and Slaves in the House of the Lord: Race and Religion in the American South, 1740–1870,* edited by John B. Boles. Lexington: University Press of Kentucky, 1988.

Minnigerode, Meade. *The Fabulous Forties, 1840–1859: A Presentation of Private Life.* New York: G. P. Putnam and Sons, 1924.

Mitchell, Reid. *All on a Mardi Gras Day: Episodes in the History of New Orleans Carnival.* Cambridge, Mass.: Harvard University Press, 1995.

Morazon, Ronald R. "'Quadroon' Balls in the Spanish Period." *Louisiana History* 14 (Summer 1973): 310–15.

Moore, Paul. "Sectarian Sound and Cultural Identity in Northern Ireland." In *The Auditory Cultural Reader,* edited by Michael Bull and Lew Black. New York: Oxford University Press, 2003.

Morris, Christopher. *Becoming Southern: The Evolution of a Way of Life, Warren County and Vicksburg, Mississippi, 1770–1869.* New York: Oxford University Press, 1995.

Morrison, Michael A. *Slavery and the American West: The Eclipse of Manifest Destiny and the Coming of the Civil War.* Chapel Hill: University of North Carolina Press, 1997.

Morrison, Michael A., and James Brewer Stewart, eds. *Race and the Early Republic: Racial Consciousness and Nation-Building in the Early Republic.* New York: Rowman and Littlefield, 2002.

Morrison, Toni. *Playing in the Dark: Whiteness and the Literary Imagination.* Cambridge, Mass.: Harvard University Press, 1992.

Morrow, Mary Sue. "Singing and Drinking in New Orleans: The Social and Musical Functions of Nineteenth-Century German Männerchöre." *Southern Quarterly* 27 (Winter 1989): 5–24.

———. "Somewhere between Beer and Wagner: The Cultural and Musical Impact of German Männerchöre in New York and New Orleans." In *Music and Culture in America, 1861–1918,* edited by Michael Saffle. New York: Garland, 1998.

Moss, Kenneth. "St. Patrick's Day Celebrations and the Formation of Irish-American Identity, 1845–1875." *Journal of Social History* 29 (Fall 1995): 125–48.

Muldrow, Blanche. "The American Theatre as Seen by British Travelers, 1790–1860." Ph.D. diss., University of Wisconsin, 1953.

Mullenix, Elizabeth Reitz. "Yankee Doodle Dixie: Performing Nationhood on the Eve of War." *Journal of American Drama and Theatre* 18 (Fall 2006): 33–54.

Murphy, Jeanette Robinson. "The Survival of African Music in America." *Popular Science Monthly* 55 (1899): 660–72.

Nagel, Joane. "Constructing Ethnicity: Creating and Recreating Ethnic Identity and Culture." *Social Problems* 41 (February 1994): 152–76.

Nagel, Paul C. *This Sacred Trust: American Nationality, 1798–1898*. New York: Oxford University Press, 1971.

Narvaez, Peter. "The Influences of Hispanic Music Cultures on African-American Blues Musicians." *Black Music Research Journal* 14 (Autumn 1994): 203–24.

Nathan, Hans. *Dan Emmett and the Rise of Early Negro Minstrelsy*. Norman: University of Oklahoma Press, 1962.

———. "The Tyrolese Family Rainer, and the Vogue of Singing Mountain-Troupes in Europe and America." *Music Quarterly* 32 (January 1946): 63–79.

Nau, John Frederick. *The German People of New Orleans, 1850–1900*. Leiden: E. J. Brill, 1958.

Needham, Maureen. "The War of the Quadrilles: Creole vs. American." In *I See America Dancing: Selected Readings, 1685–2000*, edited by Maureen Needham. Urbana: University of Illinois Press, 2002.

Neeser, Robert W., ed. *American Naval Songs and Ballads*. New Haven, Conn.: Yale University Press, 1938.

Neil, J. Merideth. *Toward a National Taste: America's Quest for Aesthetic Independence*. Honolulu: University Press of Hawaii, 1975.

Nettl, Bruno. *Folk Music in the United States: An Introduction*. Detroit: Wayne State University Press, 1962.

Newman, Simon P. *Parades and the Politics of the Street: Festive Culture in the Early American Republic*. Philadelphia: University of Pennsylvania Press, 1997.

Newton, Lewis William. "The Americanization of French Louisiana: A Study of the Process of Adjustment between the French and Anglo-American Populations of Louisiana, 1803–1860." Ph.D. diss., University of Chicago, 1924.

Nicholls, David, ed. *The Cambridge History of American Music*. Cambridge, U.K.: Cambridge University Press, 1998.

Niehaus, Earl F. *The Irish in New Orleans, 1800–1860*. Baton Rouge: Louisiana State University Press, 1965.

"Nineteenth Century Immigration, Organizations, and Churches." The Historic New Orleans Collection, New Orleans Louisiana, http://www.hnoc.org/collections/gerpath/gersect2.htm.

Nissenbaum, Stephen. *The Battle for Christmas*. New York: Vintage Books, 1996.

Nobling, Joe. *Frontier Songs of Illinois*. Moline: Illinois Writers Guild, 1989.

Nolan, J. Bennett. *Lafayette in America Day by Day*. Baltimore: Johns Hopkins University Press, 1934.

Nolt, Steven. *Foreigners in Their Own Land: Pennsylvania Germans in the Early Republic*. University Park: Pennsylvania State University Press, 2000.

Nowatzki, Robert C. "'Our Truly National Poets': Blackface Minstrelsy and Cultural Nationalism." *ATQ: Nineteenth Century Literary Quarterly* 20 (March 2006): 361–78.

Obadele-Starks, Ernest. *Freebooters and Smugglers: The Foreign Slave Trade in the United States after 1808.* Fayetteville: University of Arkansas Press, 2007.

O'Grady, Terence J. "The Singing Societies of Oneida." *American Music* 9 (Spring 1991): 67–91.

Okker, Patricia. *Our Sister Editors: Sarah J. Hale and the Tradition of Nineteenth-Century American Women Editors.* Athens: University of Georgia Press, 1995.

Ostendorf, Berndt. *Black Literature in White America.* Brighton, Sussex: Harvester Press, 1982.

———. "Literary Acculturation: What Makes Ethnic Literature 'Ethnic.'" *Callaloo* 25 (Autumn 1985): 577–86.

———. "Minstrelsy and Early Jazz." *Massachusetts Review* 20 (Autumn 1979): 574–602.

Oster, Harry. "Negro French Spirituals of Louisiana." *International Folk Music Journal* 14 (1962): 166–67.

Ownby, Ted, and Charles W. Joyner, eds. *Black and White Cultural Interaction in the Antebellum South.* Jackson: University Press of Mississippi, 1993.

Painter, Nell Irvin. "Was Marie White? The Trajectory of a Question in the United States." *Journal of Southern History* 74 (February 2008): 3–30.

Patterson, Cecil Lloyd. "A Different Drum: The Image of the Negro in the Nineteenth Century Popular Song Books." Ph.D. diss., University of Pennsylvania, 1961.

Pearce, Roy Harvey. *Savagism and Civilization: A Study of the Indian and the American Mind.* Rev. ed. Baltimore: Johns Hopkins University Press, 1967.

Peirce, Charles Sanders. "Issues of Pragmaticism." In *The Essential Peirce: Selected Philosophical Writings, Volume 2 (1893–1913),* edited by the Peirce Edition Project. Bloomington: Indiana University Press, 1998.

Perrin, William Henry. *History of Alexander, Union, and Pulasky Counties, Illinois.* Chicago: O. L. Baskin, 1883.

Perry, Lewis. *Boats against the Current: American Culture between Revolution and Modernity, 1820–1860.* New York: Oxford University Press, 1993.

Peters, Martha Ann. "The St. Charles Hotel: New Orleans Social Center, 1837–1860." *Louisiana History* 1 (Summer 1960): 191–211.

Peterson, Richard. *Creating Country Music: Fabricating Authenticity.* Chicago: University of Chicago Press, 1997.

Pieterse, Jan Nederveen. "Globalisation as Hybridisation." *International Sociology* 9 (June 1994): 161–84.

———. "Hybridity, So What? The Anti-Hybridity Backlash and the Riddles of Recognition." *Theory, Culture and Society* 18 (June 2001): 219–45.

Polk, Noel, ed. *Natchez before 1830*. Jackson: University Press of Mississippi, 1989.

Porter, James. "Convergence, Divergence, and Dialectic in Folksong Paradigms: Critical Directions for Transatlantic Scholarship." *Journal of American Folklore* 106 (Winter 1993): 61–98.

Potter, David. *The Impending Crisis, 1848–1861*. New York: Harper and Row, 1976.

Power, Richard Lyle. "A Crusade to Extend Yankee Culture, 1820–1865." *New England Quarterly* 13 (December 1940): 638–53.

Powers, David M. "The French Musical Theater: Maintaining Control in Caribbean Colonies in the Eighteenth Century." *Black Music Research Journal* 18 (Spring–Autumn 1998): 229–40.

Pratt, Mary Louise. *Imperial Eyes: Travel Writing and Transculturation*. New York: Routledge, 1992.

Price, Nellie Warner. "Le Spectacle de la Rue St. Pierre." *Louisiana Historical Quarterly* 1 (January 1918): 215–23.

Pruett, Laura Moore. "Louis Moreau Gottschalk, John Sullivan Dwight, and the Development of Musical Culture in the United States, 1853–1865." Ph.D. diss., Florida State University, 2007.

Purcell, Sarah. *Sealed with Blood: War, Sacrifice, and Memory in Revolutionary America*. Philadelphia: University of Pennsylvania Press, 2002.

Raboteau, Albert J. *Slave Religion: The "Invisible Institution" in the Antebellum South*. New York: Oxford University Press, 1978.

Rath, Richard Cullen. *How Early America Sounded*. Ithaca, N.Y.: Cornell University Press, 2003.

Rawick, Goerge P., ed. *The American Slave: A Composite Autobiography*. Westport, Conn.: Greenwood, 1972.

Rediker, Marcus. *Between the Devil and the Deep Blue Sea: Merchant Seamen, Pirates, and the Anglo-American Maritime World, 1700–1750*. Cambridge, Mass.: Cambridge University Press, 1987.

Reinders, Robert. "The Decline of the New Orleans Free Negro in the Decade before the Civil War." *Journal of Mississippi History* 24 (April 1962): 88–98.

———. *End of an Era: New Orleans, 1850–1860*. New Orleans: Pelican, 1964.

Reiss, Benjamin. *The Showman and the Slave: Race, Death, and Memory in Barnum's America*. Cambridge, Mass.: Harvard University Press, 2001.

Reps, John W. "Great Expectations and Hard Times: The Planning of Cairo, Illinois." *Journal of the Society of Architectural Historians* 16 (December 1957): 14–21.

"Review of Piccolino." *Musical Times* (February 1879): 84.

Reynolds, David S. *Beneath the American Renaissance: The Subversive Imagination in the Age of Emerson and Melville*. New York: Alfred A. Knopf, 1988.

———. *Walt Whitman's America: A Cultural Biography*. New York: Vintage Books, 1996.

Richards, Jeffrey H. *Drama, Theatre, and Identity in the American New Republic*. New York: Cambridge University Press, 2005.

Roach, Joseph. "Barnumizing the Diaspora: The 'Irish Skylark' Does New Orleans." *Theatre Journal* 50 (1998): 39–51.

———. *Cities of the Dead: Circum-Atlantic Performance*. New York: Columbia University Press, 1996.

———. "Deep Skin: Reconstructing Congo Square." In *African-American Performance and Theater History: A Critical Reader*, edited by Harry J. Elam Jr. and David Kranser. New York: Oxford University Press, 2001.

———. "Mardi Gras Indians and Others: Genealogies of American Performance." *Theatre Journal* 44 (December 1992): 461–83.

Robertson, James. "Frolics, Fights, and Firewater in Frontier Tennessee." *Tennessee Historical Quarterly* 17 (June 1958): 97–111.

Robertson, James Oliver. *American Myth, American Reality*. New York: Hill and Wang, 1980.

Robinson, Charles F. "The Louisiana Purchase and the Black Experience." In *A Whole Country in Commotion: The Louisiana Purchase and the American Southwest*, edited by Patrick G. Williams, S. Charles Bolton, and Jeannie M. Whayne. Fayetteville: University of Arkansas Press, 2005.

Rodano, Ronald. "Denoting Difference: The Writing of the Slave Spirituals." *Critical Inquiry* 22 (Spring 1996): 506–44.

Rodriguez, Junius P., ed. *The Louisiana Purchase: A Historical and Geographic Encyclopedia*. Santa Barbara: ABC-CLIO, 2002.

Roediger, David R. *The Wages of Whiteness: Race and the Making of the American Working Class*. Rev. ed. New York: Verso, 1999.

Rogers, Francis. "Jenny Lind." *Musical Quarterly* 32 (July 1946): 437–48.

Rohler, Lloyd. *Ralph Waldo Emerson: Preacher and Lecturer*. Westport, Conn.: Greenwood Press, 1995.

Rohrbough, Malcolm J. "The Art of Nostalgia: Bingham, Boone, and the Developing West." *Gateway Heritage* 11 (Fall 1990): 4–19.

Rosenzweig, Roy. "The Rise of the Saloon." In *Rethinking Popular Culture: Contemporary Perspectives in Cultural Studies*, edited by Chandra Mukerju and Michael Schudson. Berkeley: University of California Press, 1991.

Rourke, Constance. *American Humor: A Study of the National Character*. Garden City, N.Y.: Doubleday, 1953.

Ryan, Mary P. *Civic Wars: Democracy and Public Life in the American City during the Nineteenth Century*. Berkeley: University of California Press, 1997.

Sablosky, Irving. *What They Heard: Music in America, 1852–1881, From the Pages of Dwight's Music Journal*. Baton Rouge: Louisiana State University Press, 1986.

Said, Edward W. *Orientalism*. New York: Pantheon Books, 1978.

Salins, Peter D. *Assimilation, American Style*. New York: Basic Books, 1997.

Sanders, Jimy M. "Ethnic Boundaries and Identity in Plural Societies." *Annual Review of Sociology* 28 (2002): 327–57.

Sands, Rosetta. "Carnival Celebrations in Africa and the New World: Junkanoo and the Black Indians of Mardi Gras." *Black Music Research Journal* 11 (Spring 1991): 75–92.

Sanjek, Russell. *American Popular Music and Its Business: The First Four Hundred Years.* New York: Oxford University Press, 1988.

Sarna, Jonathan D. "From Immigrants to Ethnics: Towards a New Theory of 'Ethnicization.'" *Ethnicity* 5 (1978): 370–78.

Saunders, Steven, and Deane L. Root. *The Music of Stephen C. Foster: A Critical Edition.* Washington, D.C.: Smithsonian Institution Press, 1990.

Savoy, Ann Allen, ed. *Cajun Music: A Reflection of a People.* Eunice, La.: Bluebird Press, 1984.

Saxon, Lyle, Edward Dreyer, and Robert Tallant, comps. *Gumbo Ya-Ya: A Collection of Louisiana Folk Tales.* Boston: Houghton Mifflin, 1945.

Saxton, Alexander. "Blackface Minstrelsy and Jacksonian Ideology." *American Quarterly* 27 (March 1975): 3–28.

———. *The Rise and Fall of the White Republic: Class Politics and Mass Culture in Nineteenth-Century America.* New York: Verso, 1990.

Scheurer, Timothy E. *Born in the U.S.A.: The Myth of America in Popular Music from Colonial Times to the Present.* Jackson: University Press of Mississippi, 1991.

Schlereth, Thomas J. "Columbia, Columbus, Columbianism." *Journal of American History* 79 (December 1992): 937–68.

Schroeder, Walter A. *Opening the Ozarks: A Historical Geography of Missouri's Ste. Genevieve District, 1760–1830.* Columbia: University of Missouri Press, 2002.

Seeger, Charles. "Music and Class Structure in the United States." *American Quarterly* 19 (Autumn 1957): 281–94.

Sellers, Charles, ed. *The Southerner as American.* Chapel Hill: University of North Carolina Press, 1960.

Shaffer, Arthur H. *To Be an American: David Ramsay and the Making of the American Consciousness.* Columbia: University of South Carolina Press, 1991.

Shaffer, Marguerite S., ed. *Public Culture: Diversity, Democracy, and Community in the United States.* Philadelphia: University of Pennsylvania Press, 2008.

Shenkel, J. Richard. *Archaeology of the Jazz Complex and Beauregard (Congo) Square.* New Orleans: University of New Orleans Archeology and Cultural Research Program, 1980.

Shuffelton, Frank, ed. *A Mixed Race: Ethnicity in Early America.* New York: Oxford University Press, 1993.

Silber, Irwin, ed. *Songs of the Civil War.* New York: Columbia University Press, 1960.

Sillers, Florence Warfield, comp. *History of Bolivar County Mississippi.* Jackson, Miss.: Hederman Bros., 1948.

Silverman, Kenneth. *A Cultural History of the American Revolution: Painting, Music, Literature, and the Theatre in the Colonies and the United States from the* Treaty of Paris *to the* Inauguration of George Washington, *1763–1789.* New York: Thomas Crowell, 1976.

Simpson, David. *The Politics of American English, 1776–1850.* New York: Oxford University Press, 1986.

Smedley, Audrey. *Race in North America: Origin and Evolution of a Worldview.* 2nd ed. Boulder, Colo.: Westview Press, 1999.

Smith, Preserved. "Neil MacNeale, Railroad Builder of the Middle West, 1826–1897." *Mississippi Valley Historical Review* 26 (September 1939): 181–92.

Smith, Thomas Ruys. *River of Dreams: Imagining the Mississippi before Mark Twain.* Baton Rouge: Louisiana State University Press, 2007.

Smither, Nelle. "A History of the English Theatre at New Orleans, 1806–1842." Ph.D. diss., University of Pennsylvania, 1944.

Snyder, Jared. "Squeeze Box: The Legacy of the Afro-Mississippi Accordionists." *Black Music Research Journal* 17 (Spring 1997): 37–57.

Sollors, Werner. *Beyond Ethnicity: Consent and Descent in American Culture.* New York: Oxford University Press, 1986.

———, ed. *Theories of Ethnicity: A Classical Reader.* New York: New York University Press, 1996.

Somkin, Fred. *Unquiet Eagle: Memory and Desire in the Idea of American Freedom, 1815–1860.* Ithaca, N.Y.: Cornell University Press, 1967.

Sonneck, Oscar. *A Bibliography of Early Secular American Music.* Washington, D.C.: Library of Congress Music Division, 1945.

———. "Critical Notes on the Origin of 'Hail Columbia.'" *Sammelbände der Internationalen Musikgesellschaft* 3 (November 1901): 139–66.

Southern, Eileen. *The Music of Black Americans: A History.* 3rd ed. New York: W. W. Norton, 1997.

Southern, Eileen, and Josephine Wright. *African-American Traditions in Song, Sermon, Tale, and Dance, 1600s–1920: An Annotated Bibliography of Literature, Collections, and Artworks.* New York: Greenwood Press, 1990.

Sparks, Randy J. "Religion in Amite County, Mississippi, 1800–1861." In *Masters and Slaves in the House of the Lord: Race and Religion in the American South, 1740–1870,* edited by John B. Boles. Lexington: University Press of Kentucky, 1988.

Spitzer, Nicholas. "Monde Créole: The Cultural World of French Louisiana Creoles and the Creolization of World Cultures." *Journal of American Folklore* 116 (Winter 2003): 57–72.

Spletstoser, Fredrick Marcel. "Back Door to the Land of Plenty: New Orleans as an Immigrant Port, 1820–1860." Ph.D. diss., Louisiana State University, 1978.

Stepenoff, Bonnie. *From French Community to Missouri Town: Ste. Genevieve in the Nineteenth Century.* Columbia: University of Missouri Press, 2006.

Sterx, H. E. *The Free Negro in Ante-Bellum Louisiana*. Rutherford, N.J.: Farleigh Dickinson University Press, 1972.

Stevens, Harry. "Folk Music on the Midwestern Frontier, 1788–1825." *Ohio History* 57 (1948): 126–46.

———. "The Haydn Society of Cincinnati, 1819–1924." *Ohio History* 52 (1943): 95–119.

Stone, James H. "Mid-Nineteenth-Century American Beliefs in the Social Values of Music." *Musical Quarterly* 43 (January 1957): 38–49.

Stoutamire, Albert. *Music of the Old South: Colony to Confederacy*. Rutherford, N.J.: Farleigh Dickinson University Press, 1972.

Strachwitz, Chris, ed. *The American Folk Music Occasional*. New York: Oak, 1970.

Stuyvesant, George Jackson. *Early Songs of Uncle Sam*. Boston: Bruce Humphries, 1933.

Sublette, Ned. *The World That Made New Orleans: From Spanish Silver to Congo Square*. Chicago: Lawrence Hill, 2008.

Sullivan, Lester. "Composers of Color of Nineteenth-Century New Orleans: The History Behind the Music." *Black Music Research Journal* 8 (1988): 51–82.

Szwed, John. "Musical Adaptation Among Afro-Americans." *Journal of American Folklore* 82 (April–June 1969): 112–21.

Tadman, Michael. *Speculators and Slaves: Masters, Traders, and Slaves in the Old South*. Madison: University of Wisconsin Press, 1989.

Tallant, Robert. *The Romantic New Orleanians*. New York: Dutton, 1950.

Tamarkin, Elisa. *Anglophilia: Deference, Devotion, and Antebellum America*. Chicago: University of Chicago Press, 2008.

Tawa, Nicholas. *High-Minded and Low-Down: Music in the Lives of Americans, 1800–1861*. Boston: Northeastern University Press, 2000.

———. *A Music for the Millions: Antebellum Democratic Attitudes and the Birth of American Popular Music*. New York: Pendragon, 1984.

———. "The Performance of Parlor Songs in America, 1790–1860." *Anuario Interamericano de Investigacion Musical* 11 (1975): 69–81.

———. "Secular Music in the Late-Eighteenth-Century American Home." *Musical Quarterly* 61 (October 1975): 511–27.

———. "Serious Songs of the Early Nineteenth Century. Part 2: The Meaning of the Early Song Melodies." *American Music* 13 (Fall 1995): 263–94.

———. "Songs of the Early Nineteenth Century Part 1: Early Song Lyrics and Coping with Life." *American Music* 13 (Spring 1995): 1–26.

———. *A Sound of Strangers: Musical Culture, Acculturation, and the Post-Civil War Ethnic American*. Metuchen, N.J.: Scarecrow Press, 1982.

———. *Sweet Songs for Gentle Americans: The Parlor Song in America, 1790–1860*. Bowling Green, Ohio: Bowling Green University Popular Press, 1980.

———. *The Way to Tin Pan Alley: American Popular Song, 1866–1910*. New York: Schirmer, 1990.

Taylor, George Rogers. "Agrarian Discontent in the Mississippi Valley Preceding the War of 1812." *Journal of Political Economy* 39 (August 1931): 471–505.

Taylor, Joe G. "The Foreign Slave Trade in Louisiana After 1808." *Louisiana History* 1 (Winter 1960): 36–43.

Tellefsen, Blythe Ann. "'The Case with My Dear Native Land': Nathaniel Hawthorne's Vision of America in *The Marble Faun*." *Nineteenth-Century Literature* 54 (March 2000): 455–79.

Thayer, Stuart. *Annals of the American Circus, 1793–1829*. Ann Arbor, Mich.: Thayer, 1976.

Thompson, Richard H. *Theories of Ethnicity: A Critical Appraisal*. Westport, Conn.: Greenwood Press, 1989.

Thompson, Shirley Elizabeth. *Exiles at Home: The Struggle to Become American in Creole New Orleans*. Cambridge, Mass.: Harvard University Press, 2009.

Tischler, Barbra L. *American Music: The Search for an American Musical Identity*. New York: Oxford University Press, 1986.

Toll, Robert. *Blacking Up: The Minstrel Show in Nineteenth-Century America*. New York: Oxford University Press, 1974.

———. *On With the Show! The First Century of Show Business in America*. New York: Oxford University Press, 1976.

Tracy, Sterling. "The Immigrant Population of Memphis." *West Tennessee Historical Society Papers* 4 (1950): 73–82.

Travers, Len. "The Paradox of 'Nationalist' Festivals: The Case of Palmetto Day in Antebellum Charleston." In *Riot and Revelry in Early America*, edited by William Pencak, Matthew Dennis, and Simon P. Newman. University Park: Pennsylvania State University Press, 2002.

Treat, Victor Hugo. "Migration into Louisiana, 1834–1880." Ph.D. diss., University of Texas, 1967.

Tregle, Joseph G., Jr. "Creoles and Americans." In *Creole New Orleans: Race and Americanization*, edited by Arnold Hirsch and Joseph Logsdon. Baton Rouge: Louisiana State University Press, 1992.

———. *Louisiana in the Age of Jackson: A Clash of Cultures and Personalities*. Baton Rouge: Louisiana State University, 1999.

Trimillos, Ricardo D. "Music and Ethnic Identity: Strategies among Overseas Filipino Youth." *Yearbook for Traditional Music* 18 (1986): 9–20.

Trotter, James M. *Music and Some Highly Musical People*. Boston: Lee and Shepard, 1881. Reprint, New York: Johnson Reprint, 1968.

Upton, William Treat. *William Henry Fry, American Journalist and Composer-Critic*. New York: Thomas Y. Crowell, 1954. Reprint, New York: Da Capo Press, 1974.

Usner, Daniel H., Jr. *American Indians in the Lower Mississippi Valley: Social and Economic Histories*. Lincoln: University of Nebraska Press, 1998.

———. "Between Creoles and Yankees: The Discursive Representation of Colonial Louisiana in American History." In *French Colonial Louisiana and the*

Atlantic World, edited by Bradley G. Bond. Baton Rouge: Louisiana State University Press, 2005.

———. "The Frontier Exchange Economy of the Lower Mississippi Valley in the Eighteenth Century." *William and Mary Quarterly* 44 (April 1987): 165–92.

Vianna, Hermano. *The Mystery of Samba: Popular Music and National Identity in Brazil*. Edited and translated by John Charles Chasteen. Chapel Hill: University of North Carolina Press, 1999.

Volo, James, and Dorothy Denneen Volo. *The Antebellum Period*. Westport, Conn.: Greenwood Press, 2004.

Von Glahn, Denise. *The Sounds of Place: Music and the American Cultural Landscape*. Boston: Northeastern University Press, 2003.

Voss, Louis. *Louisiana's German Heritage*. Bowie, Md.: Heritage Books, 1994.

Wald, Elijah, and John Junkerman. *River of Song: A Musical Journal Down the Mississippi*. New York: St. Martin's Press, 1998.

Waldstreicher, David. *In the Midst of Perpetual Fetes: The Making of American Nationalism, 1776–1820*. Chapel Hill: University of North Carolina Press, 1997.

Walker, Daniel E. *No More, No More: Slavery and Cultural Resistance in Havana and New Orleans*. Minneapolis: University of Minnesota Press, 2004.

Walsh, Basil. *Catherine Hayes, 1818–1861: The Hibernian Prima Dona*. Portland, Ore.: Irish Academic Press, 2000.

Walters, Vernon Larry. "Migration into Mississippi: 1798–1837." Master's thesis, Mississippi State University, 1969.

Ware, W. Porter. *P. T. Barnum Presents Jenny Lind: The American Tour of the Swedish Nightingale*. Baton Rouge: Louisiana State University Press, 1980.

Warren, Louis A. *Lincoln's Youth: Indiana Years, Seven to Twenty-One, 1816–1830*. New York: Appleton, Century, Crofts, 1959.

Watson, Charles S. *From Nationalism to Secessionism: The Changing Fiction of William Gilmore Simms*. Westport, Conn.: Greenwood Press, 1993.

Watts, Edward. *An American Colony: Regionalism and the Roots of Midwestern Culture*. Athens: Ohio University Press, 2002.

———. *In This Remote Country: French Colonial Culture in the Anglo-American Imagination, 1780–1860*. Chapel Hill: University of North Carolina Press, 2006.

———. *Writing and Postcolonialism in the Early Republic*. Charlottesville: University Press of Virginia, 1998.

Weaver, Herbert. "Foreigners in Ante-Bellum Mississippi." *Journal of Mississippi History* 16 (July 1954): 151–63.

———. "Foreigners in Ante-Bellum Towns of the Lower South." *Journal of Southern History* 13 (February 1947): 62–73.

Wells, Jonathan Daniel. *The Origins of the Southern Middle Class, 1800–1861*. Chapel Hill: University of North Carolina Press, 2004.

Wells, Paul F. "Fiddling as an Avenue of Black-White Musical Interchange." *Black Music Research Journal* 23 (Spring–Autumn 2003): 135–47.

Welter, Rush. *The Mind of America, 1820–1860*. New York: Columbia University Press, 1975.

Whayne, Jeannie M. "A Shifting Middle Ground: Arkansas's Frontier Exchange Economy and the Louisiana Purchase." In *A Whole Country in Commotion: The Louisiana Purchase and the American Southwest*, edited by Patrick G. Williams, S. Charles Bolton, and Jeannie M. Whayne. Fayetteville: University of Arkansas Press, 2005.

Wheeler, Mary. *Steamboatin' Days: Folk Songs of the River Packet Era*. Baton Rouge: Louisiana State University Press, 1944.

White, Ed, ed. "Notes and Documents." *Journal of the Early Republic* 30 (Summer 2010): 319.

White, Harry, and Michael Murphy, eds. *Musical Constructions of Nationalism: Essays on the History and Ideology of European Musical Culture, 1800–1945*. Cork, Ireland: Cork University Press, 2001.

White, Richard. *The Middle Ground: Indians, Empires, and Republics in the Great Lakes Region, 1650–1815*. New York: Cambridge University Press, 1991.

White, Shane, and Graham White. *The Sounds of Slavery: Discovering African American History Through Songs, Sermons, and Speech*. Boston: Beacon Press, 2005.

Whitfield, Irene Therese. *Louisiana French Folk Songs*. Baton Rouge: Louisiana State University Press, 1939.

Whitten, David O. *Andrew Durnford: A Black Sugar Planter in the Antebellum South*. New Brunswick, N.J.: Transaction Publishers, 1995.

Whittlesey, Walter, and O. G. Sonneck. *Catalogue of First Editions of Stephen Foster (1826–1864)*. Washington, D.C.: Government Printing Office, 1915.

Wickman, Richard Karl. "An Evaluation of the Employment of Panoramic Scenery in the Nineteenth-Century Theatre." Ph.D. diss., Ohio State University, 1961.

Wilentz, Sean. *Chants Democratic: New York City and the Rise of the American Working Class, 1788–1850*. New York: Oxford University Press, 1984.

Williams, Joseph S. *Old Times in West Tennessee*. Memphis: W. G. Chenney, 1873.

Williams, Patrick G., S. Charles Bolton, and Jeannie M. Whayne, eds. *A Whole Country in Commotion: The Louisiana Purchase and the American Southwest*. Fayetteville: University of Arkansas Press, 2005.

Williams, R. Vaughan. *National Music and Other Essays*. London: Oxford University Press, 1963.

Williams, William H. A. *'Twas Only an Irishman's Dream: The Image of Ireland and the Irish in American Popular Song Lyrics, 1800–1920*. Urbana: University of Illinois Press, 1996.

Wilmer, S. E. *Theatre, Society and the Nation: Staging American Identities*. New York: Cambridge University Press, 2002.

Winans, Robert B. "Black Instrumental Music Traditions in the Ex-Slave Narratives." *Black Music Research Journal* 10 (Spring 1990): 43–53.

———. "The Folk, the Stage, and the Five-String Banjo in the Nineteenth Century." *Journal of American Folklore* 89 (October–December 1976): 407–37.

Wish, Harvey. "The French of Old Missouri, 1804–1821: A Study in Assimilation." *Mid-America: An Historical Review* (July 1941).

Witkin, Robert W. *Adorno on Music*. New York: Routledge, 1998.

Wittke, Carl. *Tambo and Bones: A History of the American Minstrel Stage*. Durham, N.C.: Duke University Press, 1930. Reprint, New York: Greenwood Press, 1968.

Wolf, Edwin. *American Song Sheets, Slip Ballads, and Poetical Broadsides, 1850–1870: A Catalogue of the Collection of the Library Company of Philadelphia*. Philadelphia: Library Company, 1963.

Wolfe, Charles. "Rural Black String Band Music." *Black Music Research Journal* 10 (Spring 1990): 32–35.

Wolfe, Richard J. *Early American Music Engraving and Printing: A History of Music Publishing in America*. Urbana: University of Illinois Press, 1980.

———. *Secular Music in America, 1801–1825: A Bibliography*. New York: New York Public Library, 1964.

Wood, Gordon S., ed. *The Rising Glory of America, 1760–1820*. Rev. ed. Boston: Northeastern University Press, 1990.

———. "The Significance of the Early Republic." *Journal of the Early Republic* 8 (Spring 1988): 1–20.

Wood, Minter. "Life in New Orleans in the Spanish Period." *Louisiana Historical Quarterly* 22 (July 1939): 642–709.

Woods, Clyde. *Development Arrested: The Blues and Plantation Power in the Mississippi Delta*. New York: Verso, 1998.

Woodward, C. Vann. *The Old World's New World*. New York: Oxford University Press, 1991.

Wright, Richardson. *Hawkers and Walkers in Early America, Strolling Peddlers, Preachers, Lawyers, Doctors, Players, and Others, from the Beginning of the Civil War*. Philadelphia: J. B. Lippincott, 1927. Reprint, New York: Frederick Ungar, 1965.

The Writer's Program. *Missouri, a Guide to the 'Show Me' State*. New York: Duell, Sloan and Pearce, 1941.

Wyatt, Lucius R. "Six Composers of Nineteenth-Century New Orleans." *Black Music Research Journal* 10 (Spring 1990): 125–40.

Yellin, Victor Fell. "Music in Early Virginia," *American Music* 20 (Winter 2002): 361–80.

Zelinsky, Wilbur. *The Enigma of Ethnicity: Another American Dilemma*. Iowa City: University of Iowa Press, 2001.

Ziff, Larzer. *Literary Democracy: The Declaration of Cultural Independence in America*. New York: Viking Press, 1981.

Index

African: dance, 125, 153, 166; in definitions of race and ethnicity, 3, 4, 111, 123; ethnicities, 4, 54, 153–54, 169; labeling as, 7, 10, 149–52, 166, 168–69; music, 114, 125, 149, 153; musicians, 113; slaves, 53, 54, 62–64, 125

African Theater Company, 170

American: composers, 35; definition of, 2–3, 6; emigrants into the region, 60–61, 70, 91; music culture as lacking, 19, 27, 30–34, 132, 140; music culture's uniqueness, 2, 36

American Revolution, results on national culture, 28, 173

American Scholar Address, 24

American Theater, 128–29, 157, 158, 162, 166

Andre, 104

Arkansas Post, 55, 80–81

Astor Place Riots, 86

authenticity: in blackface minstrelsy, 168–70; in ethnic music genres, 15, 156–60, 162–71; fabrication of, 25, 145–46, 156–70; proven through age, 29

ballrooms: in New Orleans, 81–82; number of, 79; regulated dance order in, 74, 85; in rural areas, 80; segregation in, 88–89, 123–24, 129; as sites of accommodation, 71–72, 82,

89, 93; as sites of conflict, 14, 73–77, 83–84, 90

balls: of benevolent societies, 118–19, 124; for children, 88; commemorative, 85; German, 127; as nationalizing sites, 92–93; in New Orleans, 81–84; in rural areas, 80–81; significance of, 72; during Spanish rule, 83–84. *See also* dances; quadroon balls; War of the Quadrilles

Barnum, P. T., 160, 162

Barth, Fredrik, 146

Baton Rouge: balls in, 93, 124; diverse population in, 47; Fourth of July in, 95–96; music teachers in, 132, 137, 139, 158; newspaper music in, 99, 100; performances in, 103, 162; travelers to, 47, 48

Battle of New Orleans: commemorated with a ball, 93–94; commemorated in song, 103

benevolent societies, 118–21

Bercovitch, Sacvan, 7

blackface minstrelsy, 146, 148, 163, 168–71; as African, 169; as American, 169–70; perception as authentic, 169, 170; in theater competitions, 90

Boré, Mayor, 74, 77, 79

boundaries, 5–7, 154

Brown, William Wells, 153

Buckingham, James, 22